To Protect and To Serve

David Weisburd · Thomas E. Feucht
Idit Hakimi · Lois Felson Mock
Simon Perry
Editors

To Protect and To Serve

Policing in an Age of Terrorism

 Springer

Editors
David Weisburd
Institute of Criminology
Faculty of Law
Hebrew University
Jerusalem, Israel;
Center for Evidence Based Crime Policy
George Mason University
Fairfax, VA
USA
msefrat@mscc.huji.ac.il

Idit Hakimi
Bureau of the Chief Scientist
Ministry of Public Security
Israel
idith@mops.gov.il

Simon Perry
Institute of Criminology
Faculty of Law
Hebrew University, and Israeli National Police (retired)
Jerusalem, Israel
simon.perry@mail.huji.ac.il

Thomas E. Feucht
National Institute of Justice
Washington DC
USA
Thomas.feucht@usdoj.gov

Lois Felson Mock
Retired Senior Social Scientist
Office of Research and Evaluation
National Institute of Justice
US Department of Justice
Washington DC
USA
loismock@cox.net

ISBN 978-0-387-73684-6 (hardcover)
ISBN 978-1-4419-8384-8 (softcover)
DOI 10.1007/978-0-387-73685-3
Springer New York Dordrecht Heidelberg London

e-ISBN 978-0-387-73685-3

Library of Congress Control Number: 2009926047

© Springer Science+Business Media, LLC 2009, First softcover printing 2011
All rights reserved. This work may not be translated or copied in whole or in part without the written permission of the publisher (Springer Science+Business Media, LLC, 233 Spring Street, New York, NY 10013, USA), except for brief excerpts in connection with reviews or scholarly analysis. Use in connection with any form of information storage and retrieval, electronic adaptation, computer software, or by similar or dissimilar methodology now known or hereafter developed is forbidden.
The use in this publication of trade names, trademarks, service marks, and similar terms, even if they are not identified as such, is not to be taken as an expression of opinion as to whether or not they are subject to proprietary rights.

Springer is part of Springer Science+Business Media (www.springer.com)

Acknowledgements

Like many integrative projects, this effort owes much to many beyond the small group of colleagues directly involved in it. The project grew out of a long-standing partnership between the National Institute of Justice (NIJ) and the Bureau of the Chief Scientist of the Ministry of Public Security in Israel. The formal partnership was first established in 1999 under the leadership of the then Director of NIJ, Jeremy Travis and the Ministry's Chief Scientist, Israel Barak. This partnership has been sustained and supported by key leadership in both agencies, including the Ministry's Deputy Director General, Eliezer Rozenbaum and subsequent heads of NIJ, Sarah V. Hart, Glenn R. Schmitt, and David W. Hagy. This project would not have been possible without the commitment and support of these executives.

Early decisions about the contours of this project were made with the valuable input of a team of editorial advisors. The editorial advisors included David Bayley, Gideon Fishman, Dov Lutzky, Stephen Mastrofski, Tracey Meares, and Darrel Stephens. They helped craft the specific focus of the papers to be commissioned, identified potential authors, and assisted throughout the project by keeping the editors and authors grounded in the relevant research and policy context. Their reviews of early drafts of the papers were crucial to the integration of this volume. We are indebted to their thoughtful and experienced input throughout this project. Other individuals provided additional reviews for some of the chapters, and we are grateful for their comments and suggestions. Reviewers for the project included Menachem Amir, Edward Flynn, Robert Friedmann, Meir Gilboa, Jack Greene, Gil Kerlikowske, Simha Landau, Ami Pedahzur, Dennis Rosenbaum, and Jerome Skolnick.

In October 2007, in Jerusalem, Israel, the Ministry of Public Security hosted a symposium at which drafts of the papers were presented to an international audience of experts in policing and terrorism. Comments and reactions from symposium attendees gave the authors and editors important insights that helped us anticipate important policy questions that might otherwise have gone unaddressed. In particular, we gratefully acknowledge the insights and comments from police chiefs James Bueermann (Redlands, CA), Ronal Serpas (Nashville, TN), James Corwin (Kansas City, MO), Dudi Cohen (Commissioner of the Israeli National Police), and the many symposium attendees from the Israeli National Police. Their insights and "on the ground" points of view regarding police work in an age of terrorism were invaluable to this effort.

We would also like to acknowledge others who have helped in developing this project including Brett Chapman, Marvene O'Rourke, Maggie Heisler, Winifred Reed, and Michael Hronick of the National Institute of Justice, Shomron Moyal and Yamit Barashi from the Hebrew University of Jerusalem, and Welmoed Spahr from Springer Verlag.

Finally, we owe a special debt to Kristin Miggans of the University of Maryland and Tal Jonathan from the Hebrew University of Jerusalem who acted as project coordinators and helped us manage the difficulties of international collaboration. We are particularly grateful to Ms. Jonathan who not only helped in developing all aspects of the project, but also played a key role in coordinating the completion of the book.

The work for this project was supported through a grant from the National Institute of Justice (2005-IJ-R-085). Although NIJ funding was critical for developing this project, we want to emphasize at the outset that all opinions and positions expressed by the editors and authors of the papers are their own, and do not represent the official positions or policies of the National Institute of Justice.

Contents

1 Introduction 1

2 Trends in Modern International Terrorism 11
Boaz Ganor

3 Tracking Global Terrorism Trends, 1970–2004 43
Gary LaFree and Laura Dugan

4 Cops and Spooks: The Role of the Police in Counterterrorism 81
David H. Bayley and David Weisburd

5 Police Activities to Counter Terrorism:
What We Know and What We Need to Know 101
Cynthia Lum, Maria (Maki) Haberfeld, George Fachner,
and Charles Lieberman

6 The Implications of Terrorism on the Formal
and Social Organization of Policing in the US and Israel:
Some Concerns and Opportunities 143
Jack R. Greene and Sergio Herzog

7 The Impacts of Policing Terrorism on Society:
Lessons from Israel and the US 177
Badi Hasisi, Geoffrey P. Alpert, and Dan Flynn

8 Policing, Terrorism, and Beyond 203
Thomas E. Feucht, David Weisburd, Simon Perry,
Lois Felson Mock, and Idit Hakimi

Index 225

Contributors

Geoffrey P. Alpert
Department of Criminology and Criminal Justice,
University of South Carolina, Columbia, SC, USA
geoffa@gwm.sc.edu

David H. Bayley
School of Criminal Justice, State University of New York, Albany, NY, USA
dbayley@albany.edu

Laura Dugan
Department of Criminology and Criminal Justice, University of Maryland,
College Park, MD, USA
ldugan@crim.umd.edu

George Fachner, Jr.
Administration of Justice Department, Centre for Evidence-Based Crime Policy,
George Mason University, Manassas, VA, USA
george.fachner.jr@gmail.com

Thomas E. Feucht
National Institute of Justice, Washington DC, USA
thomas.feucht@usdoj.gov

Dan Flynn
Former Savannah Police Chief/Daytona Beach Finalist for Police Chief,
danflynn@adelphia.net

Boaz Ganor
Lauder School of Government, and International Institute for Counter-Terrorism
(ICT), Interdisciplinary Center (IDC), Herzliya, Israel
ganor@idc.ac.il

Jack Greene
College of Criminal Justice, Northeastern University, Boston, MA, USA
j.greene@neu.edu

Maria (Maki) Haberfeld
Administration of Justice Department, Centre for Evidence-Based Crime Policy,
George Mason University, Manassas, VA, USA
mhaberfeld@jjay.cuny.edu

Idit Hakimi
Bureau of the Chief Scientist, Ministry of Public Security, Israel
idith@mops.gov.il

Badi Hasisi
Institute of Criminology, Faculty of Law, Hebrew University, Jerusalem, Israel
hasisi@mscc.huji.ac.il

Sergio Herzog
Institute of Criminology, Faculty of Law, Hebrew University, Jerusalem, Israel
sherzog@mscc.huji.ac.il

Gary LaFree
National Center for the Study of Terrorism and Responses to Terrorism (START),
and Department of Criminology and Criminal Justice, University of Maryland,
College Park, MD, USA
glafree@crim.umd.edu

Charles Lieberman
Administration of Justice Department, Centre for Evidence-Based Crime Policy,
George Mason University, Manassas, VA, USA
clieberman@jjay.cuny.edu

Cynthia Lum
Administration of Justice Department, Center for Evidence-Based Crime Policy,
George Mason University, Fairfax, VA, USA
clum@gmu.edu

Lois Felson Mock
Retired Senior Social Scientist, Office of Research and Evaluation, National
Institute of Justice, US Department of Justice, Washington, DC, USA
loismock@cox.net

Simon Perry
Institute of Criminology, Faculty of Law, Hebrew University, and Israeli
National Police (retired), Jerusalem, Israel
simon.perry@mail.huji.ac.il

David Weisburd
Institute of Criminology, Faculty of Law, Hebrew University, Jerusalem,
Israel; Center for Evidence Based Crime Policy, George Mason University,
Fairfax, VA, USA
msefrat@mscc.huji.ac.il

Chapter 1
Introduction

Since the turn of the century, policing in Western democracies has been faced with a new set of problems generated by global threats of terrorism. While terrorism was not a new problem for countries like the United Kingdom or Israel, especially in the United States, the idea that the police had to place terrorism as a central priority represented a radical change from what were the traditional policing duties. Prevention and control of crime and disorder, and fear of crime, had become the major concerns of police in the 1990s. And even within societies that had faced serious threats of terrorism in the past, it seemed that the idea of a service-based and community-oriented policing was overtaking concerns about terrorism and public security (Innes, 2005; Weisburd et al., 2002).

Innovations in policing during the decade of the 1990s have been impressive (Weisburd and Braga, 2006a). Reacting to a crisis that challenged the effectiveness of police strategies and the legitimacy of police in the eyes of the public, a host of new tactical and organizational strategies were implemented in police agencies in the United States, the United Kingdom, and other Western democracies. The crisis the police responded to at that time was concerned primarily with the rift between the police and the public, and a growing body of evidence that the police were not being effective in what they had defined as their primary mission – the prevention and control of crime. The changes in the United States were particularly striking, as the police rapidly adopted new programs and policies.

The police in prior decades had adopted a "standard model" of policing that looked to "one size fits all" solutions, focused exclusively on crime problems, and emphasized a professional model of policing distant from the public (National Research Council, 2004; Weisburd and Eck, 2004). The new innovations emphasized the complexity of the problems that the police faced, the broad nature of the tasks that they had to deal with, and the importance of the public in defining policing duties and aiding the police in their activities. By the turn of the century, United States policing had changed from a profession noted for its resistance to change to one that was characterized by innovation and flexibility. While the extent of change was not as great in many other Western countries, innovation in policing was common across democratic policing agencies (Griffiths et al., 2001; Leigh et al., 1998; Ratcliffe, 2002).

And as the turn of the century approached, the efforts of the police appeared to yield not just renewed support from and cooperation with the public, but a surprising drop in crime rates. In the United States, the decline in crime was so great that scholars began to refer to a "crime drop" (Blumstein and Wallman, 2000). For the police it was clear that their efforts at innovation and change had paid off (Bratton, 1998; Kelling and Sousa, 2001; MacDonald, 2008). Some scholars were more skeptical (Eck and Maguire, 2000; Harcourt, 2001; Rosenfeld et al., 2005). Nonetheless, at the dawn of the new century police professionals and many policing scholars could begin to take satisfaction at the large-scale changes in the policing "industry" (Maguire and Katz, 2002) that had been wrought in the previous decade. It seemed as if the police had emerged from the crisis of legitimacy of the prior decades with a renewed sense of mission and purpose.

But the terrorist attacks of 9/11 challenged this new sense of confidence in policing and raised a set of problems that seemed to have little connection to the innovations of the previous decade. Community policing (Cordner, 2005; Goldstein, 1987; Greene and Mastrofski, 1988; Trojanowicz, 1989) might have re-established strong links between the police and the public, but its origins had little to do with the identification of terrorist cells or the prevention of terrorist attacks. Broken windows policing (Kelling and Coles, 1996; Wilson and Kelling, 1982) might have brought disorder to a central place in the activities of police, but such disorder policing was not meant to contribute to increasing homeland security in major cities. Hot spots policing (Sherman and Weisburd, 1995; Weisburd and Braga, 2006b) was meant to deal with crime at specific places, and was not concerned with the broader and less specific threats of terrorism. Perhaps unique among police innovations of the previous decade, problem-oriented policing (Goldstein, 1979, 1990) presented a model for solving problems that could in theory be directly applied to terrorism as well as crime and disorder (see Clarke, 1992; Clarke and Newman, 2007). But importantly, its origins, as that of other innovations of the period, had much to do with developing strategies for specific crime and disorder problems and had little connection to the new terrorist threats that were emerging.

While the attacks of 9/11 caught America, and American policing, by surprise, Israeli police had already begun to focus greater attention on homeland security questions a year earlier with the outbreak of the Second Intifada. Of course, Israeli police had continually been confronted with terrorism, and its role in homeland security had been established more than two decades before as a result of a horrific terrorist attack on a school in the town of Maalot. But the Israeli police had also adopted innovations such as community policing and Compstat in the decade before (Goldshleg and Shabtai, 2002; Shalev, 1999; Weisburd et al., 2002), and many Israeli scholars thought that policing in Israel was facing fundamental changes that would move it closer to models in the United States and the United Kingdom (Shadmi, 2001; Weisburd et al., 2001).

This volume develops out of the backdrop of the new challenges that terrorism has brought to policing in Western democracies. It is a product of a decade-long research partnership between the US National Institute of Justice (NIJ) and the Ministry of Public Security, State of Israel (MoPS). This partnership, supporting work in both the social and the technological sciences, has touched on public safety issues as far ranging as corrections, forensic sciences, and domestic violence. None, however, has been more important than the agencies' shared commitment to policing research, and no aspect of policing research has emerged with greater urgency or relevance than the question of policing terrorism. Both for Israel and the United States, the question of the role of policing in responding to and controlling terrorism has become a central concern. The NIJ and the Chief Scientist's Office of the MoPS sought to bring new ideas to bear on the role of the police in the prevention and control of terrorism.

The chapters in this volume convey the perspective that the line separating terrorism from crime is imprecise and ambiguous. Specifically, they wrestle with the key question of how the government's primary institution for detecting, responding to, and preventing crime – the police – might be brought to bear on the challenge of detecting, responding to, and preventing terrorism. It also raises directly a series of questions that have often been ignored as police and policing scholars seek to reform the police to become more engaged in antiterrorism activities: What possible side effects might a specific concern with preventing and controlling terrorism have on traditional roles and responsibilities of the police? Will gains in crime fighting and control of disorder be lost as police focus more directly on homeland security? Will the gains in relationships between the police and the public be lost as the police focus on the strategic threats that terrorism raises?

The chapters that follow bring together distinguished American and Israeli policing scholars, who pool their knowledge and experience to shed light on what has happened to policing since the turn of the century, and what trends can be expected over the next few decades. The involvement of American and Israeli scholars working together provided a special opportunity to draw from the experiences of policing in each country. The tremendous innovations in policing in the United States provide a context of local police agencies linked strongly to the publics that they serve. The Israeli police experience is one of a national police agency that has been dominated much more by concern with terrorism, and accordingly provides a laboratory for assessing how an emphasis on homeland security influences the structure and functions of a democratic police organization.

The development of this volume began with a series of questions that we thought were critical to answer if police agencies were to address the new challenges brought by terrorism and increased homeland security responsibilities. To define those questions, we sought advice from distinguished policing scholars and police practitioners both from the United States and Israel who formed an editorial board for the volume (see Acknowledgments). Each chapter was critically reviewed by the editors, our editorial advisors, and independent peer reviewers representing both scholars and practitioners. In this sense, our volume benefits not only from the insights of the authors and editors, but also from key scholars and practitioners who were invited to help us develop this work.

We think that the result is a challenging and thoughtful group of essays that are linked closely and together provide a comprehensive discussion of policing terrorism in Western democracies. In the next section we introduce the chapters and the logic we used in commissioning them.

Dilemmas in Policing Terrorism and Serving the Public: Contributions of the Volume

Though our main concern is with policing terrorism, we felt that it would be impossible to address the police role without defining the nature of the terrorist threats that police in Western democracies face. Nor could we talk about the responses to terrorism without first raising questions about what terrorism was and how it relates to political and social structures in modern societies. Accordingly, Chapters 2 and 3 of the volume are concerned less with the role of the police in responding to terrorism and more with the threat of terrorism in democratic societies.

Boaz Ganor authors the second chapter, which questions the definition of terrorism and the specific social and political problems it creates for democracies. The chapter outlines the complexity of the terrorist phenomenon and suggests that it is multifaceted in nature, requiring a cohesive international and broad-based response. Drawing on psychology, economics, criminology, and other disciplines, he provides a rich theoretical context in which to examine this terrorist threat that dominates policy discourse in the United States and Israel. Ganor tests the normative frame of terrorism (when is a terrorist simply a freedom-fighter? he asks) and compares it with our frames for understanding crime. Ganor recognizes the importance of the political and ideological context for terrorism, and he underscores the special challenge of combating terrorism while preserving liberty in democratic states. In words that speak to the bilateral international framework for this volume, Ganor declares that it will take a united world community, a multidisciplinary network of terrorism-fighters to prevail: "it takes a network to defeat a network."

The third chapter provides a statistical description of trends in terrorism over the last few decades, drawing from the unique data collection on terrorist events that is being carried out by the START (National Consortium for the Study of Terrorism and Responses to Terrorism) Center at the University of Maryland. Though the events of 9/11 began a new discourse on terrorism, it would be a mistake to begin an analysis of policing and terrorism on the assumption that terrorism is a new phenomenon. A scientific examination of any phenomenon should begin with analysis of available data. Drawing on a database of more than 82,000 terrorist events over the last four decades, Gary LaFree and Laura Dugan present analyses that answer fundamental questions about the nature of terrorism and terrorist events. How can terrorist events be classified? What weapons are used? How long do terrorist organizations persist over time?

LaFree and Dugan discern patterns in these data that should be incorporated into any strategy for combating terrorism. Key findings include evidence of the very short life-span of most terrorist groups (like new business start-ups, the authors point out), the limited use of weapons of mass destruction by most terrorist groups (possibly because the complex training and handling required is beyond the grasp of many), and the changes in political stability with which terrorism appears to rise or fall (terrorism appears to be most common where states are transitioning from autocratic to democratic states, say the authors). Many readers will find LaFree and Dugan's trend analysis of terrorism extremely illuminating. One of their most surprising findings is that despite our current preoccupation with terrorism, global incidents have been on the decline since its last peak in 1993.

While many scholars and lay people take for granted the fact that the police should play a central role in the fight against terrorism, the fourth chapter authored by David Bayley and David Weisburd seeks to examine the rationale for the police role. It begins by examining the present roles that police play in counterterrorism in democratic societies. It then attempts to define the specific ways that traditional full-service police agencies can enhance the effectiveness of society in combating terrorism. While finding benefits in bringing police to attend to terrorism, the authors argue that such "high policing" functions are likely to threaten the gains of the police in establishing legitimacy in many communities, and may undermine traditional activities to control crime and disorder.

The police mission to safeguard the public is extremely broad, and police work has historically taken many forms. Are intelligence-gathering, counterterrorism, and homeland security just the latest natural developments in police work? Or does policing stand on the brink of an historic change? Drawing on several theoretical frameworks for defining and understanding policing, Bayley and Weisburd grapple with whether and how terrorism might be challenging and changing the police indelibly. "All terrorism is local," the authors note, suggesting the extent to which police concern with terrorism is similar to other "local" responsibilities of the police such as crime and disorder. At the same time, the authors give us a rich picture of the strains that police agencies face as they struggle to balance "traditional" crime-fighting, community policing, and counter-terrorism.

In Chap. 5, Cynthia Lum, Maria Haberfeld, George Fachner, and Charles Lieberman turn to the specific strategies that police agencies have developed to deal with terrorism (and the outcomes of terrorism). The key element of this chapter is an assessment of what works both in preventing terrorism and in dealing with its consequences. Do we have evidence at this time that would lead us to move in one direction or another? Have technological improvements been assessed empirically and what is known regarding their use? What types of studies are needed to define promising tactics and strategies? Using a systematic review of antiterrorism approaches and qualitative data drawn from observations in specific countries, the authors summarize existing knowledge. Unfortunately, as their chapter details, we have very little empirical data to guide the police in combating terrorism.

In Chap. 6, Jack Greene and Sergio Herzog turn to the specific problem of the impacts of fighting terrorism on police organizations. How have police agencies responded organizationally to the added responsibilities of fighting terrorism? Have they created new organizational structures, or special units to cope with the new demands of responding to terrorism and its aftermath? How has the fight against terrorism affected the allocation of personnel and of financial resources in policing? The authors argue that military and criminal justice models have traditionally been distinct in societal responses to terrorism. However, the increasing terrorist threats in this century have resulted in a new model they term the "widened criminal justice model." In this model the mission of criminal justice is expanded in the fight against terrorism through the development of "specialized units to address terrorism and intelligence issues, widening the training of police officers to include terrorism and appropriate responses to these events, expanding the use of protection devices and technology designated to confront exceptional violence, broadening cooperation between police and intelligence bodies, and, finally recruiting personnel with appropriate skills from the military." This chapter considers the implications of these changes using the United States and Israel as case studies.

In developing a book on how the police should respond to terrorism and what impacts it might have on the police mission, we thought it critical to consider the impacts of policing terrorism on communities. Police activities may have intended and unintended influences on communities and societies as a whole. Badi Hasisi, Geoff Alpert, and Dan Flynn review these issues in Chap. 7. One important role of the police is to increase a public sense of security and safety. The police succeed in fighting terrorism when the public is able to live daily lives in a "normal" fashion. But fighting terrorism may have unequal influence on different communities. For example, Arab minority communities in Israel and the United States may feel singled out in the fight against terrorism. What impact does that have on those communities, and the ability of the police to serve and protect these citizens? What issues of legitimacy are raised and what new legal problems must be addressed? Does the focus on terrorism naturally lead to a social cost in terms of service to the community in such programs as community policing? How is the legitimacy of police organizations affected both in majority and minority communities when policing terrorism becomes a priority?

In the concluding chapter, we seek not only to integrate the contributions of the preceding chapters, but also to question how policing might change in the coming decades as a result of emerging social, demographic, and technical trends. Prediction of course is always a difficult exercise, but nonetheless we thought speculation on such trends might help to put our volume in context and provide a broader context to the themes we examine.

All the chapters in the volume seek not only to review what is known today about policing terrorism, but also to define what needs to be known if we are to face the challenges of terrorism in the future while minimizing potential negative consequences for the communities that police serve and on the structure and organization of policing itself. Accordingly, the chapters in our volume include not only a description and analysis of what is, but also seek to provide a research agenda for the future. In Chapter 8, this research agenda is integrated and prioritized. We very much hope that agencies that sponsor research and scholars who carry out research consider our suggestions.

Conclusions

Despite thriving, global criminal networks, in the end, "all crime is local." Both criminals and the police are part of the fabric of everyday places: neighborhoods, markets, and communities. The same, unfortunately, is true of terrorists and terrorism. Like crime, the effect of terrorism is greatest in places where ordinary life routinely prevails: in public buildings, marketplaces, busses and bus stops, and trains and railway stations. In these everyday contexts, law-abiding citizens, criminals, and the police, may all walk the same streets with terrorists.

For many in the United States, the September 11 terrorist attacks on the World Trade Center and the Pentagon crystallized our vision of police involvement in fighting terrorism. The brave officers of the Port Authority Police, the New York Police Department, the Arlington County Police, and other local, state, and federal law enforcement agencies were on the front lines in the response to terrorism's most deadly assault on the United States soil. The heroism of these local police officers in New York City and Arlington, Virginia, was of course foreshadowed many, many times over by the Israeli National Police, where the threat and the reality of terrorism have been a continuing, almost daily reality for years.

The terrorist events of the last decade in the United States and in Israel have raised important questions about the police, their function, their operation, and their ties to the communities they are sworn to protect. How has policing changed in an age of terrorism? What new costs and challenges do the police face? What new expectations do communities hold for the police? How effective can "ordinary policing" be in the fight against terrorism? What does the future hold for the police as terrorism continues as a central challenge to democratic states like the United States and Israel? This volume aims to shed light on these important questions, and to advance both knowledge and practice on the police role in responding to terrorism. Policing in the 21st century prevents a new set of challenges for policing. We think that the chapters that follow will add to the solutions to these challenges, as scholars and practitioners work together to re-engineer policing, while maintaining the many positive trends that emerged in policing over the last few decades.

References

Blumstein, A., and J., Wallman eds. 2000. *The Crime Drop in America*. Cambridge, UK: Cambridge University Press.
Bratton, W. 1998. *Turnaround: How America's Top Cop Reversed the Crime Epidemic*. New York: Random House.
Clarke, R. V. 1992. Situational crime prevention: Theory and practice. *British Journal of Criminology*, 20:136–147.
Clarke, R. V., and G. R. Newman. 2007. Police and the prevention of terrorism. *Policing: A Journal of Policy and Practice* 1:9–20.
Cordner, G. W. 2005. Community policing: Elements and effects. In *Critical Issues in Policing: Contemporary Readings*, eds. R. G. Dunham and G. P. Alpert, Long Grove, IL: Waveland.

Eck, J. E., and E. R. Maguire. 2000. Have changes in policing reduced violent crime? An assessment of the evidence. In *The Crime Drop in America*, eds. A. Blumstein and J. Wallman, Cambridge, UK: Cambridge University Press.

Goldshleg, M., and O. Shabtai. 2002. The Compstat program in NYPD and its implementation in the Israeli Police, 1999–2000. *Police and Society*, 6:135–172 [in Hebrew].

Goldstein, H. 1979. Improving policing: A problem oriented approach. *Crime and Delinquency*, 24:236–258.

Goldstein, H. 1987. Towards community-oriented policing: Potential, basic requirements, and threshold questions. *Crime and Delinquency*, 25:236–258.

Goldstein, H. 1990. *Problem-Oriented Policing*. New York: McGraw-Hill.

Greene, J., and S. Mastrofski, eds. 1988. *Community Policing: Rhetoric or Reality?* New York: Praeger.

Griffiths, C. T., B. Whitelaw, and R. B. Parent. 2001. *Community Policing in Canada*. Scarborough, ON: Nelson Thomson Learning.

Harcourt, B. E. 2001. *Illusion of Order: The False Promise of Broken Windows Policing*. Cambridge, MA: Harvard University Press.

Innes, M. 2005. Why soft policing is hard: On the curious development of reassurance policing, how it became neighborhood policing and what this signals about the politics of police reform. *Journal of Community and Applied Social Psychology*, 15(3):1–14.

Kelling, G. L., and C. M. Coles. 1996. *Fixing Broken Windows: Restoring Order and Reducing Crime in Our Communities*. New York: The Free.

Kelling, G. L., and W. H. Sousa. 2001. *Do Police Matter? An Analysis of the Impact of New York City's Police Reforms. Civil Report 22*. New York: Manhattan Institute for Policy Research.

Leigh, A., T. Read, and N. Tilley. 1998. *Brit POP II: Problem-Oriented Policing in Practice*. London: Home Office, Policing and Reducing Crime Unit, Research, Development and Statistics Directorate.

MacDonald, H. 2008. NYPD's historic feat should quiet critics. *New York Daily News*, 8 January.

Maguire, E. R., and C. M. Katz. 2002. Community policing, loose coupling, and sensemaking in American police agencies. *Justice Quarterly*, 19:503–536.

National Research Council, Committee to Review Research on Police Policy and Practices, Committee on Law and Justice, Division of Behavioral and Social Sciences and Education. 2004. Effectiveness of police activity in reducing crime, disorder and fear. In *Fairness and Effectiveness in Policing: The Evidence*, eds. W. Skogan and K. Frydl, Washington, DC: The National Academies.

Ratcliffe, J. H. 2002. Intelligence-led policing and the problem of turning rhetoric into practice. *Policing and Society*, 12:53–66.

Rosenfeld, R., R. Fornango, and E. Baumer. 2005. Did Ceasefire, Compstat, and Exile reduce homicide? *Criminology and Public Policy*, 4:419–449.

Shadmi, A. 2001. Municipal policing in Israel: An historical necessity on the road to new policing. *Police and Society*, 5:49–70 [in Hebrew].

Shalev, O. 1999. Event coverage: A symposium of Israeli Police officers about COMPSTAT, hosting the Commissioner of NYPD, Howard Safir, which took place on June 15, 1999 in Jerusalem. *Police and Society*, 3: 143–151 [in Hebrew].

Sherman, L. W., and D. Weisburd. 1995. General deterrent effects of police patrol in crime "hot spots:" A randomized, controlled trial. *Justice Quarterly*, 12:626–648.

Trojanowicz, R. C. 1989. *Preventing Civil Disturbances: A Community Policing Approach*. East Lansing, MI: Michigan State University, National Center for Community Policing.

Weisburd, D., and A. A. Braga. 2006a. Introduction: Understanding police innovation. In *Police Innovation: Contrasting Perspectives*, eds. D. Weisburd and A. A. Braga,Cambridge, UK: Cambridge University Press.

Weisburd, D., and A. A. Braga. 2006b. Hot spots policing as a model for police innovation. In *Police Innovation: Contrasting Perspectives*, eds. D. Weisburd and A. A. Braga,Cambridge, UK: Cambridge University Press.

References

Weisburd, D., and J. E. Eck. 2004. What can police do to reduce crime, disorder, and fear? *The Annals of the American Academy of Political and Social Science*, 593:42–65.
Weisburd, D., O. Shalev, and M. Amir. 2002. Community policing in Israel: Resistance and change. *Policing: An International Journal of Police Strategies and Management*, 25:80–109.
Weisburd, D., E. Shoham, and L. Gideon. 2001. Municipal policing in Israel: Problems of efficiency, community, equality and integrity. *Police and Society*, 5:5–24 [in Hebrew].
Wilson, J. Q., and G. L. Kelling. 1982. Broken windows: The police and neighborhood safety. *The Atlantic Monthly*, March, 29–38.

Chapter 2
Trends in Modern International Terrorism

Boaz Ganor

Abstract This chapter examines some of the most widely researched trends and developments within the phenomenon of modern international terrorism, providing policy recommendations on how to counter its emerging threats – particularly that of the Global Jihad movement and "homegrown" terrorism. The magnitude of the modern terrorist threat was demonstrated by the attacks of September 11, and ever since, the field has experienced a renewal of sorts, attracting unprecedented attention by both scholars and the mainstream public. This chapter will introduce readers to the main schools of thoughts within the academic field that explain terrorism. It will also present the many disciplines applicable to the study of terrorism, demonstrating that the phenomenon is multifaceted in nature, requiring a cohesive international and broad-based response. In covering a number of dilemmas facing terrorism experts, the chapter explores the debate over a definition of terrorism, providing a proposed definition that distinguishes acts of terrorism from criminal acts. The chapter continues on to explore the phenomenon of modern terrorism, the role of traditional crime within the terror sphere, and the growing threat of Global Jihadi terrorism – including terror networks and homegrown cells and activists who have emerged as a result of the spread of radical Islamic ideology. The role of terrorism in democratic states and the economic ramifications of terrorism are also explored. Finally, the chapter ends with recommendations on how governments should effectively respond to terrorism and discuses room for further research.

Trends in Modern International Terrorism

In recent years, the academic world has witnessed a surge of research and academic programs in the field of homeland security and counterterrorism. After the attacks of 9/11, the threat of global terrorism immediately topped the international agenda.

B. Ganor
Lauder School of Government, International Institute for Counter-Terrorism (ICT), Interdisciplinary Center (IDC), Herzliya, Israel
e-mail: ganor@idc.ac.il

Growing recognition of the threat, combined with an increase in government spending, spurred the development of academic research institutions, think tanks, and new higher education programs in the study of homeland security and counterterrorism. The trend was particularly prominent in the United States, as researchers sought a basic understanding of the characteristics of terrorism and agencies sought ways to effectively cope with the phenomenon. This trend was accompanied by a significant increase in the number of researchers focusing on the phenomenon of terrorism. These researchers came from a wide array of academic disciplines, applying varied quantitative and qualitative research tools and methods in their analysis of the threat.

In understanding the phenomenon and preventing future terrorist attacks, researchers have focused primarily on understanding the rationale of terrorist organizations in general and Global Jihad organizations in particular – their cost-benefit calculations and their decision-making processes. "Trends" in terrorism have also been explored – often focusing on the introduction, transition, or prominence of a specific modus operandi or a method, such as suicide bombings, the Global Jihad movement, or the use of unconventional weapons.

Reviewing these trends and themes in terrorism – and the academic research that has accompanied them – is crucial in determining how far we have come and how far we have to go, both in terms of the governments designing and deciding on counterterrorism policy and the academics informing such decisions.

In exploring the phenomenon of modern international terrorism, this chapter will first introduce readers to the various schools of thought and academic approaches used in explaining terrorism – drawing on a wide range of disciplines and theories. Discussion will then move to one of the most basic components of the terrorism dilemma, with implications on how the term – and thus phenomenon of terrorism itself – is treated, applied, and understood by the international community – the debate over defining terrorism.

As will be demonstrated, definitions of terrorism vary widely – with equally as wide implications – yet there is still a general consensus among most leading scholars as to the essential nature of the threat. "Modern terrorism," the next theme that will be explored in this chapter, is regarded as a form of psychological warfare intended to spread fear and anxiety among the target population. This fear is translated into political pressure on decision makers to change policies in such a manner that will serve the terrorist's interests. As such, modern terrorists attempt to exploit the liberal values of democratic states, forcing governments to adhere to their demands as a result of the physical, psychological, and economic ramifications of terrorist attacks. The nature of terrorism in relation to the democratic state will be explored in a later section of this chapter as well.

As terrorist groups are usually engaged in a long war of attrition, terrorist organizations need ongoing support and funds to ensure they can maintain their activities. In fact, one of the main sources of funding for many terrorist organizations is criminal activity: smuggling, counterfeiting, extortion, and narcotics. At the beginning of the twenty-first century, the threat of international terrorism grew with the spread of Global Jihad terrorism. Made up of complex networks of hierarchal terrorist organizations, proxy and affiliate organizations, local and international terror networks, sleeper cells, and indoctrinated radical activists, all these actors share a common extreme ideology and the readiness to use violence in general – and terrorism in particular – in order to achieve their goals. The economic ramifications of these activities only further exacerbate the damage posed by terrorist attacks, another focus of terrorism research.

This dynamic terrorist phenomenon has threatened an increasing number of states while involving more terror organizations, networks, activists, and supporters worldwide. The growing level of the threat, its international scope, its lethality,[1] and the possible use of nonconventional terrorism (CBRN – chemical, biological, radiological, and nuclear weapons) necessitate future multidisciplinary research in the field and a more cohesive, international response.

Explaining Terrorism

In general, two schools of thought explaining the phenomenon of modern terrorism have emerged out of the collection of academic work within the discipline – the "psychological-sociological" school of thought and the "political-rational" school of thought. Both schools maintain that terrorism seeks to achieve political goals by instilling fear and anxiety among the target population, but each stresses a different aspect of the explanation.

The psychological-sociological school, represented most recently by scholars such as Dr. Jerrold Post (1998) and John Horgan (2005), stresses the phenomenon's psychological component, maintaining that the immediate and central goal of terrorism is to instill fear and anxiety, while its political goals are long term.

> "Terror as a clinical term refers to a psychological state of constant dread or fearfulness, associated with an abnormally high level of psych-physiological arousal. This is central to what terrorists aim to achieve, since after all, while they have some ultimate set of political objectives, it is an immediate goal of most terrorist groups to cause terror" (Horgan, 2005:14).

The psychological-sociological school addresses both the desired effect of terrorism and its root causes, relying primarily on social group dynamics and the psychological profile of an individual terrorist actor. Some early psychological explanations of terrorism have focused on the disruptive or psychopathological personalities of terrorist operatives, analyzing terrorists based on characteristics or disorders associated with violent or aggressive behaviors (De la Corte et al., 2007). Some of the common psychological characteristics that have been attributed to alleged terrorists

---

[1] Analysis of terrorist incidents over the last 35 years confirms that terrorist attacks, while arguably decreasing in quantity, are growing more deadly over time, as the number of fatalities per attack has increased (LaFree and Dugan, in this volume). Such data, however, rely on a definition of terrorism that LaFree and Dugan themselves note is relatively "inclusive." The Global Terrorism Database (GTD), on which their analysis is based, excludes "attacks on the military by guerilla organizations," but includes military targets attacked by substate actors motivated by political, economic, or social motives (See LaFree and Dugan; in this volume).

are paranoia, antisocial and narcissistic personalities (Millon, 1981; Post, 1987), lack of empathy with victims, hostility toward parents, dogmatic or ideological mentality, or a simplistic or utopian worldview (Victoroff, 2005).

At one end of the spectrum within such literature is the assertion – and at times assumption – that terrorists are to some degree psychologically "abnormal," possessing personality disorders that qualify them as insane or psychopathic (as discussed by Cooper, 1978; Hacker, 1976; Lasch, 1979; Pearce, 1977; Taylor, 1988). Despite early research providing psychological profiles of terrorists, other terrorism researchers have come to the general conclusion that there is no universal terrorist personality pattern; most terrorist operatives are not necessarily "psychopaths" (Silke, 1998), nor do they show traces of being clearly or consistently mentally ill (Crenshaw, 2000; Post, 1998; Stahelski, 2004). Early studies on the topic have been largely disproved or debunked, in fact, even within the psychological-social school of thought. Further research has shown that terrorists rarely meet the criteria for insanity,[2] but rather may possess some "particular personality dispositions" related to psychological conditions or disorders (Post, 1987).

Dr. Jerrold Post, an expert in political psychology, maintains that even though terrorists fit within the spectrum of "normality," a large number have demonstrated specific personality characteristics that indicate a minor psychopathology, such as aggression, activism, thrill seeking, an externalist psychological mechanism and factionalism. These are characteristics of narcissistic disorders and borderline personalities (Post, 1998:25–27). While Post stops short of actually diagnosing terrorists with such disorders or characteristics, he does claim they tend to have high frequency among terrorists, contributing to a uniform rhetorical style and logic (Silke, 1998:65).

According to Post, there is a unique logic that characterizes a terrorist's thought process – a "terrorist psycho-logic." Post claims that terrorists are motivated by psychological influences when they choose to conduct violent acts, as expressed in rhetoric that relies on "us versus them" and "good versus evil" dichotomies. He further claims that lodged in a terrorist's permanent logic is the notion that the regime must be toppled, which is a result of the terrorist's search for identity. In an attack against the regime, a terrorist is actually trying to destroy the inner enemy within him.

However, even as some researchers cite it as the primary cause, a terrorist's individual psychological profile is not the only significant explanation for the phenomenon of terrorism. Rather, group psychology and sociology may be significant explanatory factors behind terrorist attacks. Various researchers have cited group pressure as a variable to explain recruitment, methods of operation and involvement in terrorism (Merari, 2004). Others have applied the cult model to terrorist organizations (Morgan, 2001).

---

[2] Studies by Heskin (1984), Rasch (1979), and Taylor (1988) have all cited evidence discrediting the assumption that terrorists are psychologically "abnormal."

It is in this context that Post emphasizes the group as a framework in which a sense of belonging and importance for its members is created. He claims that ideology plays an important role in supporting a unifying environment for the group. Shared ideology justifies the group's activity and quickly transforms into the group's moral guide.

The psychological-sociological school relies, therefore, on psychological and sociological characteristics, motives, and grievances in explaining the phenomenon of terrorism. In contrast, the "political-rational" school of thought views terrorism as a rational method of operation intended to promote various interests and attain concrete political goals (Crenshaw, 2000; Hoffman, 1998; Shprinzak, 1998). Rational choice theory has been adopted by a number of terrorism researchers within this school, and maintains that terrorist action derives from a conscious, rational, calculated decision to choose one route of action over another (Crenshaw, 1992; Sandler et al., 1983; Sandler and Lapan, 1988; Wilson, 2000).[3]

Leading researcher Martha Crenshaw explains that an organization chooses terrorism among several operational alternatives in order to promote their mutual values and preferences. In making a rational calculation of the costs and benefits, terrorism is deliberately chosen as the preferred method of political activity because it is perceived to be the most effective of the operating alternatives – the benefits exceed the costs. In this context, Ehud Shprinzak similarly stressed that the phenomenon of terrorism is not the result of disturbed human activity or a random thoughtless attack. This is a process that almost always begins without violence or terrorist activity (Shprinzak, 1998:78).

Rand terrorism expert Bruce Hoffman further clarified the "rationalist" approach:

> "I have been studying terrorists and terrorism for more than twenty years. Yet I am still always struck by how disturbingly 'normal' most terrorists seem when one actually sits down and talks to them... Many are in fact highly articulate and extremely thoughtful individuals for whom terrorism is (or was) an entirely rational choice..." (Hoffman, 1998:7)

The dispute between the rationalist and psychological approach is important in understanding the root causes of terrorism, allowing experts and security professionals to identify characteristics of the threat and formulate effective counterstrategies. While the two schools may seem to fundamentally clash, an interdisciplinary explanation of terrorism may actually be the most effective way to approach the phenomenon. In a sense, these two schools can complement and complete each other.

In the Israeli setting, for example, the case of a suicide bombing is likely motivated by a combination of the rational calculations of the organization, a cost-benefit analysis made by the attackers themselves, social pressure from the attackers' peer group, and personal psychological, social, cultural, and religious motivations. The decision-making process functions on a number of levels, in which both political-rational

---

[3] For an overview of psychological, social, and rational choice theories, see Victoroff, 2005.

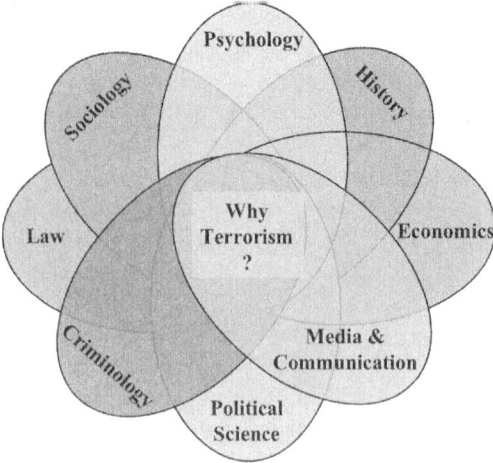

Fig. 2.1 Explanatory disciplines to terrorism

and the psychological-sociological explanations have their place, demonstrating the multidisciplinary nature of terrorism. As Crenshaw noted, even though an act of terrorism may not be wholly the result of a psychological disorder, that is not to say "the political decision to join a terrorist organization is not influenced or, in some cases, even determined by subconscious or latent psychological motives" (Crenshaw, 1998:386). It seems that only multivariable explanations based on methodologies and theories from different disciplines can adequately address the complex phenomenon of terrorism, provide explanations for the growth, development and characteristics of the phenomenon, and suggest methods for effectively dealing with terrorism (Fig. 2.1).

Explanatory Disciplines to Terrorism

Different research disciplines may be able to provide answers to fundamental questions at the core of terrorism research, such as:

Psychology

The field of psychology can provide answers to such questions as: Do terrorists have common psychological characteristics? Do terrorists have a psychological profile? Why do people become terrorists? Which people might become terrorists and which will not? Why do people join a terrorist organization and why do they leave it? When, why, and how does the personal radicalization process take place? (See Post, 1998; Raine, 1993; Hubbard, 1971).

Economics

How important are economic variables in explaining the development and motivation of terrorism? To what degree can terrorists' financial situation explain the motives for their behavior? How much does the economic factor determine the scope and characteristics of terrorism activity?[4] (See Abadie, 2004; Kahn and Weiner, 2002; Krueger and Laitin, 2008; Krueger and Maleckova, 2002; Piazza, 2006).

Sociology

How much influence does one's peer group have on the decision to join a terrorist group or the motivation to conduct acts of terrorism? How much can processes of socialization and delegitimization by society – ostracizing, discrimination, alienation, etc. – serve as variables explaining the motives of terrorism? Why does a certain population at a specific time tend to carry out terrorist attacks while another population with similar characteristics does not choose this course of action? What is the extent of the connection between terrorism and different cultures?[5] (See Bandura, 1973, 1998; Gibbs, 1989; Merari, 2004; Morgan, 2001; Webb, 2002).

Criminology

To what extent should terrorism be treated as a phenomenon in the criminal sphere? What are the differences between the characteristics of criminal and terrorist activity? What are the similarities and the differences in the organizational characteristics between terrorist and criminal organizations?[6] (See Klein et al., 2006; Klein and Maxson, 2006; Lafree, 2007).

---

[4] Several studies have focused on refuting the widely claimed link between poverty and terrorism (Harmon, 2000; Hasisi and Pedahzur, 2000; Schmid, 1983). In fact, a 2003 study by Krueger and Maleckova showed that higher-earning Palestinians were more likely to justify the use of terrorism to achieve political goals; and a 2002 study (Krueger and Maleckova, 2002) did not find a link between Hezbollah fighters and impoverished conditions – rather, they were richer and more educated than their counterparts. Another study looked at the biographies of 285 suicide bombers and found them to be richer and more educated than members of the general population (Victoroff, 2005:21).

[5] Until September 11, there were few academic studies of terrorism from a strictly sociological viewpoint. However, Bandura (1973, 1998) used social learning theory to suggest that violence follows observation and imitation of an aggressive model. Friedland (1992) cited the "frustration-aggression hypothesis" in understanding why terrorists turn to violence (as cited in Victoroff, 2005). Morgan (2001) applied the cult model to understand individual actors and group dynamics within terrorist groups.

[6] For the role of policing in counter-terrorism strategies, see Chaps. 3–5 of this volume. LaFree and Dugan (Chap. 2) also briefly discuss the comparison between rates of terrorist attacks and other types of criminal violence. The interplay and linkages between organized crime and terrorism are explored in several anthology volumes, such as Holmes (2007), among many others.

Political Science and International Relations

To what extent should terrorism be understood in rational terms (cost-benefit calculation) as an effective method intended to achieve political goals? To what extent can political terms such as sovereignty, power, authority, and social justice serve as variables to explain the phenomenon of terrorism? To what degree is the phenomenon of terrorism connected to certain ideologies or a certain form of government? To what degree does modern terrorism aim to take advantage of the liberal democratic form of government's values and traits? To what extent is the media component essential in order to explain the strategy of modern terrorism? How are the decision-making processes different in terrorist organizations than other organizations? Can terrorism be understood as a means for states to achieve their interests in the international arena? To what extent can terrorism be dealt with by using deterrent measures in general and deterring state-sponsors of terrorism in particular? (See Crenshaw, 2000; Ganor, 2005; Hoffman, 1998; Nacos, 1994).

Theology

To what extent is modern terrorism a result of religious extremism? How is incitement to terrorism carried out with the use of religious rationalizations and how can this incitement be dealt with? (See Atran, 2006; Hoffman, 1995; Juergensmeyer, 2003; Ranstorp, 1996; Rapoport, 1984).

Hence, nearly every academic research discipline has been, and will continue to be, critical in providing answers to some of the central issues that lie behind understanding the phenomenon of terrorism and the methods for dealing with it. Only this multidisciplinary approach can provide a profound understanding of the phenomenon.

The Definition of Terrorism

Growing interest in the field of terrorism and increased funding allotted to academic research and teaching budgets post-9/11 has spurred and supported the publication of hundreds of books and articles in the past few years, many professional and academic conferences, and a general flourishing of the field. Yet, six years after the world recognized the magnitude of the terrorist threat on 9/11, researchers, security professionals, politicians, jurists, and others have still not been able to agree upon its most fundamental component – *what is terrorism*?

Moreover, and somewhat surprisingly, the only consensus these individuals have reached is that it might be impossible, or even unnecessary, to reach an internationally accepted definition of terrorism.[7] Those who hold this opinion – in fact the majority in the field – usually cite the cliché "one man's terrorist is another man's freedom fighter," in order to imply that, in their opinion, the issue of definition is subjective. As such, even partial agreement regarding its content cannot be reached. Louis Henkin (1989) captured this sentiment in 1990 when he said that: "Terrorism… is not a useful legal concept."

Those who do not regard a definition as critical believe that the international system – and the security establishment in particular – can manage without consensus on the issue. They claim that terrorists, in a sense, commit regular crimes – extortion, murder, arson, and other felonies already covered by conventional criminal law. Therefore, they can be tried for committing these felonies without the need for a special criminal classification, and thus definition, for terrorism.

Needless to say, there is no shortage of proposed definitions for terrorism. Every researcher, expert, security professional, NGO, country, and politician espouses their own definition, one that likely represents a distinct world view and political stance. By the early 1980s, Schmid and Jongman had already listed 109 definitions of terrorism proposed by researchers in the field (Schmid and Jongman, 1998:5).

In their chapter in this volume, LaFree and Dugan touch upon the difficulty in reaching a consensus on a definition of terrorism given its controversial and highly politicized nature. It is within this context that they note the U.S. was reluctant to define the attacks by Contra rebels in Nicaragua as terrorism, while regarding practically all violence in Iraq and Afghanistan as such. They further note that more inclusive definitions of terrorism are often preferred by businesses or private think tanks that are collecting data for the purpose of risk assessment, as such an approach ultimately benefits their clients (LaFree and Dugan, in this volume).

Among the hundreds of definitions of terrorism that have been accepted throughout the years, some contain conceptual and phrasing problems (Hoffman, 2004:3). Many researchers note that the only certainty regarding terrorism is the pejorative manner in which the word is generally used and associated (Hoffman, 2006:23; Horgan, 2005:1). As such, when scholars, politicians, or activists describe and analyze the activities of alleged terrorist organizations, they very often use alternative terms that bear more positive connotations, such as guerilla or underground movements, revolutionaries, militias, militants, commando groups, national liberation movements, etc. (Hoffman, 2006:28).

Many in the Western world have accepted the premise that terrorism and national liberation are located on two opposite ends of a spectrum legitimizing the use of violence. The struggle for "national liberation" is, allegedly, located on the positive

---

[7] In a presentation on the definition of terrorism to the UK Parliament in March 2007, Lord Carlile quoted David Tucker from *Skirmishes at the Edge of the Empire*, stating that: "Above the gates of hell is the warning that all that enter should abandon hope. Less dire but to the same effect is the warning given to those who try to define terrorism" (See *http://www.tamilnation.org/terrorism/uk070315carlile.htm*), for a reporter's perspective see Kinsley, 2001; see also Levitt (1986), in which he claims a definition for terrorism is no easier to find than the Holy Grail.

and justified end of the violence spectrum, while terrorism is its unjust and negative polar opposite. Within this framework, it would be impossible for a specific organization to be considered both a terrorist group and a national liberation movement, as Senator Henry Jackson claims:

> "The thought that one man's terrorist is another man's freedom fighter is unacceptable. Freedom fighters or revolutionaries do not blow up buses with noncombatants; terrorists and murderers do. Freedom fighters do not kidnap and slaughter students, terrorists and murders do…" (As cited in Netanyahu, 1987:18)

There is little basis for the claim that "freedom fighters" cannot carry out acts of terrorism and murder. This approach unintentionally plays into the hands of terrorists, who claim that since they are acting to expel who they consider to be a foreign occupier, they cannot also be considered terrorists. However, many freedom fighters in modern history committed crimes and purposely targeted innocent civilians. The difference between "terrorism" and "freedom fighting" is not a subjective distinction based on the observer's point of view. Rather, it derives from identifying the perpetrator's goals and methods of operation. Terrorism is a means - a tool - for achieving an end, and that "end" can very well be liberating the homeland from the yoke of a foreign occupier. An organization can be, at the same time, both a national liberation movement and a terrorist group.

It is not the specific goal – whether "freedom fighting" or another legitimate political objective – that distinguishes a group as a terrorist organization or justifies its activities. Many groups, however, such as the Muslim World League, do not clearly make this distinction. In a special publication from 2001, the Muslim World League states that:

> "Terrorism is an outrageous attack carried out either by individuals, groups or states against the human being (his religion, life, intellect, property and honor). It includes all forms of intimidation, harm, threatening, killing without a just cause… so as to terrify and horrify people by hurting them or by exposing their lives, liberty, security or conditions to danger… or exposing a national or natural resource to danger" (Al-Mukarramah, 2001).

In presenting the activities that constitute terrorism as being committed "without a just cause," the Muslim World League's definition infers that such acts committed *with* a just cause are not considered terrorism. Such definitions are typical of attempts to create confusion between the means and the end, ultimately foiling any possibility of reaching a consensus on a definition.

Since September 11, international terrorism has emerged on the top of national and international security agendas, widely perceived as a severe and very real threat to world peace. It is a threat that necessitates international alignment and cooperation on an unprecedented level. Such a high degree of cooperation cannot be established or sustained however without agreement over the most basic common denominator – the definition of terrorism.

Outside intelligence and military circles, the effectiveness of other apparatuses essential in countering the terrorist threat is dependent upon a clear, broad, and objective definition of terrorism that can be accepted internationally. Such a definition is essential in order to: disrupt the financing of terrorism, respond to states and communities that support terrorism, prevent recruitment and incitement of terrorist operatives, and establish legal measures and guidelines to both outlawed terrorist organizations and activities, and arrest and extradite alleged terrorists. Above all else, the international community must establish a binding normative system to determine what is allowed and not allowed – what is legitimate and not legitimate – when violence is used for political objectives. A definition that would address all these requirements is:

Terrorism is the deliberate use of violence aimed against civilians in order to achieve political goals (nationalistic, socioeconomic, ideological, religious, etc.)

In defining terrorism within the above framework, it is important to note that a terrorist act would not be classified as a "regular" criminal activity warranting the application of criminal legal norms. Rather, terrorism would be viewed as an act of war, and the countermeasures mounted against it would too be conducted in accordance to the norms and laws of war.

The Israeli High Court of Justice has itself struggled with the distinction between criminal acts and acts of war, reflecting the tension facing those studying and responding to terrorism today. According to Justice Cheshin, "a judge's job is difficult. It is sevenfold as difficult when he comes to deal with a hideously murderous attack such as we have in front of us. The murderer's action is inherently – though not within the framework of or as part of the formal definition – an act of war, and an act that is inherently an act of war is answered with an act of war, in the ways of war" (Abd Al-Rahim Hassan Nazzal and others vs. the Commander of the IDF forces in Judea and Samaria, 1994). In a different verdict, the judge ruled that a "criminal code created for daily life in human society does not have an answer for the question" (Federman and others vs. the Attorney General, 1993).

The debate over whether terrorism should be considered a criminal act or an act of war remains strong among academics, NGOs, and counter terrorism professionals. Without consensus on the issue, states have applied their own policies in trying and convicting alleged terrorist suspects – whether as criminals or combatants. Despite the fact that criminal acts can consist of the same actions as terrorism – murder, arson, and extortion - terrorism, unlike an average criminal act, threatens the internal social order, personal and national security, world peace, and the economy.[8] As previously noted, acts of terrorism are intended to achieve various political goals and could thus be considered arguably more severe than criminal violations.

In addition, as international law expert and terrorism prosecutor Ruth Wedgwood has argued, criminal law may be "too weak a weapon" to counter terrorism, as destroying terrorist infrastructure and networks requires diplomacy, use of force, and criminal

---

[8] Resolution 1566 (2004) adopted by the Security Council in its 5053rd meeting, on Oct. 8 2004: "…Reaffirming that terrorism in all its forms and manifestations constitutes one of the most serious threats to peace and security. Considering that acts of terrorism seriously impair the enjoyment of human rights and threaten the social and economic development of all states, they undermine global stability and prosperity." (See: http://daccessdds.un.org/doc/UNDOC/GEN/N04/542/82/PDF/N0454282.pdf?OpenElement.)

law combined. She adds that the restrictions embedded in a criminal justice system make sense in civil society where deterrence is a factor, but this may not apply in a fight against a highly networked terrorist organization (Wedgwood and Roth, 2004).[9]

Bruce Hoffman points to a fundamental difference between a criminal and a terrorist when he asserts that while a criminal seeks personal material goals, a terrorist usually sees himself as an altruist acting for and in the name of many others (Hoffman, 2006:37). Therefore, a terrorist may be perceived as posing greater danger through his actions, since he is significantly more willing than a criminal to sacrifice in order to achieve his goals – even to the point of self-sacrifice in certain situations.

The criminal code in itself does not serve as an adequate platform to define terrorism. The laws of war are better suited as a framework for defining and dealing with terrorism, since the phenomenon is a violent action intended to achieve political goals, often involving the use of pseudo-military methods of operation. By basing the definition of terrorism on an established system of norms and laws, already included in international conventions and accepted by most of the countries in the world, the international community is more likely to reach a broad international agreement on the definition of terrorism – a basic tool in the joint international struggle against terrorism.

At the core of the Geneva and The Hague conventions are rules differentiating between two types of personnel involved in military activity: "combatants," military personnel who deliberately target enemy military personnel; and "war criminals," military personnel who, among other actions forbidden by the laws of war, deliberately target civilians. Currently, the moral differentiation between a legitimate combatant and a war criminal is based on the attacked target (military or civilian), and, at least in principle, only applies to state entities and their armies and not to substate entities.

In the Israeli setting for example, a Palestinian, considered part of a subnational group, who is involved in a deliberate attack against an Israeli military target, will receive the same treatment and punishment as a Palestinian who deliberately attacks a civilian target. Since there is no distinction made between the two, despite the difference in their targets, the degree of international legitimacy or condemnation of both cases will likely continue to be dependant on the supporter or condemner's political stance and not necessarily on the character or target of the deliberate operation – its legality under applicable rules and norms. The American government, for example, classifies attacks against its troops in Iraq as terrorist attacks, as it does the October 2000 attack against the USS Cole or the attack against the American military barracks in Dhahran (June 1996).

In fact, in an attempt to expand the definition of terrorism to include attacks against soldiers, the U.S. State Department's definition states that terrorism is the

---

[9] Ruth Wedgewood and Human Rights Watch Director Kenneth Roth debate the US's treatment of terrorist suspects – as combatants versus criminals – in a series of articles in *Foreign Affairs* (See Roth, 2004; Wedgwood and Roth, 2004).

deliberate use of violence against "non-combatant targets," which includes both civilians and military personnel not on the battle field.[10] While it is natural for victims of terrorism to adopt this broad-based definition, terrorist organizations and their supporters can legitimately argue that in seeking to achieve their political goals, they cannot reasonably be required to either not confront military personnel entirely, or do so only when they are fully armed and prepared for war. They claim that they must be given the right to attack and surprise soldiers whatever the circumstances.

In applying these considerations, the U.S. State Department's definition of terrorism could not successfully serve as a common denominator leading to international agreement. It is only in reducing the scope of the definition to the deliberate targeting of civilians – as opposed to "non-combatants" – that may solve this problem, enabling the establishment of a clear moral boundary that should not be crossed. A terrorist act would be considered, in a sense, the equivalent for a substate entity to a war crime committed by a state.[11]

During a state of war, normative principles and the laws of war forbid the deliberate targeting of civilians but allow deliberate attacks on an enemy's military personnel (in accordance with other applicable regulations). Similarly, in modern asymmetric warfare, a normative rule must be set to address limitations on *substate actors*, differentiating between guerilla warfare (violence against military personnel) and terrorism (violence against civilians) – just as the rules of war differentiate between legitimate combatants and war criminals. For the purpose of defining terrorism, it is not significant what goal the organization aspires to achieve (as long as it is political); both the terrorist and the guerilla fighter may aspire to achieve the same goals. However, they each chose a different path – a different means – in order to realize these goals.

Defining terrorism is critical in ensuring that the same normative standards currently enforced on states are applicable to nonstate actors, defining when their use of violence is permissible and when it is prohibited. Paradoxically, what is currently prohibited for states is not yet prohibited for organizations. Defining terrorism does not raise or lower the obligation of states to behave normatively and certainly does not place additional legal burdens upon them. It simply makes organizations accountable for their actions under the same value system currently obligating states.

---

[10] Terrorism is defined by the U.S. State Department as: "premeditated, politically motivated violence perpetrated against noncombatant targets by sub-national groups or clandestine agents." (from the 22 U.S.C., 2656f(d)(2); See http://www.state.gov/s/ct/rls/crt/2005/65353.htm.)

[11] The UN short legal definition of terrorism, proposed by terrorism expert Alex P. Schmid, states that an act of terrorism is the "peacetime equivalent of a war crime." While such a definition does not consider terrorism an act of war, in drawing a parallel with a war crime it notes the importance of the target (civilian vs. military) in legitimizing acts of violence. (See: http://www.unodc.org/unodc/terrorism_definitions.html.)

Reaching a broad international agreement regarding the definition of terrorism may require the international community to apply laws of war that forbid the deliberate targeting of civilians, but allow for the deliberate attack (in accordance with the other regulations) of an enemy's military personnel. The definition proposed in this chapter may be capable of eliciting a broad base of support from many countries and organizations, both because it is based on already accepted international norms, and because it seemingly provides subnational organizations the possibility of legitimately using violence in order to achieve their goals.

Such a definition would not allow for the artificial distinction that is often made between "bad" terrorism and "good" or "tolerable" terrorism. It instead adheres to the principle that "terrorism is terrorism is terrorism," no matter who carries it out – a Muslim, Christian, Jew, or member of any other religion. Terrorism would be considered an illegitimate and forbidden method of operation in all cases, under all circumstances. The ideological or cultural background of the perpetrators; and the religious, political, social or economic motives of the act; would all be irrelevant in classifying an act of terrorism.

Many view the effort to achieve a broad international agreement on terrorism as hopeless and naïve. However, Security Council Resolution 1566, which was unanimously accepted by Council members in October 2004, may be a basis for hope that countries will overcome prior disputes, rise above their own interests, and reach an agreement in the near future regarding the international definition of terrorism. Resolution 1566, without serving as the definition itself, already establishes one basic principle on which an international definition can be built. It stipulates that terrorism is a crime against civilians, which in no circumstance can be justified by political, philosophical, ideological, racial, ethnic, religious, or other considerations.[12]

Modern Terrorism

Descriptions of typical terrorist operations and their common characteristics are often included in proposed definitions of modern terrorism – particularly in those that address the fear and anxiety created by terrorist acts. In such definitions, terrorism is presented as a form of violent activity (or threat of violence) that

---

[12] Resolution 1566 (2004): "Condemns in the strongest terms all acts of terrorism irrespective of their motivation, whenever and by whomsoever committed, as one of the most serious threats to peace and security...Recalls that criminal acts, including against civilians committed with the intent to cause death or serious bodily injury or taking hostages with the purpose to provoke a state of terror in the general public or in a group of persons or particular persons intimidate a population or compel a government or an offences within the scope of and as defined in the international conventions and protocols relating to terrorism, are under no circumstances justifiable by considerations of a political, philosophical, ideological, racial, ethnic religious or other similar nature and calls upon all states to prevent such acts...". (See: http://daccessdds.un.org/doc/UNDOC/GEN/N04/542/82/PDF/N0454282.pdf?OpenElement)

intends to frighten a group of people beyond the actual victims (Horgan, 2005:1). After reviewing the development of the definition of terrorism and examining a variety of definitions, Bruce Hoffman reaches the following conclusion in his important book, *Inside Terrorism*:

> "We may therefore now attempt to define terrorism as the deliberate creation and exploitation of fear through violence or the threat of violence in the pursuit of political change… terrorism is specifically designed to have far-reaching psychological effects beyond the immediate victim(s) or object of the terrorist attack…" (Hoffman, 2006:40).

Definitions that refer to terrorism as an act intended to instill fear and anxiety in the public are generally based on the literal meaning and historical use of the term "terrorism," its application dating back to the French civil war.[13] Such definitions also rely on what is perceived to be the primary operational tactic of modern terrorism – psychological warfare – which seeks to achieve political goals by instilling fear and anxiety among its target population.

While definitions vary widely, there is a general consensus among most leading scholars as to the essential nature of the terrorist threat; researchers will rarely dispute the importance fear and anxiety play in *understanding* the phenomenon of modern terrorism. However, it is important to note that resulting fear and anxiety may not be an essential variable in *defining* a terrorist attack. In order to ensure that acts are objectively classified as terrorist attacks, an accepted definition must, in application, serve as a checklist of components.

Based on the definition proposed in the previous section, if an act is not violent, does not deliberately target civilians, or does not attempt to achieve a political goal, then it is not a terrorist attack. Adding the element of fear and anxiety to the definition – essentially putting it on the checklist of required components – significantly changes the term's application. If an attack, which would otherwise be considered an act of terrorism, does not aim to frighten, but rather only seeks to achieve concrete, tangible objectives – such as the release of prisoners or the assassination of a leading political figure – would the action not be considered terrorism? Similarly, a nuclear attack aimed at eradicating the majority of the population or contaminating an extensive area – which ultimately seeks to disable the state and prevent it from operating as an independent political entity – would be widely considered a terrorist attack, even though instilling fear and anxiety is not its primary purpose.

Since such circumstances and scenarios can reasonably exist, the "fear and anxiety element" may not be necessary in *defining* terrorism; rather, it is valuable in *explaining* the modus operandi of a significant portion of modern terrorist attacks.

---

[13] The term "terrorism" comes from the Latin *terrere*, to cause to tremble. The term became popularized during the "Reign of Terror" carried out by the revolutionary government in France from 1793 to 1794 (Juergensmeyer, 2003: 5).

Indeed, modern terrorism is not necessarily about the numbers. In fact, most modern terrorist attacks, while violent in nature, generally produce limited damage or casualties.[14] Instead, they rely on psychological warfare as a tool in achieving their goals, creating fear and anxiety among the general population. In many cases, a terrorist attack is random, aimed not at someone specific, but rather a group that shares a common trait and symbolizes the organization's broader target (Americans, Israelis, "infidels," Westerners, etc.). By simultaneously transmitting several messages, these attacks intensify the sense of anxiety felt by the target group, which leads civilians to pressure decision makers and their government into changing policies and agreeing to terrorists' demands. Some of the messages terrorist organizations aim to send through their attacks include:

1. *Uncertainty* – The randomness of the attack is supposed to instill a sense of uncertainty in the public regarding "safe behavior," prompting fear that anyone could be the next victim (Horgan, 2005:3).
2. *Vulnerability* – A terrorist attack can take place anywhere, anytime, making all citizens feel vulnerable.
3. *Helplessness* – The state's security apparatus cannot foil or prevent attacks, or protect civilians.
4. *Personalization* – You or someone close to you may not have been hurt in a recent attack, but it could very well be you the next time, since the victims have the same profile as you (Ganor, 2005:256).
5. *Disproportional price* – The price the individual must pay due to his government's policy is very high. For that reason he must act to change national/international priorities in a way that will serve the terrorist's objectives.
6. *Vengeance* – The citizen suffers due to the government's actions against the terrorist organization and its supporters, and for this reason it is in his best interest to pressure the government to avoid this activity.

Such attacks aim to create anxiety among the target group at a level disproportionate to the actual capabilities of the terrorist organization, forcing members of the target population to reprioritize and shift their concerns from that of national security to personal security. The target population perceives a growing threat from terrorism, which may be viewed by the public as largely fueled by the government's supposedly dangerous policies. As political tension and criticism against the government in the target country mount, according to the strategy of modern terrorism, the public will pressure decision makers to change their policies in a manner that will suit the interests and goals of the terrorist organizations, or call for a change in administration that will establish policies more favorable to terrorist groups.

In order to create this effect of fear, terrorist organizations often choose to escalate their activity in such a manner as to shock the public. According to Crenshaw, a review

---

[14]LaFree and Dugan note that over 53% of terrorist organizations from the Global Terrorism Database included in their study (1974–2004) have never produced a single fatality (LaFree and Dugan, in this volume).

of the history of terrorism reveals that terrorists have purposely chosen targets considered taboo or unpredictable in order to attract international media coverage (Crenshaw, 1998:14–15). The media component is central to modern terrorism's strategy. Without media coverage, a terrorist organization has little opportunity to convey its message, let alone shock or scare its target population. The success of a modern terrorist campaign is arguably dependent on the amount of publicity it receives; the "journalist and television camera are the terrorist's best friends" (Laqueur, 1987).

Terrorism and Traditional Crime

In seeking funding to support ongoing operations or infrastructure, terrorist organizations in Latin America, Europe, the Middle East, and the Far East have increasingly come to rely on "traditional" criminal activities, such as drug trafficking, counterfeiting, petty crime, human trafficking, and extortion (Vidino and Emerson, 2006; Mili, 2006). In fact, over the last three decades, law enforcement agencies have reported increased cooperation between terrorist organizations and criminal actors and activities – including attacks that have been financed through illegal crimes and suspects who have been prosecuted for crimes in which proceeds were directed to international terrorist organizations like Hezbollah and Al-Qaeda (Noble, 2003).

Growing expenses associated with terrorist activity, such as payments to organization personnel, transportation, accommodation, training, and procurement of weapons, have served as incentive for terrorist organizations to get involved in common crime. These activities only further exacerbate the danger posed by terrorist organizations to the global economy and to the safety and wellbeing of the world's population. By counterfeiting currency, for example, a terrorist organization can damage a country's economy while it raises funds. Similarly, by producing and smuggling drugs to certain countries, an organization can cause considerable harm to the local population and simultaneously finance its activities.

In the early 1970s, terrorist organizations, particularly those not supported financially by states, funded their activities through criminal activities such as bank robberies, kidnappings for ransom, and blackmail. Terrorist organizations, such as the Red Brigades in Italy, cooperated with criminal elements, enlisting them into the ranks of their organization. However, in the late 1970s and more so in the early 1980s, terrorist organizations realized that drug trafficking was far more lucrative than other routine criminal activities, leading to a phenomenon known as "narco-terrorism."[15]

Terrorist organizations have been involved in producing and selling narcotics throughout the world – in Latin America (Colombia, Peru, Cuba, Bolivia); in Asia and

---

[15] To illustrate the amount of money involved, a survey conducted by the United Nations Office for Drug Control and Crime Prevention described the production, trafficking, and sales of illicit drugs to be an estimated $400-billion-a-year industry. A 2005 UN report estimated that global drug trade generated an estimated $322 billion in 2003, greater than the gross domestic product of 88% of the countries in the world (Pollard, 2005).

the Middle East (Sri Lanka, Lebanon, Afghanistan, India, the Philippines, Pakistan); and even in Western countries such as Italy, Spain, Ireland, and the United States.

Drug trafficking by terrorist groups in Columbia is of particular concern to western governments. According to reports from the U.S. Bureau of Narcotics and Law Enforcement affairs, revenues earned from narcotics cultivation, taxation, and distribution have accounted for at least half the funding used to support terrorist activities by two of the country's largest terrorist groups – the Revolutionary Armed Forces of Colombia (FARC) and the United Self-Defense Groups of Colombia (AUC). The State Department estimates that the FARC receives $300 million a year from drug sales to finance its terrorist activities.[16]

The tri-border area (TBA), or "triple frontier" as it is known, centered along the borders of Paraguay, Argentina, and Brazil, has been widely recognized as another hotbed for terrorism financing and activity, particularly to groups such as Hezbollah and Hamas. Without strict border controls, the area serves as a haven for drugs and arms trafficking, counterfeiting, smuggling and other illegal activities. Tens of millions of dollars are estimated to have been transferred to groups through illegal remittances and other illegal activities, according to investigations by local police forces (Madani, 2002; Tri-border Transfers "funding terror," 2006).

Most terror organizations, however, are not directly involved in actually growing or producing drugs. They are tasked primarily with protecting the drugs and ensuring the safety of growers and producers. They also are active in smuggling narcotics to the marketing centers in countries where the drugs are distributed (Hudson, 2003:24). These organizations usually have a diverse network of contacts, enabling them to cross borders via indirect routes and smuggle weapons, ammunition, and various other products. Terrorist organizations can use the same routes and network used by their supporters in order to smuggle drugs.

In some cases, drugs have been used to recruit foreign activists, in a sense bribing them to execute terrorist attacks. In these cases, the activists, who are not members of the organization, are enlisted in order to carry out attacks on behalf of the terror organizations, sometimes unbeknownst to the activists themselves, in return for a regular supply of drugs.[17] In other cases, terrorist organizations supply their members with drugs in order to increase their dependence on the organization and encourage obedience to its leaders.[18] Some terrorist organizations refer to the distribution of drugs as an alternative form of attack, since drug consumption can harm the national morale and weaken the ability of the population to cope with crises.

---

[16] See Deborah McCarthy's testimony before the Committee on the Judiciary United States Senate, May 20, 2003, *"Narco-Terrorism: International Drug Trafficking and Terrorism – A Dangerous Mix."*

[17] For example, On August 28, 1971, a Dutch citizen, Henrietta Hundemeir, was arrested in Israel with a suitcase containing a timer-activated bomb with a barometric altimeter. The bomb was meant to explode in the El Al aircraft in which she herself was flying to Israel. Hundemeir was enlisted in Yugoslavia by a member of the "Popular Front for the Liberation of Palestine," who became her close friend by supplying her with drugs and using them with her.

[18] One example is the "Weatherman" organization, which was responsible for terrorist attacks in the U.S. at the end of the 1960s and the beginning of the 1970s. The group perceived drug use as a part of the revolutionary process.

Global Jihadi Terrorism

Terrorism is a dynamic phenomenon that develops over time, gradually changing its shape and activities. It is carried out by various organizations in the service of different ideologies. Despite the fact that various local terrorist groups have operated in the international arena in the past decade, there is growing recognition by scholars and the intelligence community that the current international terrorist threat does not come from organizations motivated by nationalist grievances or separatist goals (such as the IRA, ETA, Fatah, LTTE, PKK, and others). Instead, the main threat is that of radical Islamic terrorism primarily aimed at promoting a radical religious world view.[19] Such groups are motivated by what they perceive as a divine command, making them potentially more dangerous than groups motivated by other causes. Hoffman stresses that while religion was an inseparable component of many terrorist organizations in the past, the dominant motivation for their actions was political rather than religious. This is not the case with Al-Qaeda and other radical Islamic organizations today. For them, religion is the most important component defining their activities, ideology, characteristics, and recruitment methods (Hoffman, 2006:82).

According to James Thomson, "religions are very effective at guiding in-group morality and out-group hatred. They permit the take-over of groups by disenfranchised young males, they minimize the fear of death by spreading the belief in an afterlife reward for those who are dying in a holy war, etc." (Thomson, 2003:82).

Radical Islamic terrorism, part of the Global Jihad movement, includes acts perpetrated by many organizations, groups, and cells around the world. The movement is headed by Al-Qaeda, which, despite the many setbacks it has endured since September 11, 2001, is still capable of carrying out "direct attacks" through activists reporting directly to its authority or "indirect attacks" through proxy organizations – radical Islamic terrorist organizations and networks that share a similar fundamentalist Islamic ideology, aspirations, and interests. Some of these organizations, such as Egyptian, Bangladeshi, and Afghan Jihadi groups, were established by Osama bin Laden under the umbrella of his "International Islamic Front for Jihad Against Jews and Crusaders" (February 1998).

Some of these organizations have made pacts or commitments to bin Laden over the years, such as the Egyptian Al-Jama'a Al-Islamiya and the GSPC (currently referred to as Al-Qaeda of the Maghreb). However, the most significant trend of the past several years has been the phenomenon of "homegrown terrorism." Lone activists and local radical groups of Muslims, who either immigrated to Western countries

---

[19] There are also terrorist organizations that combine religious grievances with national-political motivations, such as Hamas. On the one hand, Hamas derives its ideology from the same narrative and background as Al-Qaeda, based on the early religious global ideology of the Muslim Brotherhood. At the same time though, Hamas seeks to achieve the nationalistic goal of destroying Israel and creating a Palestinian state in its place.

(first, second, or third generation) or converted to Islam in their country of origin, become inspired by the Global Jihad movement, leading them to carry out terrorist attacks.

Al-Qaeda, its allies in the Global Jihad movement, other radical Islamic terrorist organizations, and the radical Islamic networks and cells of the West, all believe in one divine mission, which calls upon them to spread their radical beliefs throughout the world (Sageman, 2004:1). In seeking to achieve this mission, they believe it is permissible and necessary to make use of violence and terrorism, and that they are fighting a "defensive war" that allows them to use drastic measures. One perspective shared by several researchers is that this defensive war is not actually pitted against American or Western imperialism, as Global Jihad organizations commonly claim. Rather, the "fight against the West" is used to help mobilize and recruit activists, arguably acting as "lip service" by Al-Qaeda. It also serves to at least express their concern over every aspect of modernization, including democratic forms of government, liberal values, and even modern technology that threaten the way of life they strive for – a radical Islamic caliphate governed by Sharia law.

It is also important to note that the threat of Global Jihad is not, as many tend to think, a war between Islam and other religions. Rather, it can be understood as a war of cultures – the culture of radical Islam against the outside world, or the culture of radical Islam against the culture of the "infidels," as Islamists call all those who do not share their world view.

Many in the radical Jihadi movement recognize that they will not be able to succeed in their worldwide campaign in the near future. Therefore they aim, as a first stage, to create localized radical Islamic revolutions, primarily in Arab and Islamic countries. In fact, the majority of Global Jihad attacks over the past several years occurred in countries of the Arab or Islamic world, such as Egypt, Jordan, Iraq, Turkey, Algeria, Morocco, Saudi Arabia, Yemen, and Indonesia. The goal of such attacks is to destabilize local regimes and create political unrest, establishing the conditions necessary for radical movements to take control of the country's government. A large percentage of these attacks target tourist destinations, serving a dual purpose – they cause Western causalities and damage a primary source of income for the targeted Muslim country.

Such attacks seriously undermine a country's ability to provide critical services to its citizens, ultimately leading to criticism, unrest, and government instability. Attacks against Western targets – such as in London, Madrid, and even on September 11th – served the same purpose; they deter Western countries from being involved in an Islamic campaign or providing military assistance and economic support to nonfundamentalist Islamic governments.

Consistent with the method of modern terrorism and Global Jihad strategy, fear of terrorist attacks felt by Americans, Brits, and other western citizens is meant to translate into pressure on decision-makers to change their policies and adopt a policy of isolationism, consequently weakening nonradical Muslim governments that would otherwise be supported by western governments. A significant achievement of this strategy was the shift in the Spanish elections following the series of terrorist attacks on four commuter trains in Madrid in March 2004, in which 191 people were killed and over 1,500 injured. The attacks came three days before general elections, apparently leading to the defeat of the incumbent party that had been leading in opinion polls. The new government decided to pull out Spanish troops deployed in Iraq. Without western support, aid, and involvement, it is difficult for nonradical Arab and Muslim governments to stay in power, which ultimately promotes the strategic goals of the Global Jihad movement.

The dynamic nature of the terrorism phenomenon has also been represented by Al-Qaeda's changing methods of operation and organizational structure. Until the September 11th attacks, Al-Qaeda operated as an organized hierarchy with a top leadership level, a mid-rank level, and a lower level of activists carrying out orders and directives from above. As such, the September 11th attacks were carried out as a result of an organized decision-making process and complex preparations over a long period of time.

However, Al-Qaeda experienced a shift in organizational structure post 9/11, partly in response to the American military campaign that followed the attacks. The occupation of Afghanistan, the destruction of the organization's administrative and operational infrastructure, loss of support from the Taliban and a significant amount of manpower, and the demolition of training camps, recruitment offices and facilities, effectively forced Al-Qaeda to change its structure and method of operation. Without autonomous territory in Afghanistan from which to operate, or freedom of movement for the organization's leaders and activists, the hierarchical structure of the organization and the control level of the organization's leadership over its activists were severely damaged.

Apart from direct, organized, and hierarchical processes of carrying out attacks, following the campaign in Afghanistan, the majority of Global Jihad attacks were carried out by affiliate organizations belonging to bin Laden's network, part of the "International Islamic Front for Jihad Against Jews and Crusaders." Other attacks were carried out by independent Jihadist organizations that actively support Al-Qaeda's world view. Such "indirect attacks" are often initiated by Al-Qaeda's leadership, and on certain occasions are even supported by Al-Qaeda on the operational level. Ultimately though, the attacks are perpetrated by organizations functioning as proxies of Al-Qaeda.

In the past several years, Al-Qaeda has undergone an additional developmental process. In addition to its reliance on proxy organizations to conduct terror attacks, Al-Qaeda has focused on spreading its ideology through international media, mosques, and Islamic community centers, and – most significantly – through the world wide web. The organization seeks to inspire young Muslims around the world, and especially in Western countries, to perpetrate attacks in their immediate environment. This phenomenon, known as "homegrown terrorism," is the current trend in radical Islamic terrorism. It works to influence the hearts and brainwash the minds of many young people around the world – first- and second-generation Muslim immigrants, converts to Islam, and others – creating a radicalization process within various Muslim communities.

This method of operation is not a substitute for direct attacks in the 9/11 model or even for indirect attacks through proxies; rather it functions in addition to these methods. Homegrown terrorism constitutes a dangerous threat to western society because it is carried out by Western citizens in their own countries. These local activists have a clear advantage over external actors: they are embedded within these societies, know the societies' weak points better than others, can move about freely, know the local language, and operate alone or as part of small local networks that are often very difficult to infiltrate.

Marc Sageman explains how such networks are assembled:

> "A group of people can be viewed as a network, a collection of nodes connected through links. Some nodes are more popular and are attached to more links, connecting them to other more isolated nodes. These more connected nodes, called hubs, are important components of a terrorist network" (Sageman, 2004:137).

As earlier noted, the internet serves as a critical modern technology that in many cases connects various nodes of a terrorist network. Radical Islamic internet websites, blogs, forums, and chat rooms create virtual radical Islamic communities, facilitating the spread of materials of incitement, supporting the radicalization process and bridging geographic barriers. The internet allows such radical activists to circumvent censorship and prepare recruits to carry out attacks. Instead of the physical training facilities it lost in Afghanistan, Al-Qaeda has begun using "cyber replacements" in order to recruit and train terrorists. The internet provides the organization direct access to a much larger pool of potential activists, all without the ability of government authorities to effectively monitor or thwart their activities (Jessee, 2006:380).

Another source of concern stemming from the dynamic processes of modern terrorism is the possible use by Global Jihad organizations of nonconventional measures (CBRN) in their attacks. Today, the world is essentially witnessing an extended process of transition from modern terrorism to postmodern terrorism.[20] This transition is already apparent in the use of various poisons by radical Islamic activists in their attacks, such as attempts to use ricin and cyanide, and even more so in the dangerous phenomenon of using chlorine in mass casualty attacks, such as in Iraq in 2007. While studies indicate that past and current use of CBRN measures or weapons of mass destruction (WMD) by terrorist groups is actually quite rare,[21] many in the intelligence and academic community expect the trend will continue and even grow as radical Islamic terrorist organizations, who see themselves as fighting a total war to save Islam from the infidels – and do not hesitate to commit suicide in carrying out their attacks – will imitate these methods in an attempt to maximize the number of casualties in their attacks and heighten anxiety among the target population (Campbell, 2000:17–49).

---

[20] For definition of post-modern terrorism see (Ganor, 2005b).

[21] Of the more than 82,000 attacks analyzed in their database study, Lafree and Dugan found only 1.3% used weapons of mass destruction, which by their adopted definition includes nuclear, biological, and chemical weapons in addition to guided missiles and sophisticated explosives intended to kill a large number of people and to create mass disruption.

Terrorism and the Democratic State

The threat posed by the Global Jihad movement is not limited to its dissemination of radical and uncompromising ideology, its willingness to commit suicide attacks, or even the possibility of its use of nonconventional weapons. Terrorist organizations pose an additional danger to liberal democratic states, which must protect the lives of their citizens while still maintaining the liberal values and democratic character of the country. Modern terrorist organizations perpetrate a large number of their attacks within the territories of democratic states or against their interests. In fact, in comparing the distribution of terrorist attacks within countries classified under four different levels of democracy (fully democratic, nearly democratic, mixed regimes, and mostly autocratic), Lafree and Dugan find that "fully democratic countries experience the most constant stream of attacks" in a comparative series.

It is in a democratic state, in which the population has the ability to change the regime or force it to change its policies to reflect the will of the people, that an act of terrorism holds the most significance. Only in a democratic state is there a mass-media free of censorship, which constitutes an essential component in modern terrorism strategy and serves to transmit a terrorist organization's various messages, particularly those of intimidation.

A state's liberal democratic values essentially limit its ability to utilize all available measures in thwarting terrorism. Terrorist organizations are aware of the fact that total efficiency in fighting terrorism, in many cases, runs contrary to democratic liberal values. A liberal democratic society is required to selectively choose measures to thwart terrorism, ensuring such measures do not harm innocent civilians or undermine values of equality among all citizens. Such measures cannot subject specific subgroups to unequal treatment on the basis of their ethnicity or religion. Freedom of movement, freedom of speech, the individual's right to protect their body and possessions – all these are pillars of a liberal-democratic society, but, in effect, they limit the measures democratic states can use in the fight against terrorism (Bandura, 1998:166).

Many view terrorism as a form of asymmetric warfare in which a nonstate actor fights a state that is relatively stronger in terms of its military, economic, and intelligence capabilities. However, contrary to the traditional David-and-Goliath style confrontation, the balance of power between the two actors does not necessarily favor the state. The state (Goliath) is actually bound and shackled by its liberal beliefs and values, and undermining these values would constitute a victory for a terror organization. The state is unable to utilize its relative advantage in cutting-edge technologies, fire power, or military and economic resources, since the fight against a terrorist group does not necessarily supply defined targets, or high-powered attacks by state actors against terrorist targets could harm those with no connection to a terrorist group. A form of reverse asymmetry is established as a result: Goliath (the state) is bound by his hands and feet, while David (the substate actor) is exempt from all moral or legal restraints.

Schmid summarizes the dilemma as follows:

> "We must make a difficult decision: do we wish to sacrifice some of our democratic values in order to be more efficient against terrorism or must we suffer a certain level of terrorism in order to preserve civil rights that we hold dear?" (Schmid, 1993:15).

It seems that the population of a democratic state is willing to tolerate a certain level of terrorism without demanding decision makers take severe steps against perpetrators, so long as terrorism serves as no more than an irritant. However, when terrorism becomes more than a nuisance – when the population's daily life is affected – massive pressure is placed on the government to use all possible means to defeat the threat (Gal-Or, 1991:144), sometimes at the risk of undermining democratic values. Therefore, in addition to the danger modern terrorism poses in terms of human lives, terror attacks can also damage a state's liberal democratic values.

The Economic Ramifications of Terrorism

Modern terrorism also has a high economic price. In examining the economic effects of mass-casualty terror attacks, one should differentiate between two types of effects – direct and indirect. Direct economic effects include, inter alia, compensation for direct damage caused by an attack, including damage to property or from personal injuries. This cost is likely to be paid by insurance companies or directly by the government through compensation payments or a national insurance system, as is customary in Israel. In addition to the direct damage, however, an attack usually causes wide-scale collateral damage that can sometimes be greater than the direct damage. This damage is generally the result of the fear and anxiety that terror attacks create among the population. The "personalization" process, which causes people to feel there is a good chance they will be the next victims of a terrorist attack, naturally influences their behavior. People may avoid traveling abroad for a certain period of time, in particular to those countries where an attack has occurred. They may also avoid air travel in general or congregating in tourist sites. One's local surroundings are perceived to be more familiar and therefore safer. Long trips may seem fraught with unnecessary danger. Such emotional effects influence world tourism and air travel.

These two industries were badly hit following the 9/11 attacks and those that occurred thereafter. In fact, they almost caused the financial collapse of several airlines and resulted in heavy economic damage to countries where tourism is considered a central source of income. As a result of such harsh blows to the tourism sector and the decrease in international flights, the leisure industry also suffered. A decline in tourism hurts restaurants, cafes, clubs, etc. The situation in Israel following the wave of terror attacks from 2000 to 2003 provides a particularly applicable case study in understanding the economic ramifications of terrorism. The process began with a halt in tourism following the terror attacks, which led to an economic recession for the entire leisure industry. The despondent mood in the business sector caused by the terror attacks quickly affected the capital market and thereafter the commercial sector. Finally, as a result of the mounting recession, the real estate sector also suffered (Melnick and Eldor, 2004:367–386).

In addition, a significant portion of a country's budget and many national resources are allocated to the prevention and defense against terrorism activities. While the cost of terrorism itself is extremely low – and is in fact becoming even lower – billions of dollars are invested in defense against terrorism (Horgan, 2005:9).

The long-term economic effects of terrorism are no less severe than the direct and indirect short-term economic ramifications. This includes severe damage to development and investment activities, such as the prevention of business expansion, identification of new markets, recruitment of personnel, etc.

One question terrorism researchers are seeking to answer is whether harming the economy is a primary or only secondary strategic goal of terrorism, and of radical Islamic terrorism in particular. Websites that serve bin Laden's followers have reiterated the influence terrorism has on the Western economy. They contend that Islam must attack the American enemy and the entire Western world exactly where it hurts the most, i.e., in their pockets. This strategy has even been dubbed "economic jihad," and its ostensible goal is not only to cause a large number of casualties, but also to trigger the collapse of the world's economic centers.[22]

The 9/11 attacks and the events that took place thereafter demonstrated the enormous damage that international terrorism can cause to the world economy, particularly in the private business sector. However, it is unknown whether or not this was bin Laden's primary goal when he initiated the 9/11 attacks. The World Trade Center (WTC) could have been chosen as a target because it served as the business hub of New York and one of the most important economic centers worldwide, or could have been selected because of the perpetrators' assessment that attacking the WTC would cause a large number of casualties and would instill fear and panic in the American population and the entire world. The twin towers may have been a symbolic target representing Western economic power, while an attack on the Pentagon would demonstrate radical Islam's ability to target the center of Western military power. A planned attack on Congress or the White House could arguably symbolize the perpetrators' ability to harm the political nerve center.

Most likely, all these goals were considered by Al-Qaeda when they chose to attack the specific targets on 9/11. The subsequent economic damage, therefore, may not necessarily have been the terrorists' primary goal. However, terrorist organizations are quick learners. They are constantly learning about their enemy – gathering information from the press, their sympathizers worldwide, and from any other possible source. Economic explanations for their actions, therefore, may have been adopted retroactively. Terrorist organizations understand that the way they

---

[22] Dr. Abd al Aziz Rantisi published a written statement on Hamas' official web site calling on Muslims all over the world to wage an "economic jihad" against the United States. Muslims must recruit their financial resources and capabilities to strike and weaken the US economy. See: Col. (res.) Jonathan Fighel, "Hamas calls for "Economic Jihad" against the U.S.", www.ict.org.il/index.php?sid=119&lang=en&act=page&id=5954&str=jonathan%20fighel

frame an attack, largely dependent on the content of their declarations following an attack, can increase their power to instill fear of future threats, ultimately advancing their goals. Many attacks in recent years have in fact been against economic, tourism, or commercial targets. Aside from the example of September 11, other such cases include the attack on a hotel in Mombassa and the firing of antiaircraft missile at an Israeli passenger plane in November 2002, the attack against tourists in Sharm-al-Sheikh (July 2005) and in Dahab (April 2006) in Egypt, an attack in a dance club in Bali (October 2005), attacks against hotels in Amman (November 2005), etc.

These attacks, as well as others, had severe economic consequences on tourism and air travel worldwide. It still appears however that the economic goal in these cases was secondary to the aim of seeking crowded venues where an attack would result in a large number of casualties. The victims' international identities and the large number of injured were meant to produce mass-media coverage. Since the victims were not local (Australians in Bali, Israelis in Mombassa, etc.), the organizations' message would reach an international audience, maximizing its impact.

Responding to Terrorism – Recommendations

Effectively coping with the phenomenon of terrorism requires local and international action on two levels – addressing both terrorists' motivation and their operational capabilities. It is a state's responsibility and duty to protect its citizens, and so it must work to reduce terrorist organizations' operational capabilities through preventative and offensive action (and sometimes also defensive action) based on intelligence resources. With the development of modern terrorism and its continuing international reach, the physical and moral damage incurred by terrorist acts has increased to such an extent that it arguably threatens the proper functioning of open society, the world economy, and the maintenance of humanitarian and liberal values – making counter-terrorism efforts all the more crucial.

Effectively countering the threat of terrorism and Global Jihad networks requires a well-coordinated and multidisciplinary campaign that takes advantage of all possible resources – intelligence, economic, security related, and diplomatic. According to Hoffman and Taw (1992), countries that have political, diplomatic, and economic ties or interests with countries that support terrorism, may not pressure them to stop granting political asylum to terrorists or allow the extradition of terrorists (1992:121).

It is important to recognize that it takes a network to defeat a network, which is only possible if the world community agrees together on the nature of the terrorist threat, prioritizing counter terrorism on their national agendas and coordinating in all their efforts. Sharing pieces of the intelligence puzzle and declaring joint sanctions on states that support terrorism – without taking into account economic considerations or diplomatic interests – is critical in developing a cohesive and effective response to terrorism. This requires not only agreement on the part of a number of states, but the advancement of international legislation against terrorism and the strict enforcement of applicable conventions and laws. As a prerequisite, the international community must agree on one international objective and comprehensive definition of terrorism, which is not broad or vague, that refers to terrorism as an outlawed method of operation that no goal can justify. Such a definition would differentiate between terrorism and other violent measures intended to achieve criminal or political aims. The implications of such efforts – which require the cooperation of the academic, security, and intelligence communities – lie in the perpetuation or termination of the threat; only when such coordination is established can the world community deal effectively with the operational capabilities of the Global Jihad movement and the modern terrorist threat.

Establishing an alliance of countries that share the common goal of effectively countering global terrorism would be one step in creating a broad-based and international response to terrorism. Such an alliance could reflect the NATO model, but, unlike NATO would include third-world, Arab and Muslim states in addition to Western countries.

In past years, the international community has in many cases been able to effectively thwart terrorist plots. A window of opportunity has been created as a result of such short-term achievements, allowing the international community to potentially deal with the roots of terrorism – the motivations that breed terrorism, propaganda and incitement to violence based on radical Islamic justifications, and the radicalization process as a whole, which has continued over generations by radical Islamic movements, organizations, and individuals all over the world.

International radical Islamic terrorism is primarily the result of a systematic process of fundamentalist indoctrination that has taken place for over two decades all over the Arab and Muslim world. It is the product of two primary factors. First, after Khomeini's revolution in Iran in 1979, the new Iranian regime's primary goal was to "export the revolution," first and foremost to Shiite Muslim populations in other countries. The regime invested tremendous amounts of resources in this venture. Second, many other resources, based on petrodollars, were invested to strengthen radical Islamic education among the Sunni-Wahabbi communities. These resources were used to establish educational, religious, and welfare services all over the Muslim world in order to provide the population with basic services. The masses, who had difficulty providing their families with basic needs, rushed to accept help from the Islamic movements, even when aid was provided only on condition that they submit to radical Islamic indoctrination.

For more than two decades, the radical Islamic movement has succeeded in establishing a solid base within many communities of the Muslim world. The movement first preached religious fundamentalism, but soon started to support and preach violence against its enemies – the "infidels" – without differentiating between Christians, Jews, or even Muslims who do not support a radical interpretation of Islam.

In order to counter the motivations behind the Global Jihad movement, the radical Islamic movement and associated political parties may need to be uprooted. This task should not be placed on the shoulders of Western states, however. Rather, it would most appropriately and effectively be a task for the pragmatic Islamic world, which is still by far the majority within the Islamic world. However, vast resources are needed in order to strengthen alternative educational, religious, and welfare systems within the Muslim world. A possible approach would be to task the West, headed by the U.S., with assisting in the development of, in essence, a new "Marshall Plan," available to pragmatic Muslim regimes. The budget for such a program could be supervised and would not intend to interfere with the religious, educational, and cultural content of the Islamic world. As such, efforts to counter radical Islamic terrorism would be based in the Muslim world, with Muslims themselves preventing the hijacking of their religion by radicals.

In recent years, the U.S. has worked to implement a plan of democratization in the Muslim world, aiming to advance reforms that would encourage democracy in the political lives of Arab and Muslim states. The premise, similar to the Helsinki Accords between the Western and Eastern blocs in 1975, was based on establishing relations between the two sides while stressing the issue of human rights. Just as with the eventual fall of the Communist regime, such democratic reforms are meant to bring about a desired regime change in Islamic states. However, the American democratization program could potentially "throw the baby out with the bath water." Demanding increased democratization in Arab and Muslim countries instead of demanding more pragmatism actually plays into the hands of the Islamic fundamentalists.

American decision makers would be better positioned if they remembered how American pressure on the Iranian Shah's regime to implement democratic reforms was a decisive factor in the fall of the regime and Khomeini's rise to power. Despite the inherent benefits of a democratic system, the U.S. must understand that imposing democratic reforms on a nation that has not gone through its own process of liberalization, pragmatism, and democratization can be dangerous and counter-productive. Forcing Arab and Muslim regimes to adopt a democratic regime and the criteria accepted in Western society could add fuel to the radical Islamic fire. It could cause the downfall of regimes that are not hostile to the west and the subsequent rise of Khomeinistic juntas that bear no resemblance to a democracy.

Efforts to eradicate radical Islamic terrorism and encourage democracy in the Muslim world should start with a long and thorough stage of pragmatic liberal education and legal restrictions on incitement to violence and terrorism. Such efforts can take place both within Muslim countries and internally in western states with large Muslim communities. Countries that host large Muslim immigrant communities can work to strengthen the moderate majority, also working to integrate and assimilate these communities and prevent discrimination against them. A host country may insist on demanding loyalty from the Muslim community, in terms of accepting the country's values, learning the language of the host country, and, above all, rejecting radical incitement to violence.

Research Implications and the Future

Academic research in the field of terrorism has been ongoing since the 1970s, but experienced a boost after 9/11, when governments began to re-evaluate the nature and level of the terrorist threat. Yet there is still significant room for further research, necessary in order to effectively counter and anticipate future threats. Comprehensive research on terrorism and counter terrorism requires multidisciplinary approaches that combine several fields within the behavioral sciences. Special emphasis should be placed on researching the radicalization process of terrorists in general and radical Islamic terrorists in particular, with specific focus on Muslim immigrants and converts. This should be combined with an ongoing effort to understand terrorists' rationale, cost-benefit evaluations, belief systems and considerations, decision-making processes, and modus operandi.

As part of this effort, exploring the direct and hidden messages sent by radical Islamic groups and movements can provide researchers significant insight into the radicalization process. The internet plays a crucial role in disseminating those messages, serving as a platform for radical virtual communities and ideology, in addition to being used for operational needs.

Within the academic field of counter terrorism, further research should also focus on gauging how much a country's counter terrorism policies and strategies stress the operational capabilities of terrorists as opposed to the motivational factors behind terrorism. The weight placed on each approach can be compared across countries. In addition, research must focus on the different forms of regional and international cooperation – both experiences and apparatuses – in order to suggest new policies for effective international cooperation regimes. In this respect, there is also a need to analyze and compare the role of the police and military in countering the phenomenon of terrorism, outlining the methods and boundaries of cooperation between these two agencies.

References

Abadie, A. 2004. *Poverty, Political Freedom, and the Roots of Terrorism*. KGS Faculty Research Working Paper Series RWP04–043. Cambridge: Harvard University.

Abd Al-Rahim Hassan Nazzal and others vs. the Commander of the IDF forces in Judea and Samaria. 1994. Israeli High Court of Justice 94/6026, verdict 48 (5):338.

Al-Mukarramah, M. 2001. *Terrorism – The Islamic Point of View. Distributed at the NGO conference in Durban*. Durban, South Africa: Muslim World League.

Atran, S. 2006. The moral logic and growth of suicide terrorism. *Washington Quarterly* 29 (2):127–147.

Bandura, A. 1973. *Aggression: A Social Learning Analysis*. Englewood Cliffs, London: Prentice-Hall.

Bandura, A. 1998. Mechanisms of moral disengagement. In *Origins of Terrorism*, ed. W. Reich, Washington, DC: Woodrow Wilson Center.

Campbell, J. K. 2000. On not understanding the problem. In *Hype or Reality? The "New Terrorism" and Mass Casualty Attacks*, ed. B. Roberts, Alexandria, VA: The Chemical and Biological Arms Institute.

Cooper, H. H. A. ("Tony") 1978. Psychopath as terrorist: A psychological perspective. *Legal Medical Quarterly* 2:253–262.

Crenshaw, M. 1992. Decisions to use terrorism: Psychological constraints on instrumental reasoning. In *Social Movements and Violence: Participation in Underground Organizations*, ed. D. D. Porta, Greenwich, London: JAI.

Crenshaw, M. 1998. The logic of terrorism: Terrorist behavior as a product of strategic choice. In *Origins of Terrorism*, ed. W. Reich, Washington, DC: Woodrow Wilson Center.

Crenshaw, M. 2000. The psychology of terrorism: An agenda for the 21st century. *Political Psychology* 21(2):405–420.

De la Corte, L., A. Kruglanski, J. de Miguel, J. M. Sabucedo, and D. Diaz. 2007. Siete principios psicosociales para explicar el terrorismo (Seven Psychosocial principles to explain terrorism). *Psicothema* 19(3):366–374.

Federman, and others vs. the Attorney General and others. 1993. Israeli High Court of Justice 93/4162.

Friedland, N. 1992. Becoming a terrorist: Social and individual antecedents. In *Terrorism: Roots, Impact, Responses*, ed. L. Howard. New York: Praeger.

Gal-Or, N. 1991. Do western societies tolerate terrorism? In *Tolerating Terrorism in the West: An International Survey*, ed. N. Gal-Or, London: Routledge.

Ganor, B. 2005. *The Counter-Terrorism Puzzle: A Guide for Decision Makers*. New Brunswick, NJ: Transaction Publishers.

Ganor, B. 2005b. The feasibility of post-modern terrorism. In *Post Modern Terrorism*, ed. B. Ganor, Israel: The Interdisciplinary Center – the International Policy institute for Counter-Terrorism.

Gibbs, J. P. 1989. Conceptualization of terrorism. *American Sociological Review* 54 (3):329–340.

Hacker, F. 1976. *Crusaders, Criminals, Crazies: Terror and Terrorism in Our Time*. New York: Norton.

Harmon, C. 2000. *Terrorism Today*. London: Frank Cass.

Hasisi, B., and A. Pedahzur. 2000. State, policy, and political violence: Arabs in the Jewish state. *Civil Wars* 3:64–68.

Henkin, L. 1989. General course on public international law, 216/IV Collected Courses (1989) 9, as referenced in Sassoli, Marco. 2006. Terrorism and war. *Journal of International Criminal Justice* 4:959–981.

Heskin, K. 1984. The psychology of terrorism in Ireland. In *Terrorism in Ireland*, eds. Y. Alexander and A. O'Day. New York: St. Martin's.

Hoffman, B. 1995. Holy terror: The implications of terrorism motivated by a religious imperative. *Studies in Conflict & Terrorism* 18(4):271–284.

Hoffman, B. 1998. *Inside Terrorism*. New York: Columbia University Press.

Hoffman, B. 2004. Defining terrorism. In *Terrorism and Counterterrorism*, eds. R. D. Howard and R. L. Sawyer, Dubuque: McGraw-Hill.

Hoffman, B. 2006. *Inside Terrorism, Revised and Expanded Edition*. New York: Columbia University Press.

Hoffman, B., and J. M. Taw. 1992. *A Strategic Framework for Countering Terrorism and Insurgency, a Rand Note; N-3506-DOS*. Santa Monica, CA: RAND.

Holmes, L. 2007. *Terrorism, Organized Crime and Corruption: Networks and Linkages*. Cheltenham: Elgar.

Horgan, J. 2005. *The Psychology of Terrorism*. London: Routledge.

Hubbard, D. G. 1971. *The Skyjacker: His Flights of Fantasy*. New York: Macmillan.

Hudson, R. A. 2003. Terrorist and Organized Crime Groups in the Tri-Border Area (TBA) of South America. Washington, DC: Federal Research Division, Library of Congress. http://purl.access.gpo.gov/GPO/LPS49424 (accessed November 2, 2008).

Jessee, D. D. 2006. Tactical means, strategic ends: Al Qaeda's use of denial and deception. *Terrorism and Political Violence* 18 (3):367–388.

Juergensmeyer, M. 2003. *Terror in the Mind of God: The Global Rise of Religious Violence*. London: University of California Press.

Kahn, J., and T. Weiner. 2002. World leaders rethinking strategy on aid to poor. *The New York Times*, 18 March, sec. A1, p. 3.

Kinsley, M. 2001. Defining terrorism: It's essential, it's also impossible. *Slate*, 5 October. http://www.slate.com/id/116697 (accessed November 19, 2008).

Klein, M. W., and C. L. Maxson. 2006. *Street Gang Patterns and Policies*. New York: Oxford University Press.

Klein, M. W., F. M. Weerman, and T. P. Thornberry. 2006. Street gang violence in Europe. *European Journal of Criminology* 3(4):413–437.

Krueger, A. B., and D. D. Laitin. 2008. Kto Kogo?: A cross-country study of the origins and targets of terrorism. In *Terrorism, Economic Development and Political Openness*, eds. P. Keefer and N. Loayza, Cambridge: Cambridge University Press.

Krueger, A. B., and J. Maleckova. 2002. *Education, Poverty, Political Violence, and Terrorism: Is There a Connection? Working Paper No. w9074*. US: National Bureau of Economic Research. http://papers.nber.org/papers/w9074 (accessed November 18, 2008).

Krueger, A. B., and J. Maleckova. 2003. Education, poverty and terrorism: Is there a causal connection? *Journal of Economic Perspectives* 17(4):119–144.

Lafree, G. 2007. Expanding criminology's domain: The American Society of Criminology 2006 Presidential Address. *Criminology* 45(1):1–31.

Laqueur, W. 1987. Terrorism and the media. In *The Age of Terrorism*, ed. W. Laqueur, London: Weidenfeld and Nicolson.

Lasch, C. 1979. *The Culture of Narcissism*. New York: Warner Books.

Levitt, G. 1986. Is terrorism worth defining? *Ohio Northern University Law Review* 13:97–115.

Madani, B. 2002. Hezbollah's global finance network: The triple frontier. *The Middle East Intelligence Bulletin* 4(1). www.meib.org/articles/0201_l2.htm (accessed November 19, 2008).

Melnick, R., and R. Eldor. 2004. Financial markets and terrorism. *European Journal of Political Economy* 20(2):367–386.

Merari, A. 2004. Suicide terrorism. In *Assessment, Treatment, and Prevention of Suicidal behavior*, eds. R. I. Yufit and D. Lester, Hoboken, NJ: Wiley.

Mili, H. 2006. Tangled webs: Terrorist and organized crime groups. *Terrorism Monitor* 4:(1). http://www.jamestown.org/terrorism/news/article.php?articleid=2369866 (accessed November 3, 2008).

Millon, T. 1981. *Disorders of Personality: DSM-III, Axis II*. US: Wiley.

Morgan, S.J. 2001. The supporters of Terrorism – Cultneurosis. In *The Mind of the Terrorist Fundamentalist*. http://www.terrorpsychology.com/supporters.htm

Nacos, B. 1994. *Terrorism and the Media: From the Iran Hostage Crisis to the World Trade Center Bombing*. New York: Columbia University Press.

Netanyahu, B. 1987. *Terrorism, How the West Can Win*. Tel-Aviv: The Jonathan Institute.

Noble, R. K. 2003. *The Links Between Intellectual Property Crime and Terrorist Financing*. Text of public testimony before the United States House Committee on International Relations, July 16, 2003. http://www.interpol.int/Public/ICPO/speeches/SG20030716.asp (accessed November 18, 2008).

Pearce, K. I. 1977. Police negotiations – new role for community psychiatrist. *Canadian Psychiatric Association Journal* 22(4):171–175.

Piazza, J. A. 2006. Rooted in poverty? Terrorism, poor economic development, and social cleavages. *Terrorism and Political Violence* 18(1):159–177.

Pollard, N. 2005. Illegal drug trade a world force – UN. *Reuters News Service*, 29 June. http://www.csdp.org/news/news/reut_un05_063005.htm (accessed November 19, 2008).

Post, J. M. 1987. Rewarding fire with fire – effects of retaliation on terrorist group-dynamics. *Terrorism* 10(1):23–35.

Post, J. 1998. Terrorist psycho-logic: Terrorist behavior as a product of psychological forces. In *Origins of Terrorism*, ed. W. Reich, Washington, DC: Woodrow Wilson Center.

Raine, A. 1993. *The Psychopathology of Crime: Criminal Behavior as a Clinical Disorder*. San Diego, CA: Academic.

Ranstorp, M. 1996. Terrorism in the name of religion. *Journal of International Affairs* 50(1):41–63.

Rapoport, D. C. 1984. Fear and trembling – terrorism in 3 religious traditions. *American Political Science Review* 78(3):658–677.

Rasch, W. 1979. Psychological dimensions of political terrorism in the Federal-Republic-of-Germany. *International Journal of Law and Psychiatry* 2(1):79–85.

Roth, K. 2004. The law of war in the war on terror – Washington's abuse of "enemy combatants". *Foreign Affairs* 83(1):2.

Sageman, M. 2004. *Understanding Terror Networks*. Philadelphia, PA: University of Pennsylvania Press.

Sandler, T., and H. E. Lapan. 1988. The calculus of dissent: An analysis of terrorist's choice of targets. *Synthese* 76(2):245–261.

Sandler, T., J. T. Tschirhart, and J. Cauley. 1983. A theoretical analysis of transnational terrorism. *American Political Science Review* 77(1):36–54.

Schmid, A. P. 1983. *Political Terrorism: A Research Guide to the Concepts, Theories, Databases and Literature*. Amsterdam: North Holland.

Schmid, A. P. 1993. Terrorism and democracy. In *Western Responses to Terrorism*, eds. A. P. Schmid and R. D. Crelinsten, London: Frank Cass.

Schmid, A. P., and A. J. Jongman. 1988. *Political Terrorism*. Amsterdam: North Holland Publishing Company.

Shprinzak, E. 1998. The psychopolitical formation of extreme left terrorism in democracy: The case of the weathermen. In *Origins of Terrorism*, ed. R. Walter, Washington, DC: Woodrow Wilson Center.

Silke, A. 1998. Cheshire-cat logic: The recurring theme of terrorist abnormality in psychological research. *Psychology Crime & Law* 4(1):51–69.

Stahelski, A. 2004. Terrorists are made, not born: Creating terrorists using social psychological conditioning. *Journal of Homeland Security* March:1–7. http://www.homelandsecurity.org/journal/Default.aspx?oid=109&ocat=1 (accessed November 18, 2008).

Taylor, M. 1988. *The Terrorist*. London: Brassey's Defense.

Thomson, J. A. 2003. Killer apes on American airlines, or how religion was the main hijacker on September 11. In *Violence or Dialogue: Psychoanalytic Insights on Terror and Terrorism*, eds. S. Varvin and V. D. Volkan London: International Psychoanalytical Association.

Tri-border Transfers "funding terror". 2006. *BBC News*, 14 Dec. http://news.bbc.co.uk/2/hi/americas/6179085.stm (accessed November 19, 2008).

Victoroff, J. 2005. The mind of the terrorist – A review and critique of psychological approaches. *Journal of Conflict Resolution* 49(1):3–42.

Vidino, L., and S. Emerson. 2006. *Al Qaeda in Europe: The New Battleground of International Jihad*. Amherst, NY: Prometheus Books.

Webb, G. R. 2002. Sociology, disasters, and terrorism: Understanding threats of the new millennium. *Sociological Focus* 35(1):87–95.

Wedgwood, R., and K. Roth. 2004. Combatants or criminals? How Washington should handle terrorists. *Foreign Affairs* 83(3):126.

Wilson, M. A. 2000. Toward a model of terrorist behavior in hostage-taking incidents. *Journal of Conflict Resolution* 44(4):403–424.

Chapter 3
Tracking Global Terrorism Trends, 1970–2004

Gary LaFree and Laura Dugan

Abstract Terrorism is a form of crime. Yet compared to most types of crime, terrorism poses unique data collection challenges. As a result, even basic descriptive questions about terrorism have been difficult or impossible to answer: What are the long-term trends in terrorist attacks? Is the number of fatalities associated with terrorist attacks increasing over time? What types of attacks are most common? What types of weapons do terrorists use most frequently? How long do terrorist groups last? In this chapter, we analyze data from the Global Terrorism Database (GTD) to provide a descriptive account of more than 82,000 domestic and international terrorist attacks that occurred between 1970 and 2004. We provide detailed information on global and country-level terrorism trends, regional characteristics of terrorism, and characteristics of the major groups that have employed terrorist methods. We also examine how terrorism rates compare to more common forms of crime. We conclude with a discussion about important research questions for the future.

Introduction

Given the extraordinary international concern raised by terrorism, it is surprising how difficult it is to produce even basic descriptive information on terrorist attacks, fatalities, strategies, and organizations claiming responsibility for attacks over time. This startling lack of information was evident in a 2003 memo from Defense Secretary Donald Rumsfeld in which he concluded that "Today, we lack metrics to know if we are winning or losing the global war on terror" (cited in: Phillips, 2007:52). Thus, it is unsurprising that despite operating in an increasingly information-rich world, most police officers are unable to access systematic data on terrorism activities that could inform their investigations (see Bayley and

---

G. LaFree (✉) and L. Dugan
National Center for the Study of Terrorism and Responses to Terrorism (START), and Department of Criminology and Criminal Justice, University of Maryland, College Park, MD, USA
e-mail: glafree@crim.umd.edu

Weisburd, Chap. 2, this volume). While a full explanation for the lack of hard data on terrorism is well beyond the scope of this essay, there is little doubt that compared to collecting data on other types of criminal violence, collecting data on terrorist violence is especially challenging.

In this chapter, we briefly examine the primary sources of data on illegal violence and discuss the difficulty of accurately recording cases of terrorist activity through these sources. We then introduce the newly constructed Global Terrorism Database (GTD), compiled from unclassified media sources. Because the GTD is the first data base to capture the full spectrum of international and domestic cases over a relatively long period of time, we carefully describe patterns of global terrorism over time, over space, and by specific characteristics of incidents, such as target types and tactics. We also provide information about the most active groups and countries over time. Finally, we examine bivariate relationships between patterns of global terrorism for countries according to their political characteristics and crime rates.

Measuring Illegal Violence

Data on illegal violence generally comes from three main sources, corresponding to the major social roles connected to criminal events: "official" data collected by legal agents, especially the police; "victimization" data collected from the general population of victims and potential victims; and "self-report" data collected from offenders and ex-offenders. In the United States, the most widely used form of official crime data has long been the Federal Bureau of Investigation (FBI)'s Uniform Crime Report. Major official sources of data on international crime include the International Criminal Police Organization (Interpol), the United Nations (UN) crime surveys, and for homicides only, the World Health Organization (WHO).

Since 1973, the major source of victimization data in the United States has been the National Crime Victimization Survey. For international data, the International Crime Victimization Survey has collected several waves of data from samples of individuals in several dozen nations around the world (Van Dijk et al., 1989). Compared to the collection of victimization data in the United States, the collection of self-report survey data has been more sporadic. Nevertheless, several major large-scale national self-report surveys now exist (Elliott et al., 1989). Similarly, several waves of an international self-reported crime study have been undertaken (Junger-Tas et al., 1994). In general, data concerning terrorist events from these three sources are either entirely lacking or face important additional limitations.

Although government departments in some countries do collect official data on terrorism (e.g., the US State Department, the Israeli Ministry of Public Security), these data face at least two major difficulties. First, terrorism data collected by government entities are suspicious either because they are influenced by political considerations, or because many fear that they might be so influenced. Of course, to some extent, this is also a problem with official data on common crimes. Police, courts and correctional officers frequently face political pressure to present their crime data in particular ways (O'Brien, 1996:183–207). However, because terrorism is especially controversial, political pressure directed at defining it in specific ways is likely to be particularly acute. Thus, the United States government was very reluctant to define actions of the Contra rebels in Nicaragua as terrorism, even though their actions often fit common terrorism definitions (LaFree and Dugan, 2007). By contrast, it seems likely that the US Government in recent years faces strong pressure to regard all violence in Iraq and Afghanistan as terrorist violence.

Second, while huge amounts of detailed official data on common crimes are routinely produced by the various branches of the criminal justice system in most nations, this is rarely the case for terrorism. For example, most suspected terrorists in the United States are not legally processed for their acts of terrorism, but rather for other related offenses.[1] So, there is no easy way to gather official data on those arrested, prosecuted or convicted of terrorist activities unless you do as Smith and Orvis (1993:661–681) have done, and assemble the data on a case by case basis. And of course, the ability to use official data to study terrorism in most other nations is even more difficult. In particular, more terrorism data are collected by intelligence agencies that operate partially or entirely outside the realm of domestic criminal justice systems. Thus, most official data collected by intelligence agents, including data from communications intercepts, surveillance, informers, defectors, interrogation of prisoners, and captured internal documents (e.g., memos, training manuals) are not readily available to researchers working in an open, unclassified environment. Still, there are important opportunities provided by official data on terrorism that have not been adequately exploited. In particular, researchers could do more to examine court records and transcripts, government reports and hearings, and unclassified intelligence reports.

Victimization data, which have played an increasingly important role in the study of common crime in the US and elsewhere, are almost entirely irrelevant to the study of terrorist activities. Several features of terrorism make it highly unlikely that victimization surveys will ever have widespread applicability. To begin with, despite the attention it gets in the global media, terrorism is much

---

[1] It is true that this situation continues to evolve. For example, in the United States in 1995, Chap. 11 3B of the Federal Criminal Code and Rules added "Terrorism" as a separate offense and the Antiterrorism and Effective Death Penalty Act was signed into law in 1996. Among other things, the 1996 act attempts to cut fundraising by those affiliated with terrorist organizations, enhances the security measures employed by the aviation industry, and expands the reach of US law enforcement over selected crimes committed abroad. Similarly, the US Patriot Act, passed in 2001, strengthens criminal laws against terrorism by adding to the criminal code terrorist attacks against mass transportation systems, domestic terrorism, harboring or concealing terrorists, or providing material support to terrorists (115 Stat. 374, Public Law 107-56-26 October, 2001). Nevertheless, it still remains the case that most of those persons who are officially designated as terrorists in the annual reports produced by the FBI are either not prosecuted at all (e.g., the likely outcome for many of those detained at the US's Guantanamo Detention Facility) or are prosecuted under traditional criminal statutes. "At the time of this publication, we have yet to see how the Obama administration will influence these procedures."

rarer than violent crime. This means that even with extremely large sample sizes, few individuals in most countries have been victimized by terrorists. Moreover, because one of the hallmarks of terrorism is that victims are often chosen at random, victims of terrorist events are unlikely to know perpetrators, making it difficult to produce details about offenders. And finally, in many cases, victims of terrorism are killed by their attackers – a problem in criminology limited to the study of homicides.

Self-report data on terrorists have been more important than victimization data, but they too face serious limitations. Most active terrorists are unwilling to participate in interviews. And even if willing to participate, getting access to known terrorists for research purposes raises obvious challenges. As Merari (1991:88–102) has put it, "The clandestine nature of terrorist organizations and the ways and means by which intelligence can be obtained will rarely enable data collection which meets commonly accepted academic standards."

But despite these limitations, collecting information on terrorist events has one considerable advantage: Terrorists, unlike most common criminals, actively seek public recognition. Jenkins (1975:16) famously declared that "terrorism is theatre" and explained how "terrorist attacks are often carefully choreographed to attract the attention of the electronic media and the international press." In fact, the media are so central to contemporary terrorist groups that some researchers have argued that the birth of modern terrorism should be directly linked to the launch by the United States of the first television satellite in 1968 (Hoffman, 1998:136–137). This invention meant that news could be transmitted for the first time from local studios back to network headquarters almost instantaneously. The fact that terrorists are specifically seeking to attract attention through the media means that media coverage can tell us far more about terrorism than other types of crime. Thus, while no responsible researcher would seriously argue that we can accurately track burglary or car theft rates by studying electronic and print media, it is a much more defensible argument to claim that we can track terrorist attacks in this way. For example, it is hard to imagine that it is any longer possible for an aerial hijacking or politically motivated assassination – even in remote parts of the world – to elude the scrutiny of the global media.

For this reason, there has been a long-standing interest in terrorist event data bases drawn from the electronic and print media. There are now a dozen or so of these data bases in existence (see LaFree and Dugan, 2007 for a review). They all rely on collecting information from some combination of wire services (including Reuters and the Foreign Broadcast Information Service [FBIS]), government reporting, and newspapers (including such purportedly global newspapers as the *New York Times* and the *London Financial Times*). Over time, the Internet has played an increasingly important role in these open source data collection efforts. And over time, these data bases have grown increasingly sophisticated. The data on terrorism presented in this chapter are drawn from the GTD, currently the largest and most extensive of these unclassified terrorism data bases. In the next section we describe the GTD in greater detail.

The GTD

The GTD originated with an extensive data collection project that began with the Pinkerton Global Intelligence Service – a relative of the famous detective agency. From 1970 to 1997, Pinkerton trained researchers to identify and record terrorism incidents from wire services, US State Department reports, other US and foreign government reporting, US and foreign newspapers, information provided by PGIS offices around the world, and data furnished by Pinkerton clients. In more recent years, Pinkerton researchers relied increasingly on the Internet. Although the coding form went through three iterations, most of the items included were similar during the entire 28 years of data collection. About 2 dozen persons were responsible for coding information over the years spanned by the data collection, but only two individuals were in charge of supervising data collection during the entire period. Most of the data collectors working for Pinkerton, including the data base managers, were retired US Air Force military intelligence personnel.

Given that their background was military, it was natural that Pinkerton used the US military definition of terrorism in selecting events for the data base:

> (t)he threatened or actual use of illegal force and violence by a non state actor to attain a political, economic, religious or social goal through fear, coercion or intimidation.

Compared to most definitions of terrorism, the military definition employed by Pinkerton throughout the data collection period is relatively inclusive. For example, compare the Pinkerton definition with the ones used by the US State Department:

> premeditated, politically motivated violence perpetrated against noncombatants targeted by subnational groups or clandestine agents, usually intended to influence an audience;

or the US FBI:

> the unlawful use of force or violence against persons or property to intimidate or coerce Government, the civilian population, or any segment thereof, in furtherance of political or social objectives.

Neither the State Department nor the FBI definition of terrorism includes threats of force. Yet as Hoffman (1998:38) points out, "terrorism is as much about the threat of violence as the violent act itself." Many, perhaps most, hijackings involve only the threatened use of force (e.g., "I have a bomb and I will use it unless you follow my demands"). Similarly, kidnappers almost always employ force to seize the victims, but then threaten to kill, maim or otherwise harm the victims unless demands are satisfied. Note also that the State Department definition is limited to "politically motivated violence." The FBI definition is somewhat broader, including social along with political objectives as fundamental terrorist aims. However, the Pinkerton definition also includes economic and religious objectives.

Perhaps the most important characteristic of the Pinkerton data is that it was not limited to international terrorism incidents. Unlike the State Department, whose mandate is to focus on international terrorism (i.e., that involving the interests and/or nationals of more than one country), and all of the other event data bases developed before 1998, the PGIS data included domestic terrorist attacks. To underscore the importance of this difference consider that two noteworthy terrorist attacks of recent years – the March 1995 nerve gas attack on the Tokyo subway system and the April 1995 bombing of the federal office building in Oklahoma City – both lack any known foreign involvement and hence were purely acts of domestic terrorism.

Based on coding rules originally developed in 1970, the persons responsible for collecting the PGIS data sought to exclude criminal acts that had no apparent political or ideological motivation and also acts arising from open combat between opposing armed forces, both regular and irregular. The data coders also excluded actions taken by governments in the legitimate exercise of their authority, even when such actions were denounced by domestic and/or foreign critics as acts of "state terrorism." However, they included violent acts that were not officially sanctioned by government, even in cases where many observers believed that the government was openly tolerating the violent actions.

In sum, the fact that these data were collected by a private corporation for a business purpose gave them some unique characteristics. Because the goal of the data collection was to provide risk assessment to corporate customers, the data base was designed to error on the side of inclusiveness. The justification was that being overly inclusive best serves the interest of clients – an employee of a corporation about to move to Colombia would be concerned about acts of violence against civilians and foreigners, even if these acts were domestic rather than international, threatened rather than completed, or carried out for religious rather than political purposes. While there is at present no universally accepted definition of terrorism, the definition used to generate the PGIS data is among the most comprehensive that we have been able to identify.

The Original GTD

In 2001 the senior author arranged to move the original hard copies of the PGIS terrorism data base to offices at the University of Maryland. During this transfer process, we discovered that 1 year of the PGIS data – 1993 – had been lost in an earlier office move. These original data were never recovered. Once the remaining data were transferred to the University, we applied for and secured funds from the National Institute of Justice (LaFree and Dugan, 2002:1–41) to computerize the data. We completed computerizing the original PGIS data in December 2005. Since then we have actively searched open sources to update, correct and extend the data. We now refer to the resulting data base – constructed on the original PGIS platform – as the GTD. In April 2006, we received additional funding from the Human Factors Division of the Science and Technology branch of the Department of Homeland Security to extend the GTD beyond 1997.

GTD Data Collection Since 2005

GTD data collection since 2005 has been conducted by a team led by Gary Ackerman and Charles Blair of the Center for Terrorism and Intelligence Studies on behalf of the National Consortium for the Study of Terrorism and Responses to Terrorism (START). We began the new data collection by creating a GTD Criteria Committee, composed of a group of international terrorism experts.[2] This committee reviewed the original PGIS criteria and made suggestions for producing a final set of data collection guidelines. This process was guided by two principles: preserving the value of the PGIS heritage data, while also making improvements in the rigor of the data collection process and the quality of the data collected. Following extensive discussion, the Criteria Committee developed a revised codebook for extending the GTD. The new procedures capture more than 120 variables and unlike the PGIS data, the new data also includes the original open source texts upon which each event is based.

Ackerman and Blair's team of 25–35 data collectors include researchers who are fluent in six language groups (English, French, Spanish, Russian, Arabic and Mandarin). The current data collection process begins by monitoring general data bases such as Lexis-Nexis (Professional) and Opensource.gov (previously FBIS). A typical day produces as many as 1,000 potential events. Data collectors are asked to review all of these events, to determine which qualify as terrorist events according to the target definition, and then to corroborate each case with at least two additional source articles. Data collectors submit all their expected cases to supervisors for review. Problematic cases are referred back to the GTD Criteria Committee for final decisions.

Current Status of the GTD

Most of our analyses in this chapter are based on the GTD for the years 1970–2004, the most recent years for which data were available when this chapter was being prepared. However, because the criteria, collection strategies and quality control procedures changed from the original data collection (1970–1997, minus 1993) to the recent data collection (1993, 1998–2004), we do not yet know the extent to which the inclusion criteria used for the original data collection matches the criteria being used today for data collection. We are in the process of reassessing the original GTD using the coding rules currently employed. Given that there are nearly 69,000 cases in the original data base, this is a major undertaking and the results of our synthesis efforts were not available at the time this chapter was being prepared. However, because we know from internal PGIS reports the total number of terrorist

---

[2] The current committee includes Gary Ackerman, Victor Asal, Martha Crenshaw, Laura Dugan, Michelle Keeney, Gary LaFree, Clark McCauley and Alex P. Schmid.

attacks in 1993 from the original data, we were able to use that figure to interpolate estimates of specific types of 1993 attacks for our temporal figures.[3] We were also able to compare the original data for 1993 to the new data collection for 1993. In the next section, we present trends from the earlier and more recent data collection and discuss the differences. For the cross-sectional results presented in this chapter, we combine the version of the two data bases that was last updated on May 7, 2007.

Characteristics of Global Terrorism, 1970–2004

In this section, we present some of the major characteristics of the terrorist events in the GTD. We consider first global trends and characteristics of terrorism, followed by regional, group-level and country-level comparisons. We then turn to comparisons between terrorist violence and criminal violence. One point that should be made obvious by this section is the rich array of details that are available for each case. While the aggregate data analysis presented here demonstrate the informative potential for policy-makers, much more detailed information is available to police officers, first responders and other law enforcement and service personnel from the web site maintained by the START Center (http://www.start.umd.edu/data/gtd/).

Global Trends

Perhaps, the most fundamental contemporary question about terrorism is whether it is increasing, decreasing or remaining stable over time. This turns out to be an extremely complex and politically volatile question to answer at this moment in history. For example, when the US State Department's *Patterns of Global Terrorism* report for 2003 was issued on 30 April, 2004, its conclusion that "worldwide terrorism had dropped by 45% between 2001 and 2003," unleashed a flood of criticism. This criticism was so intense that the name of the report was changed to "Country Reports on Terrorism," the statistical data and chronology of "significant" international terrorist events was dropped, and the US Congress mandated that starting in 2004, the terrorism statistics that

---

[3] To interpolate subsets of the total terrorist attacks for 1993, we use the following formula:

$$Attacks\ 93\ (subset) = \frac{\frac{Attacks\ 92\ (subset) \times Attacks\ 93\ (total)}{Attacks\ 92\ (total)} + \frac{Attacks\ 94\ (subset) \times Attacks\ 93\ (total)}{Attacks\ 94\ (total)}}{2}$$

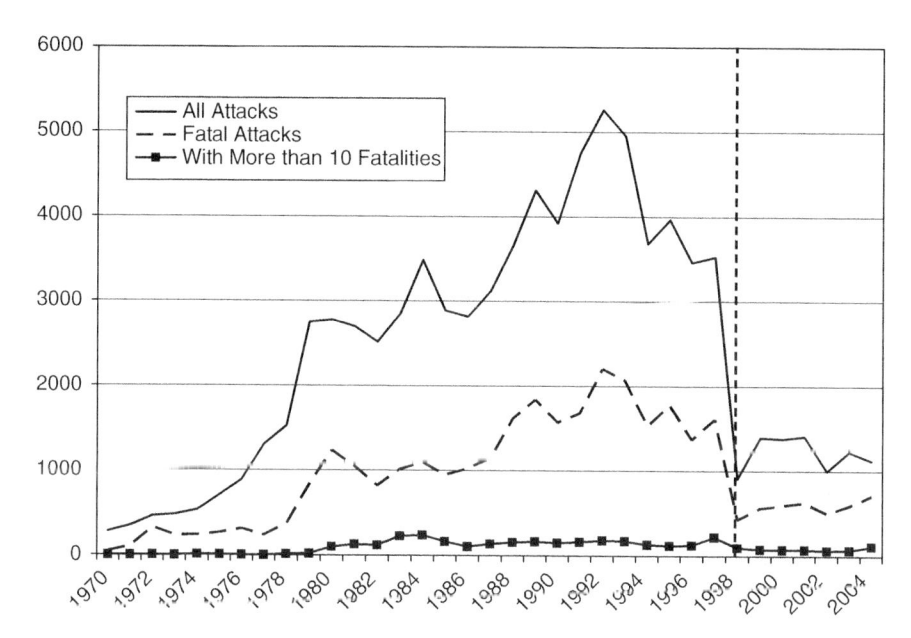

Fig. 3.1 Total attacks, fatal attacks, and attacks with more than ten fatalities, 1970–2004

had been collected by the State Department for years were henceforth to be compiled by the newly created National Counter-Terrorism Center (LaFree and Dugan, 2007).

With that example firmly in mind, we introduce here for the first time results combining trends in terrorist attacks from the original GTD with the new GTD that has been collected since 2005. Figure 3.1 compares trends in total attacks, fatal attacks, and attacks that involved more than ten fatalities from the GTD, 1970–2004. Total attacks are, of course, far more common than fatal attacks. According to Fig. 3.1, fatal attacks represent only 39.6% of total attacks and attacks including more than ten fatalities represent only 10.6% of all fatal attacks. Figure 3.1 shows that both total attacks and fatal attacks steadily increased during the 1970s and 1980s reaching a peak in both cases in 1992 (5,261 total attacks and 2,205 fatal attacks). Through 1976 terrorist attacks were relatively infrequent, with fewer than 1,000 incidents each year. But from 1978 to 1979 the frequency of attacks nearly doubled. The broad increases in attacks were characterized by smaller peaks in 1984 (3,486 total attacks, 1,100 fatal attacks) and 1989 (4,309 total attacks, 1,840 fatal attacks). After the global peak in 1992, the number of terrorist attacks declined to just over 3,500 at the end of the original data collection in 1997 – a 33% decline.

The vertical line included in Fig. 3.1 separates the first and second GTD data collection efforts. Because the two data bases have not yet been synthesized, we cannot directly compare trends before and after 1998. However, we can say that based on the original data collection, there was a major drop in total attacks and fatal attacks starting in 1993 and continuing to the end of the original data collection in 1997. We can also conclude that total attacks increased slightly from 1998 ($N = 913$) to 2004 ($N = 1,123$; a 23% rise), whereas fatal attacks increased by 65% over the same period.

The terrorism attack and fatality trends depicted in Fig. 3.1 approximate a classic boom and bust cycle with long and fairly steady increases that reach a peak in the early 1990s and then decline steadily to the end of the series in 2004. However, while these trends are based on the most extensive open source event data base yet assembled, we are simply not far enough along in the process of synthesizing the two parts of this data base to offer a conclusive judgment on how valid these estimates of terrorist attacks really are. On the one hand, the earlier data collection may have erred on the side of including attacks that did not have sufficient detail to be confidently treated as terrorist attacks. On the other hand, it could be that the new data collection strategy is so stringent that it is excluding some cases that could legitimately be classified as terrorist. Arbitrating between these two possibilities will be a major task of the START Center during the coming year.[4] We expect to release a substantially updated version of the GTD in Spring 2009.

In Fig. 3.2, we show just those attacks that resulted in more than ten fatalities, 1970–2004. As before, we include a line separating the original data base from the recent data collection efforts. Attacks involving more than ten fatalities were rare until the late 1970s. In fact, for 4 years in the 1970s there were only one or two attacks in this category. Rates increased dramatically after 1979. While the peak for total attacks and fatal attacks was 1992, the peak for attacks involving more than ten fatalities was 1984. In that year there were 240 total attacks that involved more than ten fatalities including a February 4th attack on the town of Masindi in Uganda by the National Resistance Army killing 228 people. Also on June 28 of that year an attack by the Farabundo Marti National Liberation Front (FMLN) on a dam and hydroelectric complex in El Salvador resulted in 136 deaths, including 60 members of the FMLN. After 1984 these high-fatality attacks declined in number somewhat, but hit another peak in 1997 ($N = 222$). Some of the especially lethal attacks in 1997 included a February 1st attack against Maturese villagers in Indonesia by Dayak militants leaving 300 dead, and a December 10th attack against Tutsis in a Mudende refugee camp in Rwanda by Hutus, leaving 271 dead and 227 wounded.

---

[4]In addition, the START Center recently completed in a National Institute of Justice funded project (LaFree and Dugan, 2005) with the RAND Corporation that is combining the RAND-MIPT data base and the GTD. Results from this project suggest that RAND terrorism attack counts from 1998 forward increase dramatically starting around 2003. These increases are due in large part to an exploding number of cases being classified as terrorist from Iraq and Afghanistan. (Dugan, LaFree, Cragin, and Kasupski 2008)

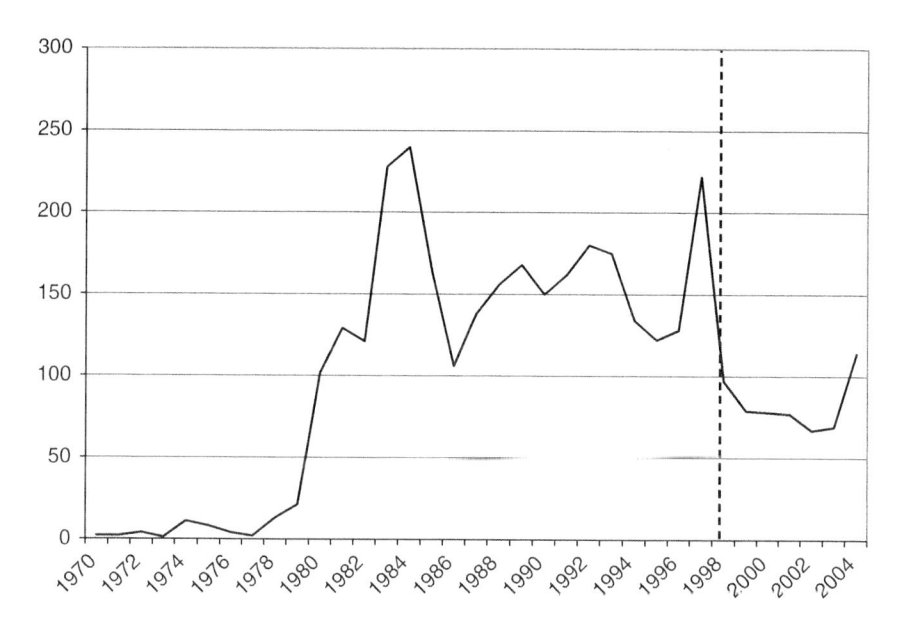

Fig. 3.2 Attacks with more than ten fatalities, 1970–2004

As with the earlier comparisons, we see a sizeable decline in the total number of cases with the new data collection in 1998 – although the drop is not nearly as steep as it was for total attacks and total fatal attacks. We also see a sizeable increase in cases with more than ten fatalities in 2004 ($N = 114$). Especially deadly cases in 2004 included a series of bombings on March 21 by the Nepalese Communist Party that left at least 500 dead. In the same year, a group of 30–35 armed Chechen rebels barricaded a school in Beslan, Russia and during an attempt to free the hostages by government authorities, 362 persons died, including many children. These patterns suggest that the correspondence between the original data and the recently collected data is greater for those more serious attacks that include multiple fatalities.

In Fig. 3.3, we present trends for just those cases where responsibility was attributed to a specific terrorist group. In general, 51% of all the attacks in the data were attributed to specific groups. Trends in attacks where groups claimed responsibility generally follow the total attack trends ($r = 0.88$). However, the trend for attacks where a specific group claims responsibility peaks in 1991 with 2,960 attacks; a year earlier than the high point for the total trend. Also, compared to the drop off between the original data and the new data for total attacks, the drop off for attacks where a specific groups claims responsibility is not as great – a likely consequence of the fact that these cases were more often included by data collectors for both data bases.

In the next figure, we examine the average number of fatalities per attack over time. Figure 3.4 shows a fairly steady increase in fatalities per attack during the 35 years spanned by the two parts of the data base. Fatalities per attack hovered around

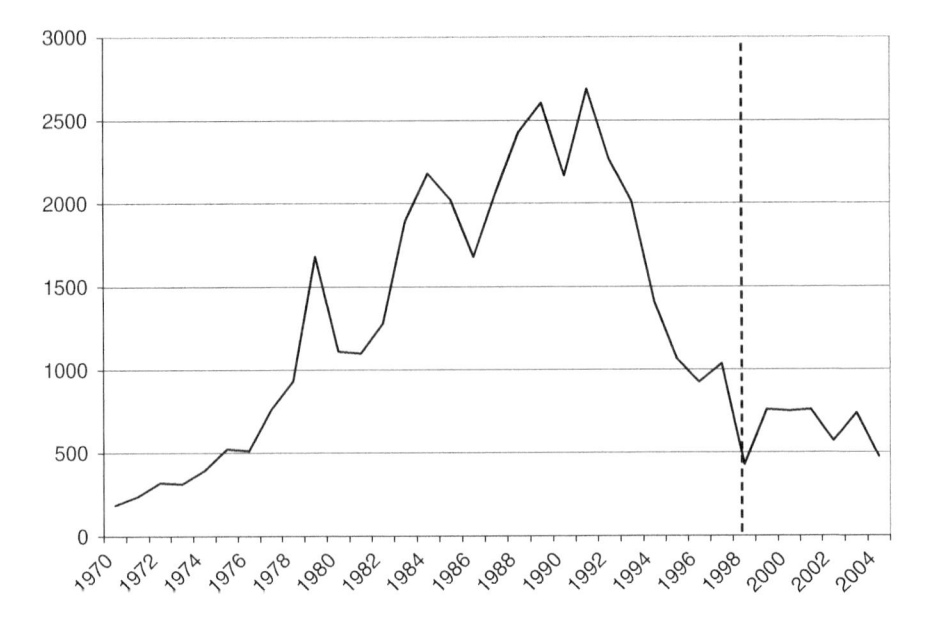

Fig. 3.3 Attacks that are attributed to a group, 1970–2004

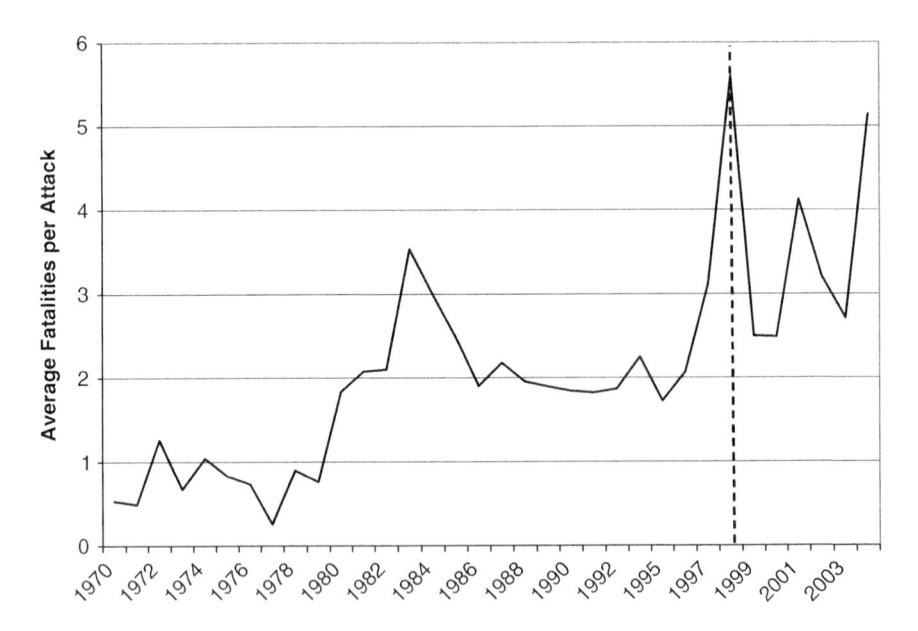

Fig. 3.4 Average fatalities per attack, 1970–2004

one for the first 10 years of data collection and then rose steeply through the early 1980s, reaching a high point of over three fatalities for every attack in 1984. After falling somewhat for the next 10 years, fatalities per attack again increased dramatically in the mid 1990s reaching a series high point of over five deaths per attack in 1998 – the first year of the new data collection. The correspondence between the original and recent data collections is much stronger here than in the earlier comparisons. While it is still unclear to what extent the high rate of fatalities in the new collection is a product of the differences in data collection or reflective of actual changes in lethality, the results are consistent with recent arguments (e.g., Enders and Sandler,) that terrorist attacks are growing more deadly over time.

The terrorist attacks in the GTD are divided into six main types: bombings, facility attacks, assassinations, kidnappings, aerial hijackings and all other (for a full description, see LaFree and Dugan, 2007). Bombings are considered to be clandestine attacks, while facility attacks (which might include bombs) are carried out openly. Major types of bombings include car bombs and other types of remote or time detonated explosions. Most facility attacks use incendiary explosives or firearms. According to Fig. 3.5, bombings are the largest single type of terrorist attack in the GTD, accounting for more than 40% of the total incidents. Facility attacks are next most common, accounting for another 34% of the incidents. Assassinations account for nearly one-fifth of the total attacks. Kidnappings account for just over

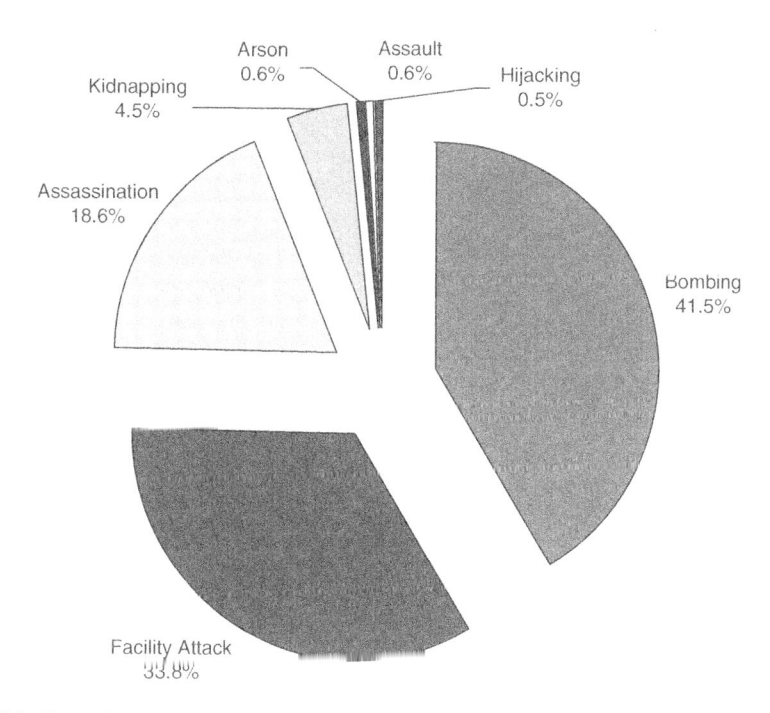

Fig. 3.5 Type of attack, 1970–2004

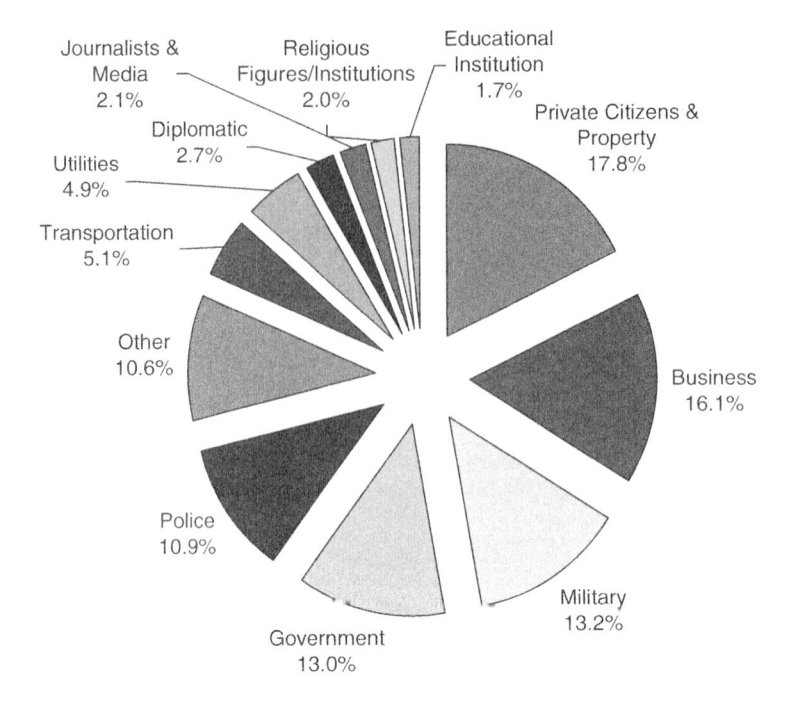

Fig. 3.6 Target type, 1970–2004

4% of total incidents. Aerial hijackings were least common, accounting for less than one-half of 1% of total incidents.

In Fig. 3.6, we examine the targets of global terrorist strikes from 1970 to 2004. We can see that there is considerable variation in terrorist targeting with no single target representing more than 18% of the total. The top three targets are private citizens and property, businesses, and military. Together, these three targets account for just under 50% of the total. Following these three in order are government, police, transportation, utilities, diplomatic, journalists and media, religious institutions or figures, and educational institutions. While the GTD excludes attacks on the military by guerilla organizations, it includes military targets that are attacked by sub state groups where there is evidence of a political motive. The "other" category here encompasses a diverse range of targets, including religious figures and institutions, non-governmental organizations, educational institutions, and tourists.

Figure 3.7 shows the primary weapons used in the commission of the terrorist incidents included in the data base. Explosives and firearms are by far the most common, accounting for more than 86% of the total. Explosives include weapons such as dynamite, car bombs, grenades, and mortars. The most common firearm types are automatic weapons, shot guns, and pistols. Fire or firebombs account for about 9% of the incidents, knives and sharp objects for just over 2% and chemical agents for one-third of 1% of all incidents. Perhaps, the most striking finding in Fig. 3.7 is the fact that the vast majority of weapons used in the terrorist attacks

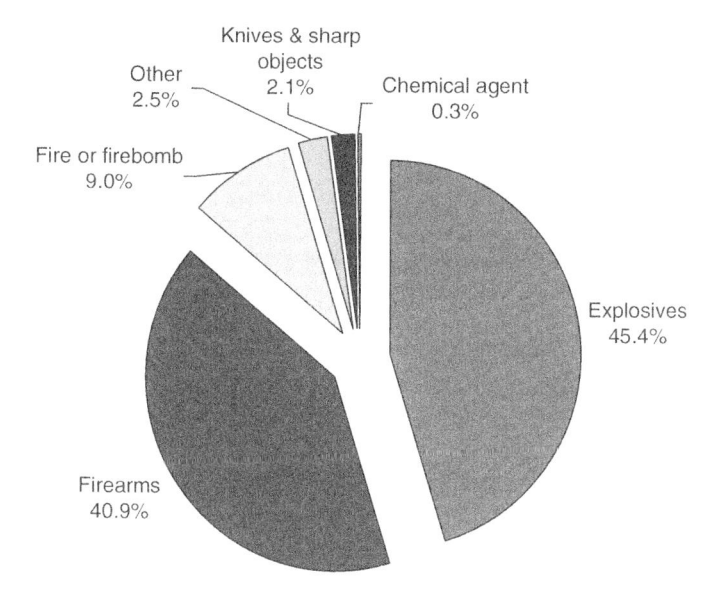

Fig. 3.7 Weapon type, 1970–2004

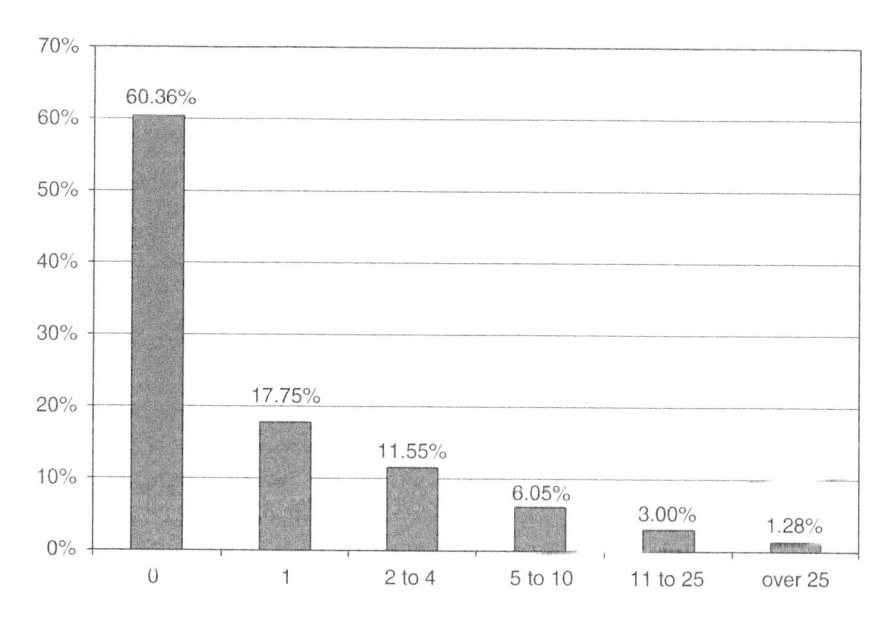

Fig. 3.8 Total fatalities per attack, 1970–2004

summarized in the GTD are readily available. More exotic weapons, like chemical agents and remotely detonated explosives are rare.

Figure 3.8 shows the distribution of fatalities by attack. Given the international publicity attached to high profile incidents such as the attacks on New York and Washington on 9/11, on London on 7/7, and on Madrid on 3/11 we are naturally primed to think of terrorist events as incredibly lethal. But Fig. 3.8 shows that nearly 61% of the terrorist attacks included in the GTD involved no fatalities. Many incidents are directed at property. Others are aimed at civilians, but fail. In many other cases terrorist groups provide a warning to civilians before striking. Twenty years ago these considerations led Jenkins (1985:12) to suggest that "terrorists want a lot of people watching, not a lot of people dead." Of course, it is still the case that 39.6% of the cases in the GTD (or 31,012 total incidents) involved at least one fatality. Incidents that are especially worrisome are the 1.28% (or 1,004 attacks) that produced more than 25 fatalities. And in fact, Jenkins (2007:119) has recently revisited his earlier statement and after reviewing the stated plans of terrorist groups operating in the early twenty-first century concluded that indeed "many of today's terrorists want a lot of people watching and a lot of people dead."

In the next section, we provide estimates of the use of weapons of mass destruction (WMD) from 1970 to 2004. In light of evolving definitions of WMD (LaFree et al., 2005; Carus, 2006; US Department of Defense, 2007:582), we examine not only nuclear, biological and chemical weapons but also guided missiles and sophisticated explosives that are intended to kill a large number of people and to create mass disruption. Following the US Department of Defense (2007:231), we defined guided missiles as direct fire weapons that travel above the surface of the earth and whose trajectory can be "altered by an external or internal mechanism." This category includes short-range, ballistic, and intercontinental ballistic missiles. The range and precision of guided missiles suggests a magnitude of lethality that indiscriminate rocket-propelled grenades, mortars, and other propelled munitions do not have. For this analysis we also distinguished between ordinary explosives and sophisticated explosives. Most explosives, when placed in confined spaces with crowds, have the capability for mass casualties that are not inherent in their design (e.g. a small pipe bomb in a crowded bus). However, the lethality of sophisticated explosives is far less dependent on the situational context in which they are deployed, either because the material used is highly powerful (e.g., Semtex) or the amount of material used is extremely large. For this analysis we included as sophisticated explosives only devices that were military grade or larger than 1,000 pounds.[5]

Figure 3.9 shows that despite our inclusive definition of WMD, attacks involving these weapons are a relatively rare occurrence. In fact, only 1,027 (1.3%) of the more than 82,000 attacks analyzed in our database used such weapons. Of these attacks, guided missiles were by far the most common, accounting for 62.8% of the total attacks. The second most common category of WMD was chemical attacks, accounting for 28.6% of the total incidents.

---

[5] We have excluded military-grade landmines from this category because their proliferation in some regions has made them relatively commonplace compared to the other types of sophisticated explosives.

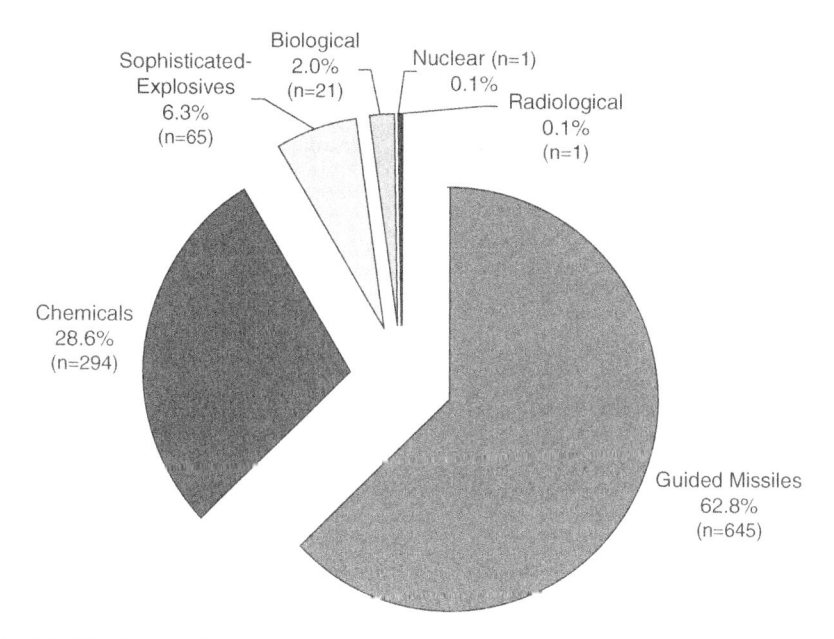

Fig. 3.9 Distribution of weapon types for WMD potential attacks, 1970–2004

As we discuss in more detail below, one of the most common forms of chemical attack in the data base was the use of butyric acid against abortion clinics in the United States.[6] Serious attacks, no doubt, but not the type of attack that most would associate with WMD. Tear gas and various poisons were also commonly used chemical agents. The next most common type of WMD was sophisticated explosives, accounting for 6.3% of the total attacks. Most of these attacks used military-grade munitions, especially C4 and Semtex. The least common types of WMD use in Fig. 3.9 were biological (two cases), and nuclear and radiological (one case each). The one radiological case involved a plot in Bellport, New York to assassinate local politicians using radioactive material. The one nuclear case involved the Ecology and Antinuclear Revolutionary Party leaving an extremely radioactive nuclear metal plaque in the mailbox of the French daily newspaper *Progress*.

---

[6] We hasten to add that our data on abortion-related attacks were far more complete for the United States than for other countries – which likely accounts for at least part of this result. Even though many attacks on abortion clinics fit the definition of terrorism being employed here, abortion-related attacks have not yet been systematically included in most open source terrorism data bases. This issue clearly requires more research attention in the future.

Regional Variations

There are also major differences in trends in terrorist attacks and fatalities across global regions. In the next series of figures we divide the world into six major regions (for a list of countries in each region, see Appendix). Figure 3.10 shows that terrorism and terrorism-related fatalities occur in Latin America nearly twice as often as in any other region of the world; more than five times as often as Sub-Saharan Africa; and more than 20 times more often than North America.[7] Europe rates second in terms of total incidents with more than 21% of all global terrorism, followed closely by Asia at nearly 20%. The Middle East/North African region follows with over 14% of the incidents, and Sub-Saharan Africa and North America account for the smallest proportion of terrorism attacks (6.4 and 1.7%, respectively).

Figure 3.10 also shows that the distribution of fatalities by region differs greatly from that of total incidents. While Latin America remains the leader in fatalities as well as in the proportion of total incidents, Asia has the second highest percentage of fatalities by region, accounting for nearly 27% of all terrorism-related fatalities. According to Fig. 3.10, while Europe is second in the proportion of attacks, it suffers relatively few fatalities as a result of these incidents, averaging less than one

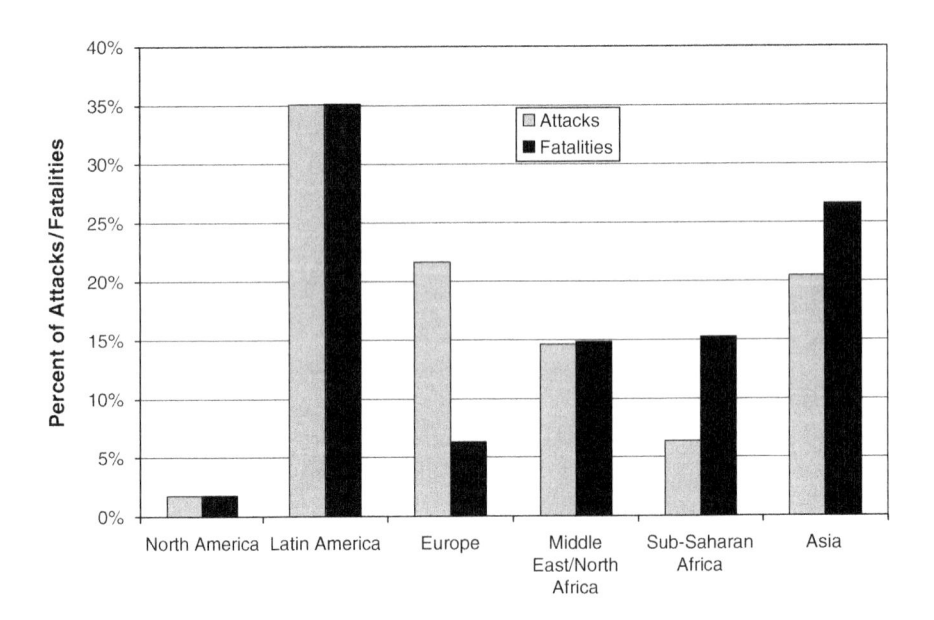

Fig. 3.10 Attacks and fatalities by region, 1970–2004

---

[7] Mexico and Puerto Rico are counted here as part of Latin America.

3 Tracking Global Terrorism Trends, 1970–2004

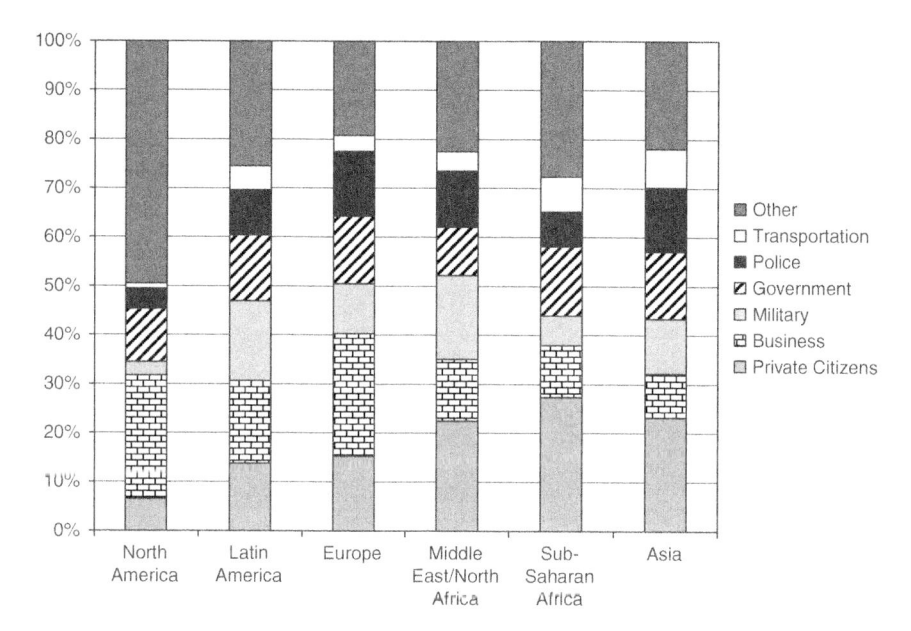

Fig. 3.11 Target type by region, 1970–2004

death (0.71) per incident. This rate is especially low compared to that for Sub-Saharan Africa which averages nearly six deaths for every terrorist attack. Thus, while the Sub-Saharan African region accounts for a relatively small proportion of total terrorist attacks, when there were attacks in this region, they were on average deadlier. The reasons for these differences remain to be explained, although part of the explanation may simply be media policies on reporting and proximate access to medical care across regions.

In Fig. 3.11, we examine target types by region of the world, emphasizing the target types that are most common. Private citizens are most likely to be targeted in Sub-Saharan Africa, Asia and the Middle East/North Africa and least likely to be targeted in North America, Latin America and Europe. A reverse pattern is found for businesses – they are most likely to be targeted in North America, Latin America and Europe and least likely to be targeted in Sub-Saharan Africa, Asia and the Middle East/North Africa. The GTD includes military targets if the attack fits the other parts of the definition provided above. In general, military targets were most common for the Middle East and North Africa and Latin America; least common in North America and Sub-Saharan Africa. Compared to the targets already discussed, government targets are more equally distributed across regions, although governments were targeted most frequently by terrorists in Sub-Saharan Africa and least frequently by terrorists in the Middle East/North African region. Police were most commonly targeted in Europe and Asia; least commonly targeted in North America.

Transportation-related targets also vary widely across the six regions. Transportation accounted for the highest proportion of attacks in Asia (8.0%) and Sub-Saharan Africa (7.1%). Attacks on transportation in North America – apart from airports and airlines – were rare, accounting for only 1.0% of all attacks. The other regions are intermediate between these extremes with transportation attacks accounting for 5.0% of all attacks in Latin America, 4.0% of all attacks in the Middle East/North Africa region, and 3.3% in Europe.

Despite the fact that the majority of target types fit into relatively few categories, the large "other" categories by region indicate substantial diversity. The region with the largest number of targets in the "other" category was North America (49.5%). Major targets in the other category for North America include abortion-related attacks (21.0%), diplomatic targets (7.4%), and airports and airlines (3.2%). The biggest single target in the other category for Latin America was utilities (10.2%). Utilities were also targeted in 6.1% of attacks in Sub-Saharan Africa and in 1.4% of the attacks in Asia. By contrast, attacks against utilities were very rare in North America, Europe, and the Middle East/North African region.

For North America, the Middle East/North Africa and Europe, a major target in the other category include diplomats (7.4% for North America, 4.1% for the Middle East/North Africa, and 3.8% for Europe). By contrast, attacks on diplomats were rare in Sub-Saharan Africa and Asia. NGOs were especially likely to be targeted in two regions: Sub-Saharan Africa (4.2%) and North America (3.2%). Most of the attacks on NGOs listed as against North America involved attacks on the UN.

In Fig. 3.12, we show the proportion of weapons used in attacks for the six regions. Overall, explosives and firearms account for the majority of cases in all six regions – a high of 91.7% of all attacks in Latin America and a low of 67.8% of all attacks in North America. In general, explosives as weapons were most common in North America (58.2%) and Europe (54.4%) and least common in Asia (37.3%) and Sub-Saharan Africa (37.9%). By contrast, firearms were most common in Asia (46.6%) and Sub-Saharan Africa (45.6%) and least common in North America (9.5%) and Europe (27.6%). Following explosives and firearms, the next most common weapon type was fire or firebombs. Fire or firebombs were most common in North America (23.0%) and Europe (14.6%) and least common in Latin America (5.5%) and the Middle East (6.0%). Knives and sharp objects were most important in the Middle East (5.9%) and Sub-Saharan Africa (5.4%).

As we saw above, chemical agents were rarely used in terrorist attacks since 1970. However, when they were used, they were far more likely to be used in North America (6.7%) than in any other region. In fact, of all the attacks with chemical agents during the period included in the data, 38% occurred in North America – largely a consequence of the use of butyric acid against abortion clinic providers.

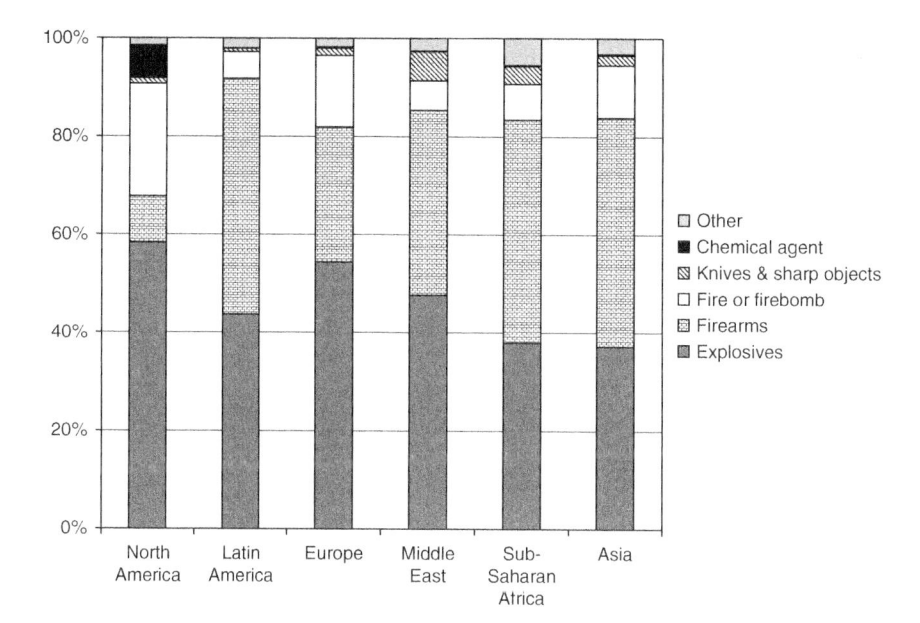

Fig. 3.12 Weapon by region, 1970–2004

Terrorist Organizations

At the time this chapter was being prepared, we had not yet finished matching terrorist groups from the original data base with those identified in the new data base. Therefore, analyses in this section are limited to the 1970–1997 data. During this period we were able to identify 1,769 separate terrorist groups in the original GTD. We gauge the longevity of groups here by measuring the amount of time from their first to their last known attack. In Fig. 3.13, we show the total number of years in which each of these groups staged known terrorist strikes. As can be seen from Fig. 3.13, nearly three-quarters of all terrorist groups ($N = 1,422$) identified in the original data base exhibited less than 1 year of time between their first known strike and their last known strike. Eighty-nine percent of the groups ($N = 1,703$) had a first strike-last strike time of 5 years or less and nearly 94% ($N = 1,791$) had a first strike-last strike time of 10 years or less. Only 24 terrorist organizations in our data base (1.3%) had a life span of more than 20 years from 1970 to 1997.

Of course the methods used here undercount the longevity of groups that began only recently – because some may have continued beyond the end of our data. Of the specific groups identified in the data base, 113 (6.5%) recorded their first strike after January 1996 (but before 1998) and 180 (10.5%) after January 1995 (but before 1998). Likewise, it is possible that a group is still functioning but that it takes a very long time between strikes. For example, other researchers (Hamm, 2007:61–62) have noted the willingness of groups like al-Qaeda to wait a considerable

[Bar chart: Years of operation for terrorist groups, 1970-1997]
- Less than 1: 74.72%
- 1 to 5: 14.77%
- 6 to 10: 4.62%
- 11 to 20: 4.62%
- over 20: 1.26%

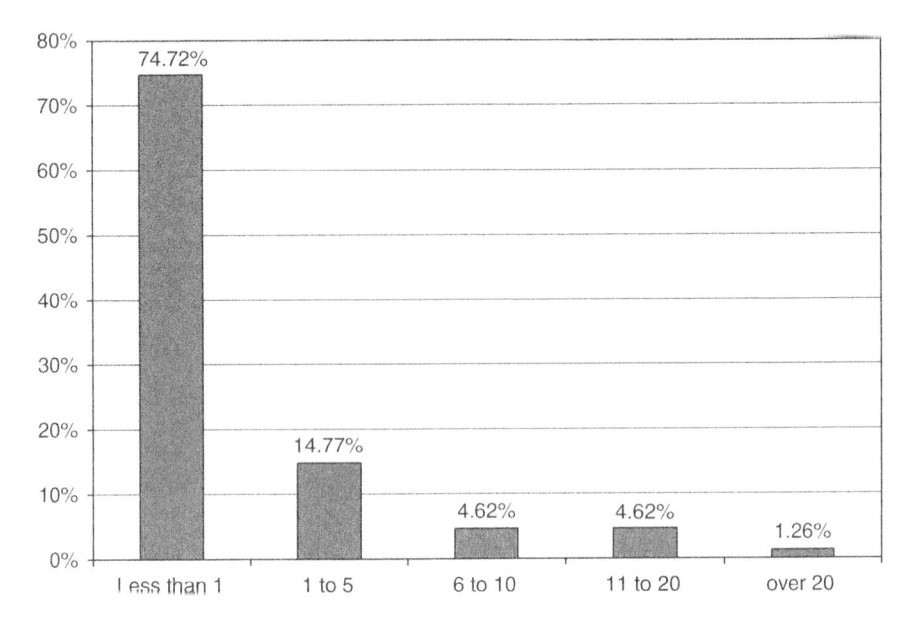

Fig. 3.13 Years of operation for terrorist groups, 1970–1997

amount of time between strikes. But even with these important caveats, the basic picture here is that the vast majority of terrorist organizations that claim responsibility for specific attacks are relatively short lived.

Another important consideration in terms of measuring the longevity of groups is whether attacks are attributed to them. In 35.5% of the cases in our data were not attributed to any group and no *specific* group was directly implicated in another 12.7% of cases. In these latter cases we were only able to attach generic group labels to the attacks – for example, "radical students" or "Sikh extremists."

But despite the methodological limitations inherent in using time between first and last claimed attack as a measure of a group's longevity, Fig. 3.13 is useful for dispelling a common stereotype about terrorist organizations: that they are long lasting. If we add up all the groups that existed for more than 10 years from 1970 to 1997 ($N = 112$) and add to this the new groups that formed and continued for the 4 years between 1994 and 1997 ($N = 112$), we have a total of 224 groups – about 11.8% of the total terrorist groups identified in the data base.[8] This is no doubt a large enough number of organizations to bring about alarm, but still does not contradict the conclusion that the vast majority of terrorist groups – like the vast majority of new businesses in the corporate world – have a very short life span.

---

[8] This calculation leaves out data for 1993.

3 Tracking Global Terrorism Trends, 1970–2004

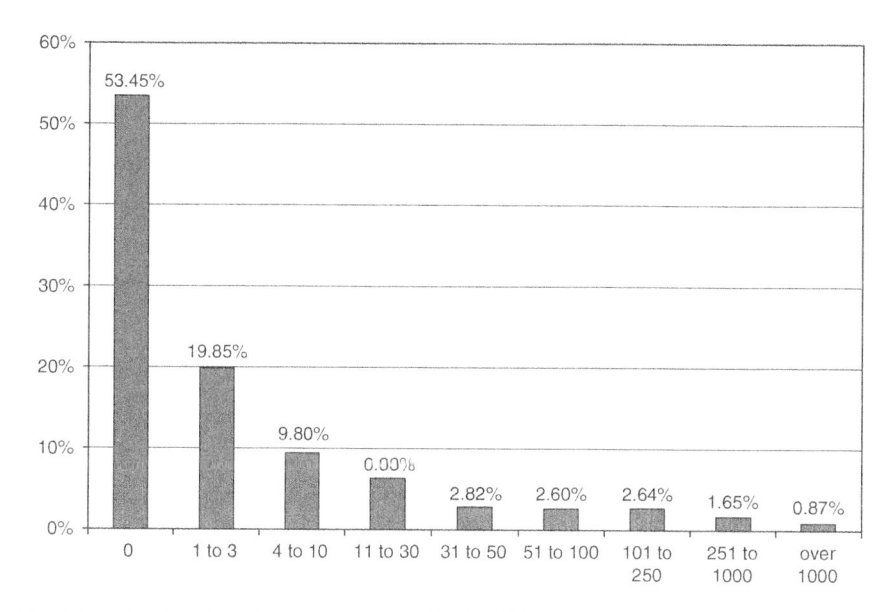

Fig. 3.14 Total fatalities for terrorist groups, 1970–1997

Bar chart values: 0: 53.45%; 1 to 3: 19.85%; 4 to 10: 9.80%; 11 to 30: 6.00%; 31 to 50: 2.82%; 51 to 100: 2.60%; 101 to 250: 2.64%; 251 to 1000: 1.65%; over 1000: 0.87%.

Another common perception about terrorist operations is that they universally produce a large number of fatalities. Figure 3.14 shows the distribution of total known fatalities claimed by the terrorist organizations in the original GTD. Given the international publicity attached to high-profile incidents we are naturally primed to think of terrorist organizations as incredibly lethal. But Fig. 3.14 shows that over 53% of the terrorist organizations in the data base never produced a single fatality. Many groups direct their attacks toward property only. Others are aimed at civilians, but fail. In many other cases terrorist groups provide a warning to civilians before striking. Of course, it is still the case that 46.6% of the terrorist organizations included in the database (or 1,074 groups) were blamed for attacks that killed at least one person.

For obvious reasons, policy makers are likely to be especially interested in the relatively small number of terrorist groups that are most active. In Table 3.1, we provide a list of the 20 most active terrorist groups from the GTD (in terms of total number of attacks claimed) from 1970 to 2004. Shining Path (Sendero Luminoso) leads the list with over 4,500 attacks from 1978 through 2004. The next highest group in terms of attacks is the FMLN. Seven additional groups in the data base claimed responsibility for more than 1,000 attacks: the Irish Republican Army (IRA), Basque Fatherland and Freedom (ETA), Revolutionary Armed Forces of Colombia (FARC), the National Liberation Army of Colombia (ELN), the Kurdistan Workers Party (PKK), the Liberation Tigers of Tamil Eelam (LTTE),

Table 3.1 Twenty most active groups, 1970–2004

Group	Attacks	First year	Last year
Shining path (SL)	4,569	1978	2004
Farabundo Marti national liberation front (FMLN)	3,353	1978	1994
Irish republican army (IRA)	2,801	1970	2003
Basque fatherland and freedom (ETA)	1,950	1970	2004
Revolutionary armed forces of colombia (FARC)	1,512	1975	2004
National liberation army of Colombia (ELN)	1,181	1972	2004
Kurdistan workers party (PKK)	1,149	1984	2004
Liberation tigers of tamil eelam (LTTE)	1,077	1979	2004
New people's army (NPA)	1,072	1970	2004
Manuel Rodriguez patriotic front (FPMR)	838	1984	1997
Tupac Amaru revolutionary movement (MRTA)	570	1984	1997
M-19 (Movement of April 19)	569	1976	1997
Corsican national liberation front (FLNC)	509	1974	2003
National union for the total independence of Angola (UNITA)	427	1978	2002
Hizballah	311	1981	2004
Movement of the revolutionary left (MIR) (Chile)	309	1976	1994
Ulster volunteer force (UVF)	276	1969	2003
African national congress (South Africa)	260	1976	1996
Dev Sol	258	1979	1996
Popular liberation army (EPL)	254	1973	1998

and the New people's army (NPA). Interestingly, eight of the 20 most active groups had no known terrorist attacks during the last 2 years of the data collection (2003 and 2004).

Among the active groups, groups that have shown a willingness to use WMD are likely to attract special interest among policy makers. In an earlier section, we used the GTD to identify all attacks that used chemical, biological, radiological, nuclear, guided missiles and sophisticated explosives from 1970 to 2004. In Table 3.2 we identify the top 20 terrorist organizations in our database that used these potential WMDs the most frequently. While some names are recognizable due to either high activity or high profile events (e.g., Hizballah, FARC, Hamas, al-Qaeda, and the Khmer Rough), others like the Dishmish Regiment and Mujahidin-e-Khalq have thus far committed relatively few attacks and generated a small number of fatalities. Yet, the majority of their attacks (86% for Dishmish Regiment and 64% for Mujahidin-e-Khalq) used at least one weapon with WMD potential. Because compared to more conventional weapons, these weapons generally require a higher level of training and infrastructure to deploy – it may be that groups who use them may be more likely to obtain and deploy more powerful WMDs in future operations.

Table 3.2 Top 20 groups that have used chemical, biological, radiation, nuclear, guided missiles or sophisticated explosives (WMD Potential), 1970–2004

Group	WMD potential attacks	Total attacks	Total fatalities
Dishmish regiment	37	43	6
Fuerzas Armadas Revolucionarias de Colombia (FARC)	34	307	1,253
Hizballah	34	311	718
Moro islamic liberation front (MILF)	29	212	580
HAMAS	28	140	446
Irish republican army (IRA)	26	2,801	1,917
Liberation tigers of tamil eelam (LTTE)	24	1,077	9,760
Taliban	20	123	298
Khmer Rouge	15	198	490
National union for the total independence of Angola (UNITA)	14	427	2,567
Mujahidin-e-Khalq	9	14	5
17 November revolutionary organization (17N)	7	15	2
al-Qaeda	7	68	3441
Kosovo liberation army (KLA)	7	56	49
National liberation army (NLA)	7	110	80
National liberation forces-Icanzo (FNL-Icanzo)	6	15	42
Basque fatherland and freedom (ETA)	5	1,812	748
Euskadi ta Askatasuna (ETA)	5	137	49
Lashkar-e-Taiba (LeT)	5	44	328
United liberation front of Assam	5	45	186

Country-Level Comparisons

In the next section, we consider country-level characteristics of the data from 1970 to 2004. We introduce this section with Table 3.3, a list of the 20 countries that were most commonly targeted by terrorists from 1970 to 2004.[9]

On the basis of substantial differences in total attacks by region that we observed above, it is unsurprising that countries vary greatly in terms of total incidents included in the GTD. The importance of Latin America as a regional source for

---

[9] Note that our analysis here includes only attacks on the soil of specific countries; we do not measure the nationality of the intended target or the nationality of the terrorist group. Thus, attacks on Turkish nationals living in France and attacks by Turkish nationals operating in France are both coded here as attacks on France. While the vast majority of all attacks within particular countries are, in fact, aimed at nationals within those countries and are committed by terrorist groups from these same countries, there is of course variation across countries and over time. We are exploring these relationships in ongoing research.

Table 3.3 Twenty countries with the most terrorist attacks, 1970–2004

Country	Attacks	Fatalities	Fatalities per attack
Colombia	6,871	13,170	1.917
Peru	6,134	13,040	2.126
El Salvador	5,556	13,764	2.477
India	3,979	12,441	3.127
Northern Ireland	3,921	2,981	0.760
Spain	3,166	1,406	0.444
Turkey	2,656	4,713	1.774
Pakistan	2,490	4,468	1.794
Sri Lanka	2,474	14,241	5.756
Philippines	2,424	6,290	2.595
Chile	2,344	232	0.099
Guatemala	2,125	5,447	2.563
Israel	2,041	1,860	0.911
Nicaragua	2,027	11,320	5.585
Lebanon	1,975	3,106	1.573
Algeria	1,677	8,376	4.995
South Africa	1,615	2,550	1.579
Italy	1,594	407	0.255
United States	1,262	2,692	2.133
France	1,255	222	0.177

terrorist attacks is underscored by the fact that the three countries with the highest number of attacks in the GTD are all Latin American: Colombia, Peru, and El Salvador. In addition, three other Latin American countries make the top 20: Chile, Guatemala, and Nicaragua. Following Latin America, Europe contains several countries that are in the top 20 in terms of total attacks: Northern Ireland (treated here as a country), Spain, Italy, and France (including Corsica). Four Asian countries are in the top 20 in terms of attacks: India, Pakistan, Sri Lanka, and the Philippines. Only three Middle Eastern/North African countries are in the top 20: Turkey, Israel, and Lebanon. South Africa and Algeria are the sole countries from Sub-Saharan Africa in the top 20 most frequently targeted countries. The United States finishes as 19th among the top 20 countries in terms of total attacks.

As international interest in terrorism has grown, researchers and policy makers have increasingly sought to understand terrorism by looking at the social, economic, and political characteristics of countries. Two commonly studied political characteristics thought to be connected with terrorist attacks within countries are the strength of democracy (Crenshaw, 1981; Chalk, 1998; Crelinsten, 1998) and the status of a country as a failed state (LaFree et al., 2007; Wilkenfeld, 2007).

Empirical connections between democracy and terrorism are far from settled, with some researchers arguing that democratic institutions inoculate countries from terrorist strikes (Sandler, 1995), others arguing that civil rights protections and the rule of law in democracies make it more difficult to prevent terrorist strikes (Eubank and Weinberg, 1994, 1998; Li, 2005) and still others (Eyerman, 1998) arguing that terrorism will be most common in countries transitioning from autocratic to democratic forms of government. A frequent related argument is that terrorist organizations exploit the openness of liberal democracies to develop and grow (Ganor, 2005, this volume).

To explore these issues in greater detail, we examined connections between country-level terrorist attacks from the GTD and the most widely examined political science measure of democracy, the POLITY 2 index (Gurr, 1974; Gurr et al., 1990; Jaggers and Gurr, 1995). Gurr et al. developed additive scales for annual rates of both democracy and autocracy for all countries of the world back to 1,800 (for a review, see LaFree and Tseloni, 2006). The democracy measure is derived from evaluations of four characteristics of national governments: (1) the competitiveness of political participation, (2) the openness of executive recruitment, (3) the competitiveness of executive recruitment, and (4) constraints on the chief executive. The POLITY 2 index ranges from −10 for fully autocratic countries to +10 for fully democratic countries. Based on this measure, we divided countries of the world into four categories: (1) *fully democratic*, for countries that received a perfect 10 points on the democracy score for the entire 27 years spanned by the original GTD; (2) *nearly democratic*, for countries that scored an average of at least 6 points on the democracy index, but received less than a full 10 points for the 27 years spanned by the GTD; (3) *mixed regimes*, for countries that scored between +6 and −6 on the Polity index, and (4) *mostly autocratic*, for countries scoring less than −6 during the entire 27 years spanned by the data.

In Fig. 3.15, we compare the distribution of terrorist attacks from the GTD from 1970 to 1997 for the four categories of democracy just identified. Figure 3.15 shows trends in

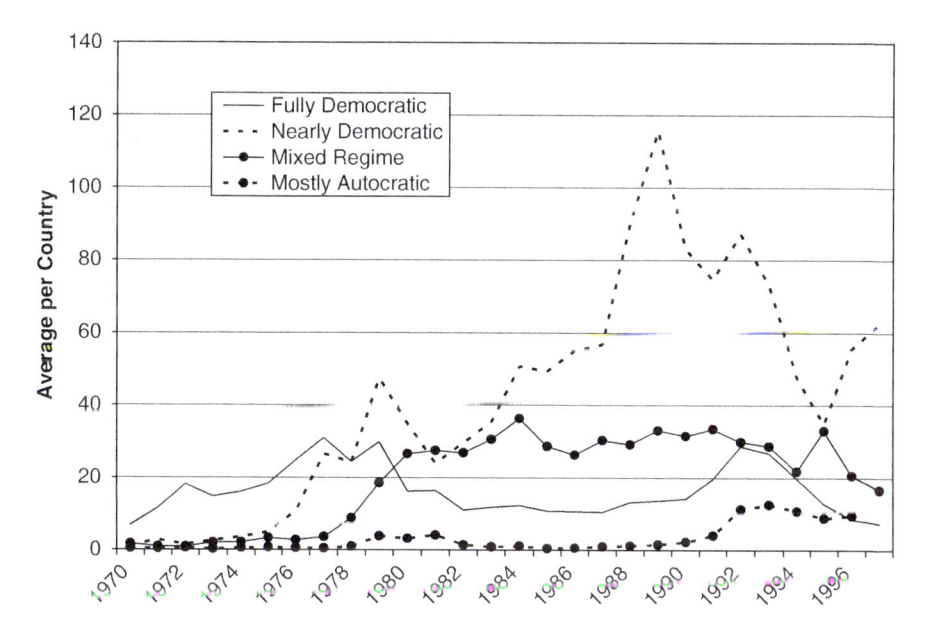

Fig. 3.15 Terrorism and democracy, 1970–1997

total terrorist attacks for fully democratic, mostly democratic, mixed and mostly autocratic countries. Perhaps, the most striking feature of Figure 3.15 is the trend line for the nearly democratic countries. Terrorist attacks within nearly democratic countries begin the series far under fully democratic countries with only 1.2 attacks on average in 1970 (only mostly autocratic countries were lower with an average of 0.46 attacks in 1970). However, the number of attacks staged in nearly democratic countries increases from the mid-1970s to a peak of 115.7 events on average per country in 1989. The mixed regime countries also begin the series at relatively low levels (1.7 in 1970) but then increase rapidly in the late 1970s. After the 1970s, they maintain a high, but steady level of attacks through to the end of the series in 1997.

Of the four democracy categories, the fully democratic countries experience the most constant stream of attacks throughout the series. They begin the series with more attacks than any other group (an average of 6.8 per country in 1970) and end the series with a similar number (an average of 7.4 per country in 1997). By contrast, the mostly autocratic countries have very low average levels of attacks until a fairly sharp upward turn starting in 1990.

Evidence of a relationship between level of democratization and terrorist activity is clearly strengthened by these results. In general, countries that stood between democracy and autocracy, classified here as nearly democratic and mixed regime, were the most prone to terrorist attacks. There is also evidence that these relationships have been changing over time. The nearly democratic countries experienced major increases in terrorist attacks from the late 1970s through the early 1990s. Attacks attributed to these countries declined somewhat afterwards, but the nearly democratic countries still ended the series in 1997 with large numbers of attacks. Mixed regime countries, the category just above the mostly autocratic category on our democracy scale, also experienced high levels of attacks throughout the series, although they did not experience the same peak in the 1980s and early 1990s that the mostly democratic countries did.

Fully democratic countries generally experienced a moderate but persistent level of attacks throughout the series. One possible explanation for the relatively moderate level of attacks in fully democratic countries might be that these countries have stronger, more robust governance structures. Research under way by Young (2007) suggests that strong states are more immune to terrorist violence.

By contrast, compared to the other democratic categories examined here, the mostly autocratic countries generally had the lowest average number of attacks. However, total attacks in the mostly autocratic countries increased considerably at the end of the series. In short, we do find important differences between terrorism attacks and fatalities and level of democracy for countries over time. However, contrary to some prior research (e.g., Eubank and Weinberg, 1994, 1998) our results show that the risk of terrorism is greatest for countries whose political structure places them between fully democratic and autocratic. In contrast, the fully democratic countries and the mostly autocratic countries face considerably less risk of terrorism. We are currently working on more detailed analysis of these issues, expecting that the relationship might depend on specific characteristics of countries that are likely to vary substantially over time.

We next examined connections between terrorist attacks from the GTD from 1970 to 1997 to a measure of failed states developed by the Political Instability Task Force (PITF), a multi-disciplinary group assembled in 1994 (Bates et al., 2006). The scope of the database collected by the PITF includes all countries with a population over 500,000 (162 countries) for the years between 1955 and 2004 (Esty et al., 1995:2).

The PITF defines state failure broadly as including "civil conflicts, political crises, and massive human rights violations that are typically associated with state breakdown" (Esty et al., 1995:1). Thus, we consider a state to have failed when it experiences one of the following types of conflict: revolutionary or ethnic war, adverse or disruptive regime transition, and genocides or politicides (homicides targeting individuals or groups based on their political affiliations). The PITF defines revolutionary wars as sustained military conflicts between insurgents and central governments, aimed at displacing regimes; ethnic wars as secessionist civil wars, rebellions, protracted communal warfare, and sustained episodes of mass protest by politically organized communal groups; genocides and politicides as sustained policies by states or their agents that result in the deaths of substantial portion of members of communal or political groups; and adverse or disruptive regime transitions as major, abrupt shifts in patterns of governance, including state collapse, periods of severe instability, and shifts toward authoritarian rule (Esty et al., 1995:2).

Because the coverage of the original GTD is from 1970 to 1997, only failures between these years were included in this analysis. Further, because one of the criteria for state failure is protracted episodes of terrorism, we excluded as indicators of state failure analysis protracted terrorism campaigns that took place in Algeria, China, Egypt, Iran, Israel, Northern Ireland/UK, Peru and the Philippines. In addition, we also excluded as indicators of state failure any direct governmental responses to such campaigns of terrorism.[10] Because both the GTD and the PITF include attacks against the military (although by different types of perpetrators), some attacks reported in the GTD could have been used by the PITF to indicate state failure.[11] To reduce possible bias due to this definitional overlap, we also excluded from the terrorism-state failure analyses any GTD attacks where the target was identified as military.

In Fig. 3.16, we compare rates of terrorist attack over time for states identified in the PITF data as "in failure" versus states not so identified. Among the 81 states in the data that experienced at least 1 year of state failure between 1970 and 1997, the mean number of years that a country was in failure was 9.3. Figure 3.16 shows that differences between the two types of states become dramatic after 1979. Prior to 1979, "out of failure" countries had, on average, more terrorism attacks each year, than in failure countries. In the 1980s, in failure states fluctuate

---

[10] It is also important to note that many of these countries had other failure problems co-occurring or occurring very closely in time to terrorism campaigns. If we determined that these other failures would have occurred independently of the terrorism episodes, we classified the country as having failed.

[11] While the GTD excludes attacks on the military by uniformed military or by guerilla organizations, it includes military targets that are attacked by sub state groups where there is a political, economic or social motive.

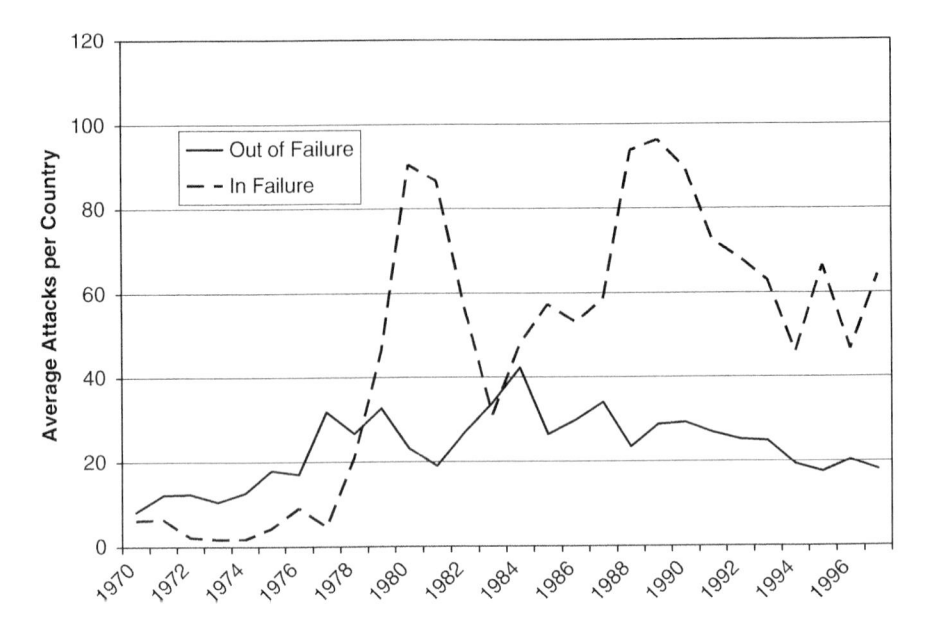

Fig. 3.16 Terrorism and state failure, 1970–1997

from a highpoint in 1980 of 90.5 attacks per year to a decade low of 31.2 attacks per year in 1983. Then, terrorism attacks for in failure countries increase to a series high in 1989 of 96.2 average attacks per country. By contrast, out of failure countries show a weak positive trend from 1977 to 1992, which includes the peak of 42.3 average incidents per country in 1984. After 1984, the trend steadily declines. The large differences in magnitude between states in and out of failure for most of the series after 1979 is consistent with the conclusion that states are especially vulnerable to terrorism while experiencing state failure.

It is also worth noting that during the 1970s, countries in failure had virtually no recorded terrorist attacks in the GTD. In fact, total event counts for in failure countries during the years 1970 through 1977 were fewer than ten. A partial explanation for these striking differences might be media bias: perhaps failed states during these years had less media coverage, resulting in undercounting in open source terrorism data bases such as the GTD. We are exploring this possibility in ongoing research.

Terrorism and Violent Crime

Given that terrorism is a form of violent criminality, there has been some interest in comparing rates of terrorist attacks to other types of criminal violence, especially at the cross-national level. However, as with other empirical issues related to terrorism, this ends up being a challenging exercise. At present, the three major sources of longitudinal, cross-national crime data are the International Criminal Police Organization (Interpol), the UN, and the WHO. The strengths and weaknesses of these three data sources are reviewed elsewhere (Neapolitan, 1997; LaFree, 1999; Aebi et al., 2003), and hence we only summarize major conclusions here. Substantial variation across countries in legal definitions has increasingly lead researchers (Archer and Gartner, 1984; Lynch, 1995) to rely on homicide data in cross-national comparative research. Both Interpol and the UN survey collect homicide data from criminal justice agencies in member nations. WHO homicide data are based instead on cause of death reports submitted by participating nations. There is now substantial agreement (Kalish, 1988; Neapolitan, 1997; Messner and Rosenfeld, 1997) that among the three major cross-national homicide data sources, WHO data are the most valid and reliable.

However, a major limitation of WHO homicide victimization data is that they are only consistently available for a small proportion of the world's countries. We were able to assemble annual time-series data from WHO on homicide victimization rates per 100,000 residents for 28 countries from 1970 to 1997. We included only countries with complete data for the entire series. Because Iceland had no homicides for several years, it was impossible to compute a meaningful measure of relative difference between Iceland and other countries and we excluded it. Rates for Israel are reported only for the Jewish population. Several political changes affected the geographical boundaries, and hence the homicide rates of the nations included. We examine rates for Czechoslovakia until the political breakup of 1992 and for the Czech Republic only thereafter. We examine rates for the Federal Republic of Germany (West Germany) prior to unification with the German Democratic Republic in 1990 and for the unified country thereafter.

As is universally true in this type of research, the sample is heavily dominated by North American and West European nations, which comprises 18 countries (64%) in the sample. In addition, the sample includes one Latin American/Caribbean country, three East European countries, four countries from the Western Pacific, one from Africa, and one from the Middle East.

Figure 3.17 compares mean homicide rates to total terrorist attacks from 1970 to 1997. The two series are significantly correlated ($r = 0.54$; $p = 0.003$). Homicide rates trend upward throughout most of the series with a series high point in 1992. By contrast, total terrorist attacks for the same countries move steeply up from 1970 before reaching a series peak in 1979. Following this high point terrorist attacks decline into the late 1980s before hitting another smaller peak in 1993. From that point until the end of the series, terrorist attacks, like homicide rates, show considerable decline.

Discussion and Conclusions

In this paper we presented for the first time a combined analysis of the GTD from 1970 to 2004. Although we had not finished synthesizing the original GTD collection and the more recent GTD collection when this chapter was being prepared, our

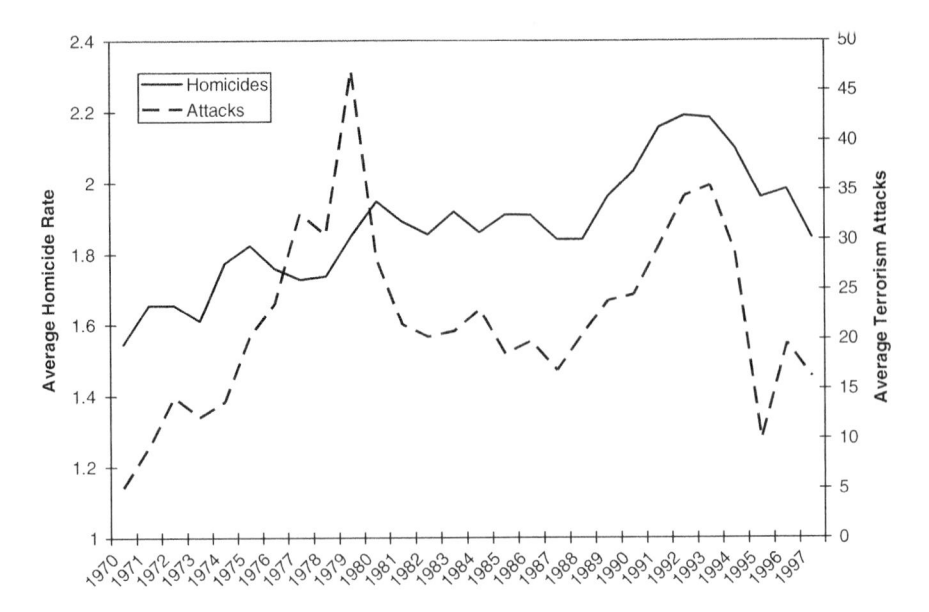

Fig. 3.17 Average homicides and terrorism attacks, 1970–1997

preliminary analysis suggests that terrorism attacks began to increase steadily during the 1970s and 1980s, reaching a peak in the early 1990s and then declining considerably before the end of the twentieth century. However, our current data collection for GTD and our work on a companion research project with RAND (Dugan et al. 2008) both suggest that the widening scope of hostilities in Iraq and Afghanistan in the early part of the twenty-first century is likely to force these rates to increase substantially after 2004.

We have found several patterns in the data that should inform the research community, policy-makers and law enforcement. If we were to profile typical terrorism over the 34-year period, we would argue that most terrorism is most often non-lethal, using relatively simple, unsophisticated weaponry. Bombings are by far, the preferred mode of attack, and private citizens and businesses are targeted most often. But of course, many cases do not fit this profile. In order to properly understand terrorism, one must appreciate the variance found in the less common cases.

For instance, while the most common terrorist attack produces no fatalities, the average number of fatalities per terrorist attack has continued to increase over time. Changes in the number of fatalities per attack are closely correlated with changes in the location of terrorist attacks. In particular, as attacks have become more common in Sub-Saharan Africa and Asia and less common in Europe, the average number of fatalities per attack has also steadily increased. The change can also be linked to changing strategies employed by terrorist groups. Thus, while groups like the IRA and ETA have often avoided mass casualty attacks, groups that have become more active in recent years, such as the LTTE and al-Qaeda have actively sought high fatality attacks.

Despite the attention devoted to complex attacks based on highly sophisticated weaponry, the typical terrorist attack has been relatively simple and has rarely involved difficult to obtain weaponry. Bombings, facility attacks and assassinations are by far the most common forms of terrorism. Kidnappings are rare and aerial hijackings are rarer still. The vast majority of incidents involved explosives, firearms or firebombs. Fortunately, chemical, biological, radiological, and nuclear weapons have thus far been extremely rare.

As noted above, the most common targets are private citizens and property, businesses, and the military. Government agents or facilities, police, transportation, utilities, diplomatic, journalists and media, religious institutions or figures, and educational institutions are less common. Yet, when we examine regional distributions, we uncover important variations across the globe.

Contrary to common perceptions, most terrorist organizations last only a short time. The few that persist over longer periods of time naturally receive the most attention. More than half of terrorist attacks where a group claims responsibility result in no fatalities. By contrast, over 5% of attacks by terrorist groups produced more than 100 fatalities and just under 1% produced more than 1,000 fatalities. It is of course the threat of these especially deadly attacks that raises the greatest concern.

Terrorism trends at the country level are closely related to other political trends. In general, countries that stand between democracy and autocracy and countries whose social and political institutions are in a state of failure were the most prone to terrorist attacks. There is also evidence that these relationships are growing stronger over time. Countries midway between full democracy and autocracy and countries in a state of failure both experienced major increases in terrorist attacks from the late 1970s through the early 1990s. In short, we do find important connections among terrorism attacks, democracy levels, and state failure for countries over time. We are currently working on more detailed analysis of these issues, expecting that these relationships may depend on specific characteristics of countries that are likely to vary substantially over time.

Ironically, the media savvy nature of terrorism makes it easier to track than more common crimes through publicly open sources. WHO homicide data are generally regarded as the gold standard in cross-national comparative criminology research. Our comparison of terrorist event data and WHO homicide data for 28 countries from 1970 to 1997 showed that, indeed, there is a significant positive relationship between country-level terrorist attacks and homicide rates over time. We plan to explore these connections in more detail in ongoing research.

Our efforts to track trends in global terrorism for this volume have raised a number of serious gaps in our understanding of terrorism that we want to emphasize in closing. First, it is imperative that governments develop more accurate and valid methods for tracking terrorism over time. Krueger and Laitin (2004:9) points out that the US State Department is the only Cabinet-level agency in the US government that has no in-house statistician office. Imagine fighting cancer with no data on how many people contract cancer. Or imagine crafting a responsible policy on unemployment with no data on the number of people without jobs. Criminology has long struggled to develop valid measures of crime. But, while data collection in criminology is also challenging, policy makers and law enforcement officials can now draw on a wealth of official statistics as well as national and international victimization and self report surveys – data sources that do not exist for terrorism.

Second, in his examination of academic research on terrorism, Merari (1991:89) emphasizes the importance of in-depth studies of specific terrorist organizations, including their ideology, motivation, structure, demographic characteristics and decision making mechanisms. Indeed, data bases like the GTD and RAND's MIPT (for a review, see LaFree and Dugan, 2007) are greatly improving our understanding of terrorist attacks. However, these data bases are not organized to answer direct questions about the characteristics of terrorist organizations. While the operational aspects of terrorist behavior are routine subjects for intelligence analysts and criminal justice professionals, the information collected is often anecdotal and unsystematic. In the absence of valid empirical data, a host of important questions about terrorism remain unanswered. How do terrorists groups make operational planning decisions? How do time horizons, risk thresholds, perceptual biases, and other decision-making factors affect these decisions? Do these factors vary according to the structural make-up of groups, for example small self-organizing groups versus large well-organized groups? How well do they meet their mid-term and long-term goals? How do terrorist strategies relate to criminal activities? What determines when terrorists will resort to ordinary crimes? Can some identified set of "precursor" crimes predict potential or actual terrorists? What accounts for the selection of tactics, such as weapon selection? When and why do groups employ or condone suicide attacks? When and how do tactics change, whether through innovation or imitation? How can criminal justice processing be used to prevent, mitigate or punish terrorist activity? What types of investigation, prosecution, and punishment are most effective against terrorism?

Third, unlike research on criminal justice polices and practices, there is a startling lack of social science research on how anti-terrorism and counter-terrorism efforts impact the behavior and activities of terrorists or potential terrorists. We need to have a much better idea of which of our policies for countering terrorism are working, which are not and which are making things worse. Even basic questions in this area have not been adequately addressed. How can we measure the success of counter- and anti-terrorist measures? What have been the short- and long-term impacts on terrorist activity of counter-terrorist initiatives taken at the local, national, and international levels? Which initiatives have fostered terrorist group deterrence and desistence, and which have led to defiance and innovation by groups? Do specific initiatives have a consistent or a variable effect on different terrorist groups? To what extent do counter-terrorism initiatives alienate communities? Many of these questions need to be addressed in an environment where terrorist organizations are themselves evolving. For example, effective counter-terrorist strategies may be very different for hierarchically organized terrorist groups than for loosely organized networks.

Fourth, much of the research work on terrorism that has been completed to date has been aimed at transnational terrorism – events that target a different country than the home country of the offenders. This has been the case despite the fact that attacks launched by domestic terrorist groups likely outnumber international terrorist attacks by as much as seven to one (LaFree and Dugan, 2007). Until recently, none of the open-source terrorist event data bases included domestic attacks. However, with the creation of databases like the GTD this situation is rapidly changing. In many ways, the challenges of domestic terrorism for researchers, policy makers and law enforcement officials are very different than the challenges posed by transnational terrorists. In particular, the possibility of home grown terrorism raises issues about the mechanisms that lead individuals and groups to adopt terrorist methods against their own country. What is the nature of this process for individuals and groups and how is it differentially affected by different political, social, and economic factors? Just as importantly, what are the processes by which these radicalization processes can be reversed or disrupted? And how can societies counter the ideological arguments of extremists and bring about decreases in support for and commitment to terrorist behavior? Issues like these strike at the heart of long-standing concerns in democratic societies about how to balance security issues with privacy and civil liberties issues.

And finally, just as important as understanding terrorism is understanding the most effective methods for responding to terrorism. That is, not only do we need to know more about how to prevent terrorism, we also need to know far more about how the negative effects of terrorism can be mitigated by our responses to it. Responses to terrorism raise a whole series of critical research concerns. How resilient are communities to the threat of terrorism? What are the most effective strategies for enhancing resilience? What can federal and state government do to increase resilience and what should local communities be encouraged to do? How should federal and state government most effectively encourage communities to act on their own to enhance their resilience? What role can non-governmental institutions play in bolstering the levels of resilience? How do countries, states, and communities respond to large-scale terrorism in the long term? Do social or political changes wrought by terrorism persist? If so, how do societies adapt and if not, how quickly does a return to the *status quo ante* occur, and is the *status quo ante* always the preferred outcome?

In short, there are currently major gaps in our understanding of terrorism and the best methods for countering it. Nevertheless, there is also clear evidence that researchers and policy makers are seeking answers to fundamental questions with an unparalleled sense of urgency.

Acknowledgment Support for this work was provided by the National Institute of Justice (NIJ), grant number 2002-DT-CX-0001 and the Department of Homeland Security (DHS) through the National Center for the Study of Terrorism and Responses to Terrorism (START), grant number N00140510629. We would like to thank Erin Miller, Susan Fahey and Brandon Behlendorf for assistance with data analysis. Any opinions, findings, and conclusions or recommendations in this document are those of the authors and do not necessarily reflect the views of NIJ or DHS.

Appendix: Countries listed under each region

Region	Countries/territories
North America	Canada, the French territory of St. Pierre and Miquelon[a], and the United States
Latin America	Anguilla[a], Antigua and Barbuda[a], Argentina, Aruba[a], Bahamas[a], Barbados[a], Belize[a], Bermuda[a], Bolivia, Bonaire[a], Brazil, Cayman Islands[a], Chile, Colombia, Costa Rica, Cuba, Curacao[a], Dominica[a], Dominican Republic, Ecuador, El Salvador, Falkland Islands[a], French Guiana[a], Grenada[a], Guadeloupe[a], Guatemala, Guyana, Haiti, Honduras, Jamaica, Martinique[a], Mexico, Montserrat[a], Nicaragua, Panama, Paraguay, Peru, Puerto Rico[a], Saba[a], St. Barthelemy[a], St. Eustatius[a], St. Kitts and Nevis[a], St. Lucia[a], St. Maarten[a], St. Martin[a], St. Vincent and the Grenadines[a], Suriname[a], Trinidad and Tobago, Turks and Caicos[a], Uruguay, Venezuela, and the Virgin Islands (British and USA)[a]
Europe	Albania, Andorra[a], Armenia, Austria, Azerbaijan, Belgium, Bosnia-Herzegovina, Bulgaria, Byelarus, Croatia, Czech Republic, Denmark, Estonia, Finland, France, Georgia, Germany, Gibraltar[a], Greece, Greenland[a], Hungary, Iceland, Ireland, Italy, Kazakhstan, Kyrgyzstan, Latvia, Liechtenstein[a], Lithuania, Luxembourg, Macedonia, Malta[a], Isle of Man[a], Moldova, Monaco[a], Netherlands, Norway, Poland, Portugal, Romania, Russia, San Marino[a], Serbia- Montenegro (Yugoslavia), Slovak Republic, Slovenia, Spain, Sweden, Switzerland, Tajikistan, Turkmenistan, Ukraine, United Kingdom, and Uzbekistan
Middle East and North Africa	Algeria, Bahrain, Cyprus, Egypt, Iran, Iraq, Israel, Jordan, Kuwait, Lebanon, Libya, Morocco, Oman, Palestine[a], Qatar, Saudi Arabia, Syria, Tunisia, Turkey, United Arab Emirates, and Yemen
Sub-Saharan Africa	Angola, Benin, Botswana, Burkina Faso, Burundi, Cameroon, Cape Verde[a], Central African Republic, Chad, Comoros, Congo, Djibouti, Equatorial Guinea, Eritrea, Ethiopia, Gabon, Gambia, Ghana, Guinea, Guinea-Bissau, Ivory Coast, Kenya, Lesotho, Liberia, Madagascar, Malawi, Mali, Mauritania, Mauritius, Mozambique, Namibia, Niger, Nigeria, Reunion[a], Rwanda, Sao Tome and Principe[a], Senegal, Seychelles[a], Sierra Leone, Somalia, South Africa, Sudan, Swaziland, Tanzania, Togo, Uganda, Zaire, Zambia, and Zimbabwe
Asia	Afghanistan, Australia, Bangladesh, Bhutan, Brunei[a], Cambodia, China, Cook Islands[a], Fiji, French Polynesia[a], Guam[a], Hong Kong[a], India, Indonesia, Japan, Kiribati[a], Laos, Macao[a], Malaysia, Maldives[a], Marshall Islands[a], Micronesia[a], Mongolia, Myanmar, Nauru[a], Nepal, New Caledonia[a], New Zealand, Niue[a], North Korea, Northern Mariana Islands[a], Pakistan, Palau[a], Papua New Guinea, Philippines, Samoa (USA)[a], Singapore, Solomon Islands[a], South Korea, Sri Lanka, Taiwan, Thailand, Tonga[a], Tuvalu[a], Vanuatu[a], Vietnam, Wallis and Futuna[a], and Western Samoa[a]

[a] These countries are not part of the POLITY 2 database and are excluded from the data used to create Fig. 3.14. However, incidents from these countries are used to produce the other figures in the paper

References

M.F. Aebi, M. Killias, and C. Tavares. 2003. Comparing Crime Rates: The International Crime (Victim) Survey, the European Sourcebook of Crime and Criminal Justice Statistics, and INTERPOL Statistics. In: H. Kury (ed). *International Comparison of Crime and Victimization*. pp. 22–37 *International Comparison of Crime and Victimization*. Ontario: de Sitter.

D. Archer and R. Gartner. 1984. *Violence and Crime in Cross-National Perspective*. New Haven: Yale University Press.

R.H. Bates, D.L. Epstein, J.A. Goldstone, T.R. Gurr, B. Harff, C.H. Kahl, M.A. Levy, M. Lustik, M.G. Marshall, T.M. Parris, J. Ulfelder, and M.R. Woodward. 2006. *Political Instability Task Force Report: Phase IV Findings*. Mclean, VA: SAIC.

D.H. Bayley and D. Weisburd. 2008. The Role of Police in Counter-terrorism. Forthcoming.

W.S. Carus. 2006. *Defining "Weapons of Mass Destruction."* Center for the Study of Weapons of Mass Destruction, National Defense University.

P. Chalk. 1998. The response to terrorism as a threat to liberal democracy. *Australian Journal of Politics and History* 44:373–388

R.D. Crelinsten. 1998. The discourse and practice of counter-terrorism in liberal democracies. *Australian Journal of Politics and History* 44:389–413.

M. Crenshaw. 1981. The causes of terrorism. *Comparative Politics* 13:379–99.

Department of Defense. 2007. *Joint Publication 1–02*, Department of Defense Dictionary of Military and Associated Terms, 12 April 2001 (as amended through 12 July, 2007).

Dugan, Laura, Gary LaFree, Kim Cragin, and Anna Kasupski. 2008. *Building and Analyzing an Open Source Comprehensive Data Base on Global Terrorist Events*. A Final Report to the National Institute of Justice for Grant # 2005-IJ-CX-0002.

L. Dugan, G. LaFree, and A. Piquero. 2005. Testing a rational choice model of airline hijackings. *Criminology* 43:1031–1065.

D.S. Elliott, D. Huizinga, and S. Menard. 1989. *Multiple Problem Youth: Delinquency, Substance Abuse, and Mental Health Problems*. New York: Springer.

W. Enders and T. Sandler. 2006. *The Political Economy of Terrorism*. Cambridge: Cambridge University Press.

D.C. Esty, J. Goldstone, T.R. Gurr, P.T. Surko, and A.N. Unger. 1995. *Working Papers: State Failure Task Force Report*. McLean, Virginia: Science Applications International Corporation.

W. Eubank and L. Weinberg. 1994. Does democracy encourage terrorism? *Terrorism and Political Violence* 6:417–435.

W. Eubank and L. Weinberg. 1998. Terrorism and democracy: what recent events disclose. *Terrorism and Political Violence* 10:108–118.

J. Fyerman. 1998. Terrorism and democratic states: soft targets or accessible systems. *International Interactions* 24:151–170.

B. Ganor. 2005. *The Counter-Terrorism Puzzle: A Guide for Decision Makers*. New Brunswick: Transaction.

T.R. Gurr. 1974. Persistence and change in political systems, 1800–1971. *American Political Science Review* 68:1482–1504.

T.R. Gurr, K. Jaggers, and W. Moore. 1990. The transformation of the western state: the growth of democracy, autocracy, and state power since 1800. *Studies in Comparative International Development* 25:73–108.

M.S. Hamm. 2007. *Terrorism as Crime*. New York: New York University Press.

B. Hoffman. 1998. *Recent Trends and Future Prospects of Terrorism in the United States*. Santa Monica: Rand.

K. Jaggers and T.R. Gurr. 1995. Tracking democracy's third wave with the polity data. *Journal of Peace Research* 32:469–482.

B.M. Jenkins. 1975. International Terrorism: A New Model of Conflict. In: D. Carlton and C. Schaerf (eds). *International Terrorism and World Security*. London: Croom Helm.

B.M. Jenkins. 1985. *International Terrorism: The Other World War*. Santa Monica, CA: RAND Corporation, R–3302-AF.

B.M. Jenkins. 2007. *The New Age of Terrorism.* National Security Research Division, RAND. http://www.rand.org/pubs/reprints/2006/RAND_RP1215.pdf. (accessed November 5, 2008).

J. Junger-Tas, G-J. Terlouw, and W.K. Malcolm (eds). 1994. *Delinquent Behavior among Young People in the Western World: First Results of the International Self-Report Delinquency Study, Studies on Crime and Justice.* Amsterdam: Kugler.

C.B. Kalish. 1988. *International Crime Rates: Bureau of Justice Statistics Special Report.* Washington, DC: Government Printing Office.

A. Krueger and D. Laitin. 2004. Misunderstanding terrorism. *Foreign Affairs* 83:8–13

G. LaFree. 1999. Homicide: Cross-National Perspectives. In: M.D. Smith and M.A. Zahn (eds). *Studying and Preventing Homicide: Issues and Challenges.* pp. 115–139, Thousand Oaks, CA: Sage.

G. LaFree and L. Dugan. 2002. *The Impact of Economic, Political, and Social Variables on the Incidence of World Terrorism, 1970 to 1997.* Grant proposal to the National Institute of Justice, Department of Justice.

G. LaFree and L. Dugan. 2005. *Building and Analyzing a Comprehensive Open Source Database on Global Terrorism Events, 1968 to 2005.* Grant proposal to the National Institute of Justice, Department of Justice.

G. LaFree and L. Dugan. 2007. Introducing the global terrorism data base. *Terrorism and Political Violence* 19:181–204.

G. LaFree and A. Tseloni. 2006. Democratization and crime: a multilevel analysis of homicide trends in 43 nations, 1950 to 2000, *Annals of the American Academy of Political and Social Science* 605:26–49.

G. LaFree, L. Dugan, and D. Franke. 2005. The interplay between terrorism, nonstate actors, and weapons of mass destruction: an exploration of the Pinkerton database. *International Studies Review Forum* 7:155–158.

G. LaFree, L. Dugan, and S. Fahey. 2007. Global Terrorism and Failed States. In: J.J. Hewitt, J. Wilkenfeld, and T.R. Gurr. *Peace and Conflict.* pp. 39–54, Boulder: Paradigm.

Q. Li. 2005. Does democracy promote or reduce transnational terrorist incidents? *Journal of Conflict Resolution* 49:278–297.

J. Lynch. 1995. Crime in International Perspective. In: J.Q. Wilson and J. Petersilia (eds). *Crime.* pp. 11–37, San Francisco: ICS.

A. Merari. 1991. Academic research and government policy on terrorism. *Terrorism and Political Violence* 3:88–102.

S.F. Messner and R. Rosenfeld. 1997. Political restraint of the market and levels of criminal homicide: a cross-national application of institutional-anomie theory. *Social Forces* 75:1393–1416.

J.L. Neapolitan. 1997. *Cross-National Crime: A Research Review and Sourcebook.* Westport, Connecticut: Greenwood.

R.M. O'Brien. 1996. Police productivity and crime rates: 1973–1992. *Criminology* 34:183–207.

Z. Phillips. 2007. A feel for numbers. *Government Executive* 1:51–60.

T. Sandler. 1995. On the relationship between democracy and terrorism. *Terrorism and Political Violence* 7:1–9.

B.L. Smith and G.P. Orvis. 1993. America's response to terrorism: an empirical analysis of federal intervention strategies during the 1980s. *Justice Quarterly* 10:661–681.

US State Department. 2003. *Patterns of Global Terrorism.* Washington, DC: Government Printing Office.

J. Van Dijk, P. Mayhew, and M. Killias. 1989. *Experiences of Crime across the World: Key Findings of the 1989 International Crime Survey.* The Hague, The Netherlands: Ministry of Justice.

J. Wilkenfeld. 2007. Unstable States and International Crises. In: J. Hewitt, J. Wilkenfeld, and T.R. Gurr (eds). *Peace and Conflict 2008.* pp. 67–78, Boulder, CO: Paradigm.

J. Young. 2007. *State Capacity and Political Violence.* University of Maryland, Unpublished manuscript.

Chapter 4
Cops and Spooks: The Role of the Police in Counterterrorism

David H. Bayley and David Weisburd

Abstract This chapter examines the role of full-service or general-duties policing in combating terrorism. In particular we are concerned with whether the counterterrorism activities of covert intelligence gathering and disruption are playing a larger role in the activities of police agencies today, and if so to what extent such a role is impacting the services that police are expected to provide in Western democracies. We begin with a comparison of national structures for conducting counterterrorism in Western democracies. Then, we explore the impact of counterterrorism post 9/11 on policing and specify specific factors that affect the strength of its impact. Finally, drawing heavily on information from the United States and Israel, the chapter discusses arguments for and against the involvement of police in covert terrorism prevention. Overall, we conclude that general duties police agencies should be cautious in adopting a strong counterterrorism function.

The catastrophic events of September 11, 2001, in the United States dramatically focused the attention of the world on the threat of terrorism. In fact, it launched what has been called the "global war on terrorism." This war is being fought by many agencies of government, military and civil, as well as by private security agencies and businesses. Its impact has been felt especially by the police, who, in most countries, bear primary responsibility for maintaining public safety. The impact has been especially strong in the United States where, as the International Association of Chiefs of Police (IACP) observed, homeland security "towers above" all other agendas (*Post 9–11 Policing*, 2005). Even countries that had organized to fight terrorism much earlier than 9/11, such as Great Britain, Germany, and Israel, raised their alert levels and reappraised their preparedness.

Although few people would argue that the police should not be involved in counterterrorism, their precise role is unclear and indeed controversial. Some are concerned that expanding the police role in counterterrorism will change the character

---

D.H. Bayley (✉) and D. Weisburd
School of Criminal Justice, State University of New York, Albany, NY, USA
e-mail: dbayley@albany.edu

of policing in democratic states. In particular, that police will emphasize covert prevention of terrorism to the neglect of publicly visible policing of individual criminal victimization (Kempa et al., 2004; O'Reilly and Ellison, 2006). Policing of this kind has been called "high policing" (Brodeur, 1983, 2003, 2007).

High policing has two distinguishing features – its substantive focus and its methods. High policing targets what might be called macrocrimes, that is, crimes that are considered threats to society in general, such as drug trafficking and illegal immigration, as opposed to microcrimes that affect only individuals (Bayley, 2006). In high policing, prevention is the key objective, utilizing the tactics of covert intelligence gathering, surveillance, and disruption. "Low policing," by contrast, emphasizes prevention through visible patrolling and deterrence through the application of criminal law. High policing differs sharply from the standard practices of normal or low-policing because it is less transparent, less accountable, and less careful with respect to human rights (Crelinsten, 1998; Loader, 2002; Sidel, 2004; Thacher, 2005; Wilkinson, 2001). In general, high policing encourages a top-down command structure and changes the orientation of police from servicing to controlling the population.

At the same time, other people argue that full-service or general-duties policing should play a large role in counterterrorism, indeed, that it has unique advantages in a war on terror that should be exploited (Henry, 2002; Innes, 2006; Kelling, 2004; Kelling and Bratton, 2006). For example, general-duties policing provides unprecedented access to communities. Properly focused, it can obtain information about activities that are the precursors of terrorism. Furthermore, by being responsive to the mundane concerns of individuals, it raises the likelihood that the public will assist the police by providing information or accepting direction in the event of disasters. More particularly, routine policing can build bridges to communities that may shelter or give rise to terrorists. In short, the activities of low policing are not a distraction from counterterrorism but an essential "force multiplier."

So two questions about the future of policing arise out of the new emphasis on counterterrorism post 9/11. First: what has happened to policing since 9/11? In particular, has high policing replaced low policing? Second: what is the appropriate role for uniformed, full-service policing in counterterrorism? Should it undertake high policing? What are the advantages and disadvantages of doing so?

We cannot answer these questions fully in this chapter. That would require a large-scale comparative assessment in many countries. We will, however, begin to explore answers to them by (1) describing national structures for conducting counterterrorism in leading democracies; (2) exploring the current impact of counterterrorism on policing; (3) specifying factors that affect the strength of this impact, especially the impingement of high policing on low policing; and (4) examining arguments for and against the involvement of normal police in terrorism prevention.

While we do not think it is necessary to define terrorism, it is necessary to state what we mean by counterterrorism. Counterterrorism will be used as a synonym for high policing, that is, it will refer to the covert activities of intelligence gathering and disruption directed against people considered to be terrorists. When we speak of police, we will be referring to agencies of law enforcement that operate exclusively within a country. This stipulation is necessary in order to distinguish police from the military whose unique responsibility is to protect countries from external threats. We will also confine our examination of terrorism's impact only to the public police, that is, to agencies of law enforcement that are authorized and maintained by government (Bayley, 1985). The impact of counterterrorism on private agencies is an important topic in its own right because they have a growing role in counterterrorism from intelligence gathering to prevention, damage mitigation, and postevent investigation (O'Reilly and Ellison, 2006). Indeed, there are even private companies that specialize in high policing (ArmorGroup, Control Risks Group, Kroll, and Risk Advisory Group).

National Models of Counterterrorism

We begin by asking who has responsibility for counterterrorism in Western democracies. In particular, is counterterrorism assigned to specialized agencies or to the police? If counterterrorism is a responsibility of the police, how are they organized to carry it out? Is it assigned to a dedicated unit or carried out by all personnel along with their other responsibilities? Finally, in large police organizations is counterterrorism concentrated at central levels of the organization or delegated to subordinate commands, especially dispersed geographical commands?

Most countries have specialized agencies entirely separate from the police that engage in counterterrorism abroad – collecting information, penetrating potential terrorist and/or criminal groups, and taking preventive action. Such agencies rarely have exclusive jurisdiction for intelligence gathering abroad, but are supplemented by military as well as other civil agencies. Some of the specialized foreign intelligence agencies are actually run by the military, as in Italy (SISMI) and Sweden (MUST). Although these agencies are important in the global war on terrorism, they are outside our purview because they are not police agencies. They do not have authority, by and large, to operate within the boundaries of their country (Table 4.1).

What, then, is the division of labor with respect to counterterrorism within countries and, especially, is it a responsibility of police? In our review of democracies, the responsibility for counterterrorism – clandestine intelligence collection and disruption – is

Table 4.1 National models for foreign intelligence in western-style democracies

National Models: foreign Intelligence	
Australia	Australian secret intelligence service (ASIS)
France	The general directorate for external security (DGSE) (Replaced the Direction de Documentation Exterieure et de Contre Espionnage (SDECE) in 1984)
Germany	Federal intelligence service (BND) Bundesnachrichtendienst
India	Research and intelligence wing (RAW)
Israel	Mossad
Italy	Intelligence and military security service (SISMI)
Japan	Public security investigation agency (PSIA) (Koan Chosa Koancha)
Sweden	Militära Underrättelse-och SäkerhetsTjänste (MUST)
United Kingdom	MI6
United States	Central intelligence agency (CIA)

distributed domestically in three ways: (1) to a national agency specializing in counterterrorism, (2) to one or more national police services, and (3) to all police agencies at any governmental level. These modes of organization are not exclusive but may coexist in the same country (Table 4.2).

Table 4.2 National models for counterterrorism: Domestic Organizations

National Models: domestic organization		Intelligence	Disruption	Arrest/ detention
1. Specialized national				
Australia	Australian security intelligence organization (ASIO)	+	+	Limited
Canada	Communications security establishment (CSE)	+	−	−
	Canadian security intelligence service	+	?	−
France	Direction de la Surveillance due Territoire (DST)	+	?	?
Germany	Federal office for the protection of the constitution (Bundesamt fur Verfassungsschutz – BfV)	+	−	−
India	Intelligence bureau (IB)	+	?	?
Israel	Shin Bet	+	−	−
Italy	Intelligence and military Security service (SISMI)	+	+	+
	The intelligence and democratic security service (SISDE)			
Japan	Public security investigation agency (PSIA) (Koan Chosa Koancha)	+	+	+
Netherlands	Binnelandse Veiligheiddient (BVS)	+	?	?
Spain	National intelligence center Centro Nacional de Inteligencia (CNI)	+	+	+
Sweden	National security service (Sakerhetspolisen) (SAPO)	+	+	+
United Kingdom	MI5	+	+	−
2. Specialized stratified		There are no cases of countries creating specialized counterterrorism agencies at subnational levels separate from the police		
3. National police				
(a) Single agency				
	Australia: Australian federal police	+	+	+
	Canada: RCMP	+	+	+
	Germany: Federal criminal investigation office (Bundesktiminalamt) (BKA)	+	+	+
	Israel: national police	+	+	+
	India: central bureau of investigation (CBI)	+	+	+
	Japan: national police agency	+	+	+
	Sweden: Swedish police services	−	−	−
	United States: FBI	+	+	+

(continued)

Table 4.2 (continued)

National Models: domestic organization		Intelligence	Disruption	Arrest/ detention
(b) Multiple agencies				
	France: police nationale	+	+	+
	Gendarmerie			
	Italy: Guardia de Pubblica	+	+	+
	Sicurezza			
	Carabinieri			
	Spain: national police corps (Cuerpo National de Policia)	+	+	+
	Civil guard (Cuerpo de la Guardia)			
4. Police: stratified				
Australia	7 state/territory police forces	+	+	+
Canada	REMP on contract to provinces and municipalities	+	+	+
	Two provincial police (Ontario, Quebec)	+	+	+
	200 municipal Police			
Germany	State police (Landerpolizei)	+	+	+
India	State police	+	+	+
	Municipal police in several large cities			
Japan	49 Prefectural police	+	+	+
United Kingdom	43 Local police forces	+	+	+
United States	17,000 state and local police forces	+	+	+

All the countries in our review have created an agency that specializes in collecting domestic intelligence about potentially violent subversion – Australia (ASIO), France (DST), Israel (Shin Bet), Japan (PSIA), the United States (FBI). At the same time, they vary in their powers to take preventive action. Some do intelligence gathering only, such as the Canadian Security Intelligence Service (CSIS), Israel's Shin Bet, and Britain's MI5. They would not, then, fit common definitions of a police organization, which involves the application of constraint to individuals, as in arresting. Undoubtedly many of these services also undertake clandestine action to disrupt potentially violent subversion without invoking the power of arrest or detention. Information about these activities, and their legal status, is limited. A crucial topic for future research into comparative counterterrorism is the degree of visibility required under law with respect to proactive counterterrorism actions.

Some national counterterrorism agencies do have full police powers and can detain, arrest, and submit for prosecution – India's Central Bureau of Investigation (CBI), Italy's Intelligence and Democratic Security Service (SISDE), Japan's Public Security Investigation Agency (PSIA), Spain's National Intelligence Center (CNI), Sweden's National Security Service (SAPO). For this reason, they should be regarded as police forces that specialize in counterespionage. As is the case with foreign intelligence, domestic intelligence gathering is often supplemented by nonpolice agencies. These agencies tend, for the most part, to be associated with defense establishments.

In our review, all national, that is, centralized, police services engage in counter terrorism with the exception of Sweden. Counterterrorism in Sweden is the exclusive responsibility of the National Security Service (Sakerhetspolisen – SAPO). In other words, with one exception, centralized agencies of national government created expressly to be police, in the sense of being responsible for enforcing the law, also engage in counterterrorism. Their activities may be supplemented by specialized militarized counterterrorism "strike forces," such as the UK's Security Air Service, America's Delta Force, Canada's Task Force 2, France's Groupe d'"intervention de Gendarmerie Nationale (GIGN), Germany's Grenzschutzgruppe 9 (GSG-9), and Spain's Grupo Especial de Operaciones (CEO).

All countries that authorize the creation of police at subnational, decentralized levels require them to undertake counterterrorism operations. Indeed, all subnational counterterrorism is carried out by police. There are no cases of agencies specializing in counterterrorism at subnational levels. Thus, the police in all federal systems have counterterrorism responsibilities. The police in centralized systems may also delegate counterterrorism functions to subordinate levels of command for reasons of operational effectiveness. This occurs, for example, in France, Japan, and Israel. The UK is a special case. It does not have a federal system of government, nor does it have a national police force, but all its 43 police forces have a dedicated intelligence capability (Special Branch) and, since 2004, a "Counter Terrorist Security Advisor."

In the United States, most of its 17,000 state and local police do not have specialized counterterrorism units. All police, however, undertake covert surveillance of some sort, generally as a part of crime control. Since 9/11, state and local police have been encouraged to participate in "Joint Terrorism Task Forces" led by the FBI. There are now approximately 100 of these, 65 established after 9/11 (Maguire and King, 2006). Several of the larger American police forces collect their own foreign intelligence through liaison officers posted abroad. New York City, for example, has officers permanently assigned to London, Lyon, Tel Aviv, Hamburg, Madrid, and Toronto (Skolnick, 2005).

In sum, police in all democratic countries, centralized and noncentralized, are authorized to engage in high as well as low policing. The extent to which they actually do so varies widely and, as we shall now see, is not well researched.

The Impact of Counterterrorism on Police

There is universal agreement among police officials, academics, and other observers that terrorism has sharply impacted the activities of full-service police departments since 9/11. This is true not only in the United States but also for police agencies around the world, even those with longer histories of dealing with terrorist threats.

Unfortunately, these assessments are for the most part unsystematic both in terms of the activities examined and the range of cases studied. As one would expect, most of the writing available in English about impact comes from the

United States (Anonymous, 2006; Kaplan, 2006; Kerlikowske, 2006; Marks and Sun, 2007; Skolnick, 2005). Even that, however, is limited. As the IACP observed, there is "very little information, suggesting that the areas of inquiry had not been addressed for scholarly study, or even popular treatment in print" (*Post 9–11 Policing*, 2005). It also noted that funding agencies of the US government, which are the most likely sponsors of such research, appear not to be planning studies of counterterrorism's impact on police.

The IACP's own survey of changes in policing as a result of terrorism showed that 86% of forces reported operational or policy changes since 9/11 (2005). Most of these (48%) were in strategic planning with respect to national alerts, WMD response, risk assessment, and first-responding procedures. The other major areas of impact were in training, equipment, reorganization, redeployment, and interagency collaboration.

According to other observers, counterterrorism in the sense of high policing is still not a high priority in local American law enforcement agencies. For example, few have created specialized counterterrorism units (O'Hanlon, 2005). This is not surprising, considering that the average size of an American police department is 42 sworn officers (Pastore and Maguire, 2003). By and large, local law enforcement does not have the capacity to undertake intelligence gathering focusing on terrorism, nor could it analyze the information that might be collected (Riley et al., 2005). Most intelligence about terrorism comes from federal sources, apart from a few large cities like New York and Los Angeles.

The impact of terrorism on policing, however, involves more than high policing. Besides collecting intelligence and undertaking preventive actions, counterterrorism involves limiting the damage from terrorism and investigating, arresting, and prosecuting those who have done it (Bradley and Lyman, 2006).It is important to remember that all terrorist attacks are local. This means that although some counterterrorism functions can be made the responsibility of dedicated units deployed at centralized levels of organization, police on the ground will necessarily become involved wherever terrorism strikes or is likely to strike. Counterterrorism impacts, then, almost all levels of policing to some degree.

If the police are to be effective in the war on terrorism, there are at least ten categories of police activity that could properly be considered counterterrorism.

(1) Covert detection
(2) Disruption/dismantling of terrorist plots
(3) Risk analysis
(4) Target hardening
(5) Community mobilization for prevention
(6) Protection of important persons and infrastructure
(7) Emergency assistance at terrorist incidents
(8) Order maintenance when terrorism occurs
(9) Mitigation of terrorist damage
(10) Criminal investigation of terrorist incidents

Because the ways in which police may become involved in meeting the threat of terrorism are so varied and complex, a complete checklist of information required

Table 4.3 Data categories for assessing police involvement in high-policing functions

1. Creation of new organizational units.
2. Enhancement of existing functions to deal with terrorism (intelligence, protection, first responding, criminal investigation).
3. Increased funding explicitly for counterterrorism.
4. Reallocation of internal resources (money and people) to new counterterrorism duties.
5. Reorientation of traditional operations to counterterrorism requirements (crime analysis, patrol, use of informants, community crime prevention).
6. Changes in crime-intelligence targeting, especially to new groups (Muslims, illegal immigrants).
7. Increased interagency planning and coordination.
8. Acquisition of specialized equipment for counterterrorism (personal hazmat protection gear, bomb-sniffing dogs, command-control technology).
9. Changes in the legal authorizations of the police with respect to human rights and procedural guarantees.
10. Unplanned expenses, in particular, overtime, sick leave, injuries, stress management, and line-of-duty deaths attributable directly to terrorism.

for determining the impact of the war on terror on policing would be very long. In order to make the job of comparing terrorism's impact on policing manageable, we propose the following *select* list of critical indicators, based on reports of the major adaptations made following 9/11 (Table 4.3).

Because changes enacted in response to terrorism are usually labeled as such, information about most of these items can be collected from either documents or interviews. We think that systematic data collection of this sort is essential to understand the changes that have emerged in policing in democracies as a result of terrorism.

Factors Affecting the Impact of Counterterrorism on Police

Terrorism does not impact the status and prominence of high policing in all police forces equally. We suggest that there are six factors that determine whether a police force alters its activities to include a greater number of high-policing functions.

1. *Local Incidents of Terrorism.* Because terrorist violence is frightening and traumatic, it requires visible response from government, the police, and other emergency services. In countries where terrorist threats are serious and where the attacks are common, high policing is likely to have a much larger place in police operations. This is clearly the reason why Israel and the UK have a long history of police involvement in homeland security and counterterrorism functions. In Israel for example, the police received their official mandate of responsibility for homeland security in 1974 following a particularly horrific terror attack at an Israeli school in Ma'alot and the more general rise of Palestinian terror. In the UK, the rise of Irish Republican terrorism played a major role in pushing the police into high-policing practices in the late nineteenth century (Critchley, 1967).

   After a dramatic terror attack the public will not accept business-as-usual, even if the probability of attack locally is low. This explains why there was a sudden growth of high-policing practices after 9/11. The IACP's survey of changes in policing as a result of terrorism showed that 86% of forces reported operational or policy changes after 9/11 (*Post 9–11 Policing*, 2005).

Furthermore, after a dramatic terror attack police responses will be affected by perceptions of local vulnerabilities. The greater the number of likely targets for terrorism, the greater will be preparations made by local police. Three-fourths of American police departments conducted risk assessments after 9/11, compared with only one-fourth that did so before (Davis et al., 2004). This variable probably correlates with size of jurisdiction, although not perfectly. Some very small jurisdictions may contain critical infrastructure such as nuclear plants or transportation hubs.

2. *The Structure of Police Organization*. The higher the governmental level at which police are organized, the more likely it is that preventive counterterrorism will be undertaken. Police agencies that are organized at a national level, such as the Israeli or the French, appear to take on high-policing tasks with greater ease than police organized in a decentralized way. As a corollary to this, it seems likely that local police which are decentralized units within a national organization are more likely to undertaken high-police functions than those which are independent.

This principle is clearly illustrated in the United States. The IACP survey found that 95% of state agencies reported change after 9/11, 85% of municipalities, and 77% of county sheriffs (*Post 9–11 Policing*, 2005). Another American study found that 75% of state law enforcement agencies had specialized counterterrorism units versus only 15% at local levels (Riley et al., 2005).

3. *The Size of the Police Unit*. Specialization of function can only take place in organizations of scale. This would explain in part why national police agencies in our survey are more likely to have specialized units that deal with high-policing functions. One American study found that participation in joint federal/state/local terrorism task forces increased with the size of the local police agency (Riley et al., 2005).

4. *Time under Threat*. Terrorism will have a greater impact on policing the longer a country has experienced it. Looking only at the period since World War II, Great Britain passed antiterror legislation in 1974, amending it in 1989, 2000, 2001; France, 1986; Germany, 1976, 1978; Israel, 1945, 1977, 1980, 2002, 2003, 2005; Italy, 1975, 1980; Spain 1980. The United States, however, only recently faced the prospect of major terrorism at home, which is reflected in antiterrorist legislation in 2001 and 2006. Before that, terrorism affected the police episodically in well-documented cycles of mobilization, alleged abuses of power, critical public reaction, and return to the status quo ante (Halperin et al., 1976; *History of Police Intelligence Operations, 1880–1975*, 1976; Wilson, 1978). When two American presidents were killed by Anarchists in the late nineteenth century (Garfield and McKinley), American police intensified their surveillance of European immigrants. Attorney General Palmer arrested hundreds of alleged subversives during the "Red Scare," 1919–1920, following the Russian revolution. And the FBI's COINTELPRO operations 1956–1968

attempted to destroy the Communist party and other "subversive" organizations, among them the civil rights movement, the United Farmworkers Party, and the Committee to Abolish the HUAC following widespread violence in American cities in the mid-1960s and the growing anti-Vietnam War demonstrations and occasional bombings.

5. *Intolerance of Political Dissent.* Acceptance of high policing occurs more frequently in countries where dissent is not tolerated, whether for ideological, cultural, or political reasons (Bayley, 1985). Authoritarian governments, notably, view dissent as a threat and therefore treat it with the tactics of high policing.

   This principle is clearly complex and is mitigated by the other pressures that we have identified earlier. In England, which has longer experience with democracy than any modern nation, high policing in the form of Special Branch has been a part of local policing since the 1880s. In Israel, in turn, where significant dissent is tolerated in the political realm, often by groups challenging the legitimacy of the government, high policing is perhaps more prominent at the local level than in any other democratic regime. In both the UK and Israel, responses to terrorism have often led to strong criticism of violations of human rights and democratic principles undertaken in the name of national security (*UK Human Rights: A Broken Promise*, 2006; Ganor, 2002; Great Britain Home Office, 2006; Haubrich, 2003; Michaelsen, 2005).

6. *Legal Mandates and Financial Encouragement.* In countries which allow subnational levels of government to develop autonomous police forces, such as federal systems (Brazil, India, Australia, Germany, the United States), local police may be required to modify their operations by national laws, administrative directive, or inducements of money. For example, governments may enact new requirements for port security, protection of chemical and nuclear plans, or standards for participating in joint law-enforcement programs (*The Role of 'Home' in Homeland Security*, 2003). Similarly, local police agencies may emphasize counterterrorism because resources have been made available to do so (Howitt and Pangi, 2003). Davis and colleagues report a positive correlation in the United States between counterterrorism preparedness and the availability of federal funding (2004).

   Financial encouragement may, however, have limits. A study by the Urban Institute, Washington, DC, found that grants made by the Office of Community Oriented Police Services did not cause police departments to establish community policing unless local police had already decided that they wanted to do so (Moore et al., 1999). A begrudging response may be true as well for counterterrorism funding, although it seems reasonable to expect that counterterrorism funding will more powerfully alter the shape of policing because failure to adapt could be so catastrophic.

   In sum, the threat of terrorism impacts almost all police agencies in one way or another. Centralized and higher-level police agencies will engage more in specialized counterterrorism intelligence gathering and surveillance (high policing) than local ones. But most will be affected by the need to analyze risk and to respond to terrorist attacks, to maintain order, to relieve distress, and to investigate incidents. The extent to which they do so is only partly under their control.

Subordinate police in decentralized systems will have greater control over their adaptations than police in centralized systems. But even the police in decentralized systems may find themselves powerless in the face of directives, mandates, and events.

Advantages to Using General-Duties Police for High Policing

It is obvious that full-service police agencies can make essential contributions to the war on terrorism in terms of preparedness planning, threat analysis of critical infrastructure, target protection, first-responding, order-maintenance, and postevent criminal investigation. Although not all frontline police agencies can do all these things unassisted, their expertise and resources must be used. They are the first line of defense with respect to these tasks. The more difficult question is whether general-duties police can contribute usefully to the distinctive actions of high policing, namely, intelligence collection, disruption, and apprehension. In this and the next section, we will examine the advantages and disadvantages of their doing so.

Low policing can contribute to high policing in six distinct and important ways.

1. *The Benefits of Scale and Diffusion of Generalized Police Agencies in Local Communities.* Uniformed police have more opportunities to observe activities that may be associated with terrorism than specialists, especially specialists not deployed routinely in local areas. In the United States, for example, there are approximately 708,022 full-time sworn police officers compared with 11,633 FBI Special Agents only about 2,200 of whom work directly on terrorism (Maguire and King, 2006). In order to utilize these additional eyes and ears helpfully in the war on terrorism, police officers need to be trained to recognize likely terrorists or precursor terrorist activities (Howard, 2004; Posen, 2001).

    It has been estimated, for example, that one out of five Americans 16 years of age and older have one face-to-face contact with police each year. (Hickman and Reaves, 2002). This amounts to almost 44 million contacts, 20 million of them in traffic stops. Timothy McVeigh, for example, was arrested and subsequently tried for the Oklahoma City bombing after being stopped by a Michigan State Trooper for having an invalid license plate (Runge, 2003). Mohammad Atta was given a ticket by Broward County, Florida, sheriff's deputies for driving without a license 4 months before the attack on the World Trade Towers. Because he skipped his court appearance, a warrant was issued for his arrest (Maguire and King, 2006). Two days before 9/11, a Maryland State Trooper stopped Ziad S. Jarra, who was on a CIA "watch" list, for speeding in Pikesville, Maryland. Although hindsight is always wiser than foresight, these examples show the remarkable extent of routine contact that police have with criminals, including potential terrorists. Traffic stops can also uncover other activity associated with terrorism, such as the transportation of explosives. We now know that several of the 9/11 hijackers had previous contact with local police. In May 2001, Nawaf al-Hazmi reported an attempted robbery in Fairfax, Virginia, but declined to press charges.

The same is true in Israel. In 2006, for example, a young Palestinian raised the suspicion of two Israeli patrol officers near the old city in Jerusalem. He was stopped, questioned, and an explosive device was found in the bag he was carrying (Ranodi, 2006).

2. *The Utility of Local Knowledge and Intimate Contacts with Local Communities.* Police have access to information within communities that cannot be obtained by more remote, specialized intelligence agents (Clutterbuck, 1994; Loyka et al., 2005; Lyons, 2002; Wardlaw, 1982). For example, they have more detailed knowledge of facilities that provide resources to terrorists, such as flight-training schools, explosives manufacturers, and providers of nitrogenous fertilizers (Rees, 2006). Even more important, their routine activities put them in a position to observe activism among radical groups, the distribution of inflammatory literature, the movements of radical leaders, and people acting suspiciously near critical infrastructure (Davies and Plotkin, 2005).

Local police are especially useful in cultivating informative relations with marginalized communities that may harbor, often unwittingly, potential terrorists (Lyons, 2002). Because the usefulness of the police contacts depends on the trust they have engendered with local populations, their access is likely to be greater with relatively well-to-do communities than with others. This can be a serious handicap for counterterrorism intelligence gathering. The implication, however, is not that local police should not try, but that the "soft" strategies associated with community policing may play a critical, even unique, role in terrorism prevention, especially in disadvantaged communities.

This insight is being acted on by the London Metropolitan Police which has developed a program of local reassurance and contact after the terror attack on London transport on July 7, 2005. Called "Safer Neighborhoods," it deploys approximately 4,000 police and civilian Police-Community Service Officer teams in all of London's 624 wards. Each team consists of one sergeant, two police officers, and from three to six PCSOs. Although the MET has also upgraded its high-policing capability, it has notably enhanced its contact with communities rather than allowing uniformed operations to be reduced. In the words of its Commissioner, Sir Ian Blair, national security requires neighborhood security.

3. *Identification of Links between Ordinary Crime and Terrorism.* Analysis of ordinary crime patterns may reveal activities associated with terrorism, such as the theft of explosives, biological cultures, or protective clothing; the fraudulent use of personal identification; trafficking in drugs and people; and money laundering (Loyka et al., 2005; O'Hanlon, 2005) In Israel, for example, the police often work with the Military Police in investigating thefts of army equipment in part because of possible links to terrorism (Hare'l, 2006; Rofe'-Ofir, 2007; Shikler, 2007; Yamin-Volbowitz, 2007). As George Kelling observes, once terrorists are inside the country, "police – not the FBI or CIA – have the best tools for detecting and prosecuting these crimes" (Howard, 2004).

4. *Ease of Building Local Partnerships with Business and Private Security.* Local police are best positioned to develop partnerships in terrorism detection and protection with businesses and the growing private security industry (Howard, 2004). These can be mobilized to protect important facilities and also to provide information about the purchase of chemicals and protective clothing as well as short-term rentals, especially for cash, of apartments, storage facilities, and motor vehicles. The potential for a strong police/private security link in combating terrorism is especially apparent in Israel where the police are heavily involved in approving security measures and supervising security agencies responsible for protecting malls, entertainment venues, and other public spaces (Weisburd et al., forthcoming).

5. *The Benefits of General Duties Policing in Narrowing Down Local Investigations of Terrorist Threats.* By drawing on local knowledge, intelligence specialists can narrow their surveillance, interrogations, and penetration more quickly on likely suspects. As the FBI has found in the United States, they often have more leads than they can adequately investigate. Local knowledge as well as the investigatory manpower available to local police can quickly reduce these to the most promising.

6. *Advantages in Blending in Specific Local Communities.* Local police may also be better able to work undercover without detection, perhaps off a federal watchlist, than agents brought in from afar (Hart and Rudman, 2002; Travis, 1999). This depends, of course, on the size of the jurisdiction because officers in small jurisdictions may be too well known to work effectively undercover.

7. *Recruitment of Informers.* Because of their leverage over criminals, local police can recruit and monitor informants better than outside agents (Clutterbuck, 1994). As Richman observes, "Every felony arrest is an intelligence opportunity and should be recognized as such" (2004–2005). Kelling and Bratton (2006) observe that when Israeli police officers come into contact with criminal suspects, their first priority is gathering intelligence while the prosecution of the case is secondary, and no incident is considered too minor for this.

Disadvantages to Using General-Duties Police in High Policing

Although there are some advantages to using local police for high policing, there are also distinct disadvantages both for policing generally and for counterterrorism in particular.

1. *The Costs of Investing Scarce Resources In Counterintelligence.* Because police resources are limited, enhancing intelligence gathering capability by general-duties police through surveillance, covert penetration, and the use of informers may lead to the neglect of other important police responsibilities. In other words, there may be significant opportunity costs. This downside of high policing is particularly evident in Israel, where the impact of high policing on the ability of police to respond to crime problems has become a commonly voiced concern among police managers (Fishman, 2005; Weisburd et al., forthcoming). Indeed, high policing has come to be seen by some as supplanting low-policing activities.

Whatever the short-term gain of high policing for police agencies, there can be an eventual public backlash to a growing emphasis on high policing. If local police begin to withdraw resources from activities that provide perceptible services to the public, such as uniformed patrolling, responding to calls-for-service, school liaison programs, and traffic regulation, public regard and support for the police may decline. This in turn can undermine the public's willingness to think of themselves as partners in preventing terrorism. Paradoxically, then, diversion of resources to high policing can jeopardize the comparative advantage that local police have in counterterrorism. This can be particularly damaging with respect to the very communities that high-policing needs to focus on, such as transients, disadvantaged people, minority groups, and recent immigrants.

At the same time, it is important to bear in mind that the public in all public-safety emergencies looks for easily understandable solutions, something it can grasp that seems uniquely fitted to the task. In the war on terrorism, high policing is that solution, the "silver bullet" in the war on terror. In the short run, therefore, the public may applaud the development of local high policing and fail to notice a diversion of resources away from normal police service.

2. *The Attractiveness of Counterterrorism as Compared with Traditional Service-Oriented Policing.* Although high policing is undoubtedly needed in the war on terror, its injection into local policing can produce tunnel vision that undermines creativity in traditional areas of policing. For example, by opening up a "sexy" new career track, counterterrorism can lure ambitious officers away from the core activities that have connected policing to the communities they serve. Specialization in antiterrorism and homeland security conveys status inside the police and may become a promising promotion track. It is instructive that when community policing was promoted in the 1980s and 1990s, many officers thought its community-engaging activities were not "real police work," preferring to work more high-profile rapid response vehicles and to become detectives (Braga and Weisburd, 2006 ; Weisburd et al., 2002; Weisburd and McElroy, 1988). Similarly, we believe that may be a tendency for officers to choose high policing over traditional low policing

3. *High Policing and Violations of Civil Liberties.* As previous campaigns of counter-espionage have shown, high policing is difficult to control. Because protection from terrorism is so obviously a righteous cause, high policing can lead to the infringement of human rights, particularly the procedural protections of due process, and to the overzealous and sometimes illegal monitoring of speech, thought, and association. Big Brother replaces "serve and protect." The Israeli police have been the subject of repeated investigation and criticism (Stein, 2001; Yashuvi, 1990). The New York City Police Department is still under a consent decree with respect to civil liberty violations that predate 9/11. And the Denver Police Department has recently negotiated an agreement with the American Civil Liberties Union about the actions of its intelligence bureau (Richman, 2004, 2005).

The problem is that a single episode of thoughtlessness or overreaching may undermine public trust. Perception is everything. The loss of public confidence is especially costly for the success of counterterrorism itself if it increases the alienation of minority and immigrant communities.

4. *Challenges to Community Perceptions of Police Legitimacy.* High policing changes the mindset of officers from service to suspicion, where people are viewed as suspects to be watched rather than individuals to be helped. Kelling and Moore (1989) have argued that American police evolved during the twentieth century through three distinct periods of reform – professionalism, constitutionalism, and community involvement. By implication, if covert counterterrorism by local police is not handled very carefully, it could push the clock back, undoing decades of community consultation and involvement, collaborative problem solving, and adherence to the rule of law.

The general point is that legitimacy is the bedrock of successful policing, whether in the control of ordinary crime or of terrorism. It can be lost by acts of omission as well as commission on the part of police. Using frontline police as high police can, ironically, jeopardize the very advantages that local policing has in the war on terror.

Conclusion

It is impossible to say with confidence whether the war on terrorism has changed the character of policing in developed democracies, in particular whether high policing has significantly impacted low policing. The evidence is fragmentary and impressionistic. It appears that specialized capabilities, especially for intelligence gathering and analysis, have been augmented in all countries. It is not at all clear how much traditional frontline policing in the form of uniformed patrol, response to calls-for-service, and criminal investigation has been affected.

If we ranked the countries of our sample along a continuum from transformative impact to no impact at all, our impression is that general policing has been affected most in Israel and least in the United States. Despite 9/11, American police seem still be to searching for their role in counterterrorism. After convening three executive roundtables, the IACP observed that they had "failed to identify a body of promising practice information that even began to approach what was needed…or, more important, to supply the field with hoped for response to post 9/11 change and conditions" (*Post 9–11 Policing*, 2005:4).

Among the other English-speaking democracies, Great Britain seems to have adapted its policing more to the requirements of counterterrorism due largely to the terrorism associated with the "troubles" in Northern Ireland during the last 35 years. Australia, Canada, and New Zealand, cluster toward the American end and India tends more to the intermediate position. Countries in Western Europe range somewhere in the middle of this continuum.

The critical question is whether a shift to high policing, especially by general-duties police agencies, in Western democracies should be applauded or prevented. As we have pointed out, there are reasons why uniformed, general-duties police should take on a greater role in the prevention and control of terrorism, in addition to their inevitable role in responding to terrorist events and ameliorating their impacts. Local police can be enormously helpful in detecting terrorist-related activity, building bridges to informants in critical communities, and in coordinating security responses between public and private agencies. At the same time, acting as high police may come at a cost that policy makers and the public should be aware of. It may lead to a decline in crime-prevention services to the general public and undermine the investigation of ordinary crime, thereby separating the police from the population in general and reducing the possibility of obtaining useful information about terrorist activities.

Taking stock of the advantages as well as the disadvantages of using general-duties police in counterterrorism, we believe that they can contribute more by focusing and finetuning their standard operations than by creating specialized high-policing capabilities. Customary activities by regular police represent a unique capacity for intelligence gathering while, at the same time, serving as the frontline for risk assessment and first responding. But to do all this, the police will have to be cautious. There is no free lunch, and significant involvement by local police in high policing can come at a significant cost. This suggests that low policing and high policing should be conducted by separate personnel and perhaps by different levels of police. Such an approach would prevent high policing from overwhelming the low-police functions that are crucial for the development of police legitimacy, thus serving the objectives of public safety against all threats, ordinary crime and disorder as well as terrorism.

Acknowledgments We would like to thank Tal Jonathan, Gali Aviv, Rochelle Schnurr, and Kristen Miggans for their assistance in the preparation of this manuscript. We owe a special debt to Tal Jonathan and Simon Perry for their comments and suggestions regarding high-policing strategies.

References

D.H. Bayley. 1985. *Patterns of Policing*. New Brunswick, NJ: Rutgers University Press.
D.H. Bayley. 2006. *Changing the Guard: Developing Democratic Police Abroad*. New York, NY: Oxford University Press.
J.M. Bradley and R.L. Lyman. 2006. The public safety model: A homeland security alternative. *The Police Chief* 73(3):24–27.
A.A. Braga and W. David. 2006. Problem-oriented policing: The disconnect between principles and practice. In: D. Weisburd and A.A. Braga (eds) *Police Innovation: Contrasting Perspectives*. Cambridge, UK: Cambridge University Press.
J-P. Brodeur. 1983. High and low policing: Remarks about the policing of political activities. *Social Problems* 30(5):507–520.
J-P. Brodeur. 2003. Democracy and secrecy: The French intelligence community. In: J-P. Brodeur, P. Gill, and D. Tollborg (eds) *Democracy, Law and Society*. Aldershot, UK: Ashgate.
J-P. Brodeur. 2007. High and low policing in post-9/11 times. *Policing* 1:25–37.
R. Clutterbuck. 1994. *Terrorism in an Unstable World*. New York: Routledge.
R.D. Crelinsten. 1998. The discourse and practice of counter-terrorism in liberal democracies. *Australian Journal of Politics and History* 44(3):389–413.

T.A. Critchley. 1967. *A History of Police in England and Wales, 1900–1966*. London: Constable.

H.J. Davies and M.R. Plotkin. 2005. *Partnership to Promote Home Security*. Washington, DC: Office of Community Oriented Police Service and Police Executive Research Forum.

L.M. Davis, J.K. Riley, G. Ridgeway, J. Pace, S.K. Cotton, P.S. Steinberg, K. Damphousse, and B.L. Smith. 2004. *When Terrorism Hits Home: How Prepared are State and Local Law Enforcement?* Santa Monica, CA: RAND Corporation.

G. Fishman (ed). 2005. *Balanced Police Action Between Terror and Maintaining Public Order: A Summary of an Era and Challenges for Coming Years*. Jerusalem, Israel: The Israel Democracy Institute [In Hebrew].

B. Ganor. 2002. *Israel's counter-terrorism policy: Efficacy versus liberal-democratic values 1983–1999*. PhD dissertation, The Hebrew University of Jerusalem [In Hebrew].

Great Britain Home Office. 2006. *Counter-Terrorism Policy and Human Rights: Prosecution and Pre-Charge Detention, the Government Reply to the Twenty-Fourth Report from the Joint Committee on Human Rights*. London: The Stationery Office.

M. Halperin, J. Berman, R. Borosage, and M. Christine. 1976. *The Lawless State: The Crimes of the U.S. Intelligence Agencies*. New York, NY: Penguin Books.

A. Hare'l. 2006. The theft of 48 weapons from an IDF base was solved. *Walla News*, 2 April. http://news.walla.co.il (accessed December 2007). [In Hebrew].

G. Hart and W.B. Rudman. 2002. *America Still Unprepared – America Still in Danger*. New York, NY: Council on Foreign Relations.

D. Haubrich. 2003. September 11, anti-terror laws and civil liberties: Britain, France and Germany compared. *Government and Opposition* 38(1):3–28.

V.E. Henry. 2002. The need for a coordinated and strategic local police approach to terrorism: A practitioner's perspective. *Police Practice and Research* 3(4):319–336.

S. Herzog. 2003. Border closures as a reliable method for the measurement of Palestinian involvement in crime in Israel: A quasi-experimental analysis. *International Journal of Comparative Criminology* 3(1):18–41.

M.J. Hickman and B.A. Reaves. 2002. Local police and homeland security: Some baseline data. *Police Chief* 69:83–85, 88.

History of Police Intelligence Operations, 1880–1975. 1976. Gaitherburg, MD: International Association of Chiefs of Police.

P. Howard. 2004. *Hard Won Lessons: How Police Fight Terrorism in the United Kingdom*. New York, NY: Manhattan Institute for Policy Research. http://www.manhattan-institute.org/pdf/scr_01.pdf (accessed December 2007).

A.M. Howitt and R.L. Pangi. (eds). 2003. *Countering Terrorism: Dimensions of Preparedness*. Cambridge, MA: MIT Press.

M. Innes. 2006. Policing uncertainty: Countering terror through community intelligence and democratic policing. *The Annals of the American Academy of Political and Social Science* 605:222–241.

D.E. Kaplan. 2006. The spy next door. *U.S. News and World Report*, 8 May, pp. 41–49.

G. Kelling. 2004. Introduction: Do police matter? In: P. Howard (ed) *Hard Won Lessons: How Police Fight Terrorism in the United Kingdom*. New York: Manhattan Institute. http://www.manhattan-institute.org/pdf/scr_01.pdf (accessed December 2007).

G.L. Kelling and W.J. Bratton. 2006. *Policing Terrorism*. New York: Manhattan Institute. http://www.manhattan-institute.org/html/cb_43.htm (accessed December 2007).

G.L. Kelling and M.H. Moore. 1989. From political to reform to community: The evolving strategy of police. In: J.R. Greene and S.D. Mastrofski (eds) *Community Policing: Real or Rhetoric*. New York, NY: Praeger.

M. Kempa, S. Philip, and W. Jennifer. 2004. Policing communal spaces: A reconfiguration of the 'Mass Private Property' hypothesis. *British Journal of Criminology* 44(4):562–581.

R.G. Kerlikowske. 2006. *Safe at Home? Policing the Hometown in the Era of Homeland Security, November 20, 2006. The Patrick V. Murphy Lecture Series on Perspectives on Police Leadership*. New York: John Jay College of Criminal Justice.

I. Loader. 2002. Policing, securitization and democratization in Europe. *Criminal Justice* 2(2):125–153.

S.A. Loyka, D.A. Faggiani, and C. Karchmer. 2005. *Protecting Your Community from Terrorism: Strategies for Local Law Enforcement. Volume 4 – The Production and Sharing of Intelligence.* Washington, DC: Office of Community Oriented Police Service and the Police Executive Research Forum.

W. Lyons. 2002. Partnerships, information and public safety: Community policing in a time of terror. *Policing* 25(3):530–542.

E.R. Maguire and W.R. King. 2006. Federal-Local Law Coordination in Homeland Security. In: B. Forst, J. Greene, and J. Lynch (eds.) *Security and Justice in the Homeland: Criminologists on Terrorism.* (Forthcoming 2010).

D.E. Marks and I.Y. Sun. 2007. The impact of 9/11 on organizational development among state and local law enforcement agencies. *Journal of Contemporary Criminal Justice* 23(2):159–173.

C. Michaelsen. 2005. Derogating from international human rights obligations in the 'War against Terrorism'? A British-Australian perspective. *Terrorism and Political Violence* 17:131–155.

M.H. Moore, D. Thatcher, F.X. Hartmann, and C. Catherine. 1999. *Case Studies of the Transformation of Police Departments: A Cross-Site Analysis.* Washington, DC: Urban Institute Press.

M.E. O'Hanlon. 2005. *The Role of State and Local Governments in Homeland Security.* Washington, DC: US Senate and Brookings Institution.

C. O'Reilly and G. Ellison. 2006. 'Eye Spy Private High' re-conceptualizing high policing theory. *British Journal of Criminology* 46(4):641–660.

A.L. Pastore and K. Maguire. 2003. *Sourcebook of Criminal Justice Statistics.* Washington, DC: Bureau of Justice Statistics.

B.R. Posen. 2001. The struggle against terrorism: Grand strategy, strategy, and tactics. *International Security* 26(3):39–55.

Post 9–11 Policing: The Crime-Control-Homeland Security Paradigm – Taking Command of New Realities. 2005. Alexandria, VA: International Association of Chiefs of Police. http://www.theiacp.org/pubinfo/finalpost911policing.pdf (accessed December 2007).

D. Ranodi. 2006. At the last minute: A terror attack was prevented in Jerusalem. *MSN News*, 17 July. www.business.msn.co.il/news (accessed December 2007). [In Hebrew].

D.M. Rees. 2006. Special focus: Post-September 11 policing in suburban America. *Police Chief* 73(2):72–77.

D. Richman. 2004–2005. The right fight: Enlisted by the feds, can police find sleeper cells and protect civil rights, too? *Boston Review* 29.

K.J. Riley, G.F. Treverton, J.M. Wilson, and L.M. Davis. 2005. *State and Local Intelligence in the War on Terrorism.* Santa Monica, CA: Rand Corporation.

S. Rofe'-Ofir. 2007. Suspicion: A soldier stole weapons and sold them to Palestinians. *Yediot Aharonot*, 7 March. www.ynet.co.il (accessed December 2007). [In Hebrew].

J.W. Runge. 2003. Traffic law enforcement and homeland security. In: R.L. Kemp (ed) *Homeland Security: Best Practices for Local Government.* Washington, DC: International City/County Management Association.

O. Shikler. 2007. A terrorist group that attempted kidnapping was arrested. *News First Class*, 12 March. www.nfc.co.il (accessed December 2007). [In Hebrew].

M. Sidel. 2004. *More Secure, Less Free.* US: The University of Michigan.

J.H. Skolnick. 2005. Democratic policing confronts terror and protest. *Syracuse Journal of International Law and Commerce* 33:191–212.

Y. Stein. 2001. *Torture of Palestinian Minors in the Gush-Etzion Police Station.* Israel: B'Tselem. http://www.btselem.org/Download/200107_Torture_of_Minors_Eng.rtf (accessed December, 2007).

D. Thacher. 2005. The local role in homeland security. *Law and Society Review* 39(3):635–676.

The Role of 'Home' in Homeland Security: The Federalism Challenge. 2003. Albany, NY: Rockefeller Institute of Government.

J. Travis. 1999. *Inventory of State and Local Law Enforcement Technology Needs to Combat Terrorism*. Washington, DC: National Institute of Justice.

UK Human Rights: A Broken Promise. 2006. Amnesty International. http://web.amnesty.org/library/pdf/EUR450042006ENGLISH/$File/EUR4500406.pdf (accessed December, 2007).

G. Wardlaw. 1982. *Political Terrorism: Theory, Tactics, and Counter-Measures*. New York, NY: Cambridge University Press.

D. Weisburd and J. McElroy. 1988. Enacting the CPO role: Findings from the New York City pilot program in community policing. In: J.R. Greene and S.D. Mastrofski (eds) *Community Based Policing: Rhetoric or Reality*. New York: Praeger.

D. Weisburd, T. Jonathan, and S. Perry. Forthcoming. The Israeli model for policing terrorism: Goals, strategies and open questions. *Criminal Justice and Behavior*.

D. Weisburd, S. Orit, and A. Menachem. 2002. Community policing in Israel: Resistance and change. *Policing: An International Journal of Police Strategies and Management* 25(1):80–109.

P. Wilkinson. 2001. *Terrorism versus Democracy: The Liberal State Response*. UK: Frank Cass.

J.Q. Wilson. 1978. *The Investigators: Managing FBI and Narcotics Agents*. New York, NY: Basic Books.

T. Yamin-Volbowitz. 2007. Suspicion: Israeli companies assisted in funding terror organizations. *Maa'riv*, 25 February. www.nrg.co.il (accessed December 2007). [In Hebrew].

N. Yashuvi. (ed). 1990. *Violence against Minors in Police Detention*. Israel: B'Tselem. http://www.btselem.org/Download/199006_07_Violence_against_Minors_Eng.doc (accessed December 2007).

Chapter 5
Police Activities to Counter Terrorism: What We Know and What We Need to Know

Cynthia Lum, Maria (Maki) Haberfeld, George Fachner, and Charles Lieberman

Abstract This study seeks to answer the question "What are police doing to counter terrorism?" We use a multistep process to unearth these global tendencies of police responses. First, we review existing studies which have surveyed police agencies about their counterterrorism activities. To supplement this existing research, we then report preliminary findings from three new studies currently underway by the authors and others. We conclude by providing an agenda for future research and action given this exercise. Specifically, the one major lesson that emerges that influences our agenda is: Despite the proliferation and spending on police counterterrorism efforts, very little is known about the nature and effectiveness of police counterterrorism strategies. Clearly, building the knowledge and a research infrastructure to support such knowledge with regard to police counterterrorism strategies is an essential and currently missing component of this research and action arena.

What Are Police Doing to Counter Terrorism?

At first, there seems to be a flurry of answers to this question that include buzzwords such as "interagency partnerships," "biochemical hazard sensory equipment," "intelligence gathering and information sharing," "joint terrorism tasks forces," "threat and risk assessments," "guarding critical infrastructure," and "undercover investigations and surveillance." Especially since the attacks in the United States on September 11th, law enforcement agencies across the world have increasingly examined, discussed, developed, or revised technologies, tactics, strategies, interagency agreements, standard operating procedures, and other policy

---

C. Lum (✉), M. Haberfeld, G. Fachner, and C. Lieberman
Administration of Justice Department, Center for Evidence-Based Crime Policy,
George Mason University, 10900 University Blvd., MS 4F4, Manassas, VA 20110, USA
e-mail: clum@gmu.edu

options in an effort to prepare for, assess the risk of, and prevent future events of terrorism. Like the list of counterterrorism activities more generally (see Lum et al., 2006b), law enforcement options seem profuse and are often matched by increases in spending and resource allocation.[1]

At the same time, the search for the answer to the question of "what are police doing?" is complicated by many factors. First, the pressures for politicians and practitioners to respond quickly creates an environment of layers upon layers of rhetoric, ideas, clichés, debates, and assertions that may or may not be supported by actual tangible, effective, useful, or legal actions. Additionally, policing itself is multilayered; at any point in time agencies may be engaged in discussions, strategies, or tactics at varying levels of intensity or combination that may directly or indirectly address terrorism. Existing activities used for other purposes might now be co-opted as counterterrorism strategies. Furthermore, the secrecy and mythology that surrounds police efforts generally, and even more so regarding concerns of "high policing" of which counterterrorism is a part (see Bayley and Weisburd, this volume; Brodeur, 1983), make it difficult to ascertain what police are really doing. Resource allocations to homeland security efforts are often general, vague, and politically motivated, and guessing police response from these monetary allocations can be misleading. All these factors can obscure our understanding of the law enforcement response to terrorism.

Not only do we *not* have a clear idea of what activities police are engaged in, but there is also a lack of empirical research that documents police activity or scientifically evaluates interventions. The lack of empirical information makes sifting through the rhetoric difficult, while the scattered, vague, multiuse and co-opted nature of existing programs makes generalizations elusive. While we may know what a specific agency at a specific point in time is doing to respond to or prepare for a particular terrorism-related concern, it is more difficult, to grasp the tendencies and themes of law enforcement or to know with some certainty if such responses are effective. Consequently, listing all possible police responses or reporting upon activities of single agencies can also result in hyperbole.

In this murky environment of rhetoric and reality, and because we have an overall social science goal of improving the evaluation and understanding of police counterterrorism efforts, we approach this chapter using a broad, global, and thematic approach while at the same time, providing specific examples to illustrate themes of police response. Taking a thematic perspective has two advantages. First, such an approach can provide a sense of the strategic (more general and long term) and tactical (more specific and on-the-ground) responses, tendencies, and priorities of a nation or region's law enforcement apparatus in countering terrorism, without

---

[1] In the United States, of the recent appropriation of $34 billon allocated to homeland security, "key investments" included moneys to improve local, state, and federal law enforcement and first responder prevention, preparation, response, coordination, and training activities (See Summary: 2008 Homeland Security Appropriations by the US House of Representatives, Committee on Appropriations http://appropriations.house.gov/pdf/HomelandHP.pdf).

diverting the reader's attention with descriptions of esoteric programs not being widely implemented. Second, a thematic approach may contribute to building an evidence-based research infrastructure for counterterrorism (Lum et al., 2006b) by illuminating common dimensions of the prevention or response mechanisms of seemingly different interventions and by exposing what further information is needed to determine "what works." Such information can in turn provide decision makers with more informed clues about what we already know could be effective in countering terrorism or what needs further knowledge and testing (Lum and Koper, forthcoming).

To unearth these global tendencies of police responses, we combine past and current research. First, we review three existing studies which have surveyed police agencies about their counterterrorism activities. While such studies have only focused on American policing agencies, they provide some sense of the depth and nature of seemingly diverse, distinct, or esoteric counterterrorism responses across multiple jurisdictions and layers of law enforcement. We then report preliminary findings from a new study of United States police agencies conducted by Lum and Fachner which asks questions not included on previous surveys in order to extract general themes of police responses to countering terrorism. Haberfeld and Lieberman then engage this thematic discussion by applying, comparing, and contrasting their international research of qualitative observations of police agencies in six European nations that they conducted for a separate National Institute of Justice project (Haberfeld et al., forthcoming). We also discuss David Weisburd's research on counterterrorism activities conducted by the Israeli Police.

One major conclusion emerges in our exercise: despite the proliferation and spending on police counterterrorism efforts, very little is known about the nature and effectiveness of police counterterrorism responses and strategies. This point has already been pre-empted by the Campbell Collaboration systematic review on counterterrorism interventions conducted by Lum et al. (2006a). In that review and meta analysis, of the over 20,000 pieces of literature the authors found which discussed terrorism, only seven studies included evaluations of counterterrorism interventions using at least moderately rigorous scientific methods. None of these studies specifically focused on law enforcement approaches. From this lesson, we highlight three needs for a research agenda in this area: (1) a greater understanding of what police are doing to counter terrorism, (2) scientific evaluations of those efforts, and (3) the building of a research infrastructure to support (1) and (2).

Existing Research on Police Counterterrorism Activities

We begin by examining existing studies that have surveyed multiple law enforcement agencies about their counterterrorism activities to gain a general understanding of the tendencies of law enforcement efforts. Such studies stand in contrast to opinion and thought pieces that either suggest what should be the priorities of law enforcement or which describe a specific program within an individual agency.

Currently, the best available general assessments include a series of studies by the RAND Corporation on the terrorism preparedness of state and local law enforcement agencies in the United States (Davis et al., 2004; Riley and Hoffman, 1995), a study undertaken by the Council of State Governments and Eastern Kentucky University (2006), and the most recent Law Enforcement Management and Administrative Survey conducted in 2003 by the US Department of Justice, Bureau of Justice Statistics (2006).[2]

The Rand Studies on State and Local Law Enforcement Preparedness

In 2002, the RAND Corporation conducted a survey of local and state law enforcement counterterrorism preparedness (Davis et al., 2004) as a post-September 11th update to a previous study (see Riley and Hoffman, 1995). The 2002 survey, of which we direct our focus, reports on law enforcement preparedness after September 11th, but prior to the creation of the US Department of Homeland Security. In both surveys, RAND questioned hundreds of US law enforcement agencies about their counterterrorism response, soliciting information on resource allocation, threat perceptions, vulnerabilities, and preparedness activities. The authors also analyzed relationships between the agency size, perception of risk, levels of funding, and preparedness. To select agencies for their study, Davis et al. employed a two-stage sampling approach similar to the method used by Riley and Hoffman in 1995, which used a combination of expert opinion, population size, and purposeful and random sampling techniques.[3] In total, 325 agencies were sampled and 78% responded.

Davis et al. (2004), found evidence of increased law enforcement activity since September 11th (especially in state and larger county jurisdictions) in three main areas: risk assessments and emergency response planning, interagency coordination, and personnel and resource reallocation. With regard to risk assessments and emergency planning, the vast majority of responding police agencies had conducted these between 2000 and 2002 (82% of all state agencies and 73% of all local agencies), although the exact nature of such assessments is unknown. Likely connected with such assessments was the counterterrorism activity of developing written response plans to prepare for future attacks, which included coordinating with other agencies. Interestingly, Davis et al. (2004), report that 60% of state agencies and

---

[2] We decided to exclude the International Association of Chiefs of Police's "Post 9–11 Policing Project" report (International Association of Chiefs of Police, 2005), as it was more focused on understanding the priorities, perceptions, and feelings of law enforcement executives with regard to how September 11th affected change (both positive and negative) in their agencies.

[3] See Davis et al. (2004:4–8, 129–137) (Appendix A) for a full description of that study's methodology.

only 35% of their local counterparts felt it was their responsibility to create such written documents.

According to this study, US law enforcement agencies have also more regularly engaged in the general and often ambiguously defined counterterrorism activity of "interagency cooperation." Such coordination usually involves agencies receiving some kind of guidance, training, or education from federal law enforcement agencies such as the Federal Bureau of Investigation or Joint Terrorism Task Forces (JTTFs) (see US Department of Justice, 2004) or establishing communication channels with other agencies. Larger agencies at the state or metropolitan level also tend to be more involved and proactive in interagency activities than small agencies. Notably, despite this widespread assertion of interagency cooperation, *every* state police agency and the vast majority of local organizations who responded to the RAND study stated that there were limitations to interagency communications and interoperability. In combination, these answers may hint at the ambiguous nature of such activities, despite an overall willingness to cooperate.

Finally, the RAND study indicated that US agencies have responded to terrorism by reallocating personnel and resources. For example, in response to September 11th and at least for large agencies, more personnel have been allocated to conduct emergency planning for terrorism. Additionally, a large majority of state agencies (77%) claimed to have specialized counterterrorism units (although only 16% of local agencies have the same). However, it should be noted that Davis et al. found that such specialized units are less often engaged in actual investigations or deterrence activities than in more general "liaising" activities with other law enforcement organizations or in data collection and analysis.

Although the RAND studies were designed to assess one type of law enforcement response to terrorism – preparation activities (rather than implementation of surveillance, deterrence, and technological tactics) – Davis et al. (2004) and Riley and Hoffman (1995) provide a sense of some of the tendencies of law enforcement's counterterrorism activities. Particularly, "counterterrorism" in the United States often involves more long-run and strategic planning activities that could be interpreted as somewhat general, ambiguous, and vague. There are also differences in the capacity for, interest in, and engagement of these activities by state and local jurisdictions, which indicate how different types of jurisdictions view their counterterrorism roles and responsibilities in relation to the broader law enforcement community.

Council of State Governments/Eastern Kentucky University Study

A second source for understanding police responses to terrorism is a study conducted by the Council of State Governments and Eastern Kentucky University (2006), herein called the "CSG/EKU study." The aim of this study was to gauge how the terrorist attacks of September 11th affected the operations and organization of law enforcement agencies by probing agencies about their allocation of resources, interagency relationships, interactions with the private sector, and involvement in homeland security initiatives. Seventy-three statewide law enforcement agencies in the United States (state police, highway patrol, and general investigative bureaus) were surveyed, as well as 400 local police and sheriff agencies.[4] Eighty-four percent of the state law enforcement agencies responded, while 58.5% of the large agencies and 35% of the smaller agency sample answered the survey.

Similar to the findings from RAND, the CSG/EKU study indicates that state agencies were more likely to reallocate resources for infrastructure security, special events, intelligence gathering and analysis, and terrorism-related investigations than local or smaller agencies. Local agencies also expressed more interest in training and technical assistance from state agencies who in turn felt overwhelmed by such requests. There were a few new findings compared to Law Enforcement Management and Administrative Statistics (LEMAS) (discussed later) and RAND worth noting. For instance, 60% of state agencies reported an increase in their interactions with corporate security and private companies after September 11th (a trend found also with large local agencies), indicating an interest in involving private, non-governmental entities in local law enforcement counterterrorism activities. Another finding from this survey was that local agencies are devoting more resources to airport and port security, whereas state agencies tend to focus on border security concerns. This interesting nuance may indicate that although small, local agencies often are seen and see themselves as low-risk jurisdictions, these agencies may be those in which borders, ports, airports, points of entry, or other critical infrastructure might be located and therefore may warrant stronger attention.

Law Enforcement Management and Administrative Statistics (LEMAS) Survey

The third existing source of knowledge about police counterterrorism responses is the most recently published LEMAS survey, conducted in 2003 by the Bureau of Justice Statistics of the US Department of Justice (see US Department of Justice, 2006).[5] The LEMAS survey is administered approximately every 3 years to document a wide range of police organizational characteristics and activities, and the 2003 survey marked the first time police agencies were asked about their counterterrorism activities. The 2003 LEMAS presents three advantages that can supplement the RAND studies. First, it is given to a substantial sample of agencies in the US, including all agencies with 100 or more sworn officers (denoted here as "large") and a representative sample of agencies with fewer than 100 officers ("small"). Second, LEMAS traditionally enjoys a high response rate (of the 3,154

---

[4] These 400 agencies included the 200 largest police agencies in the United States and a random sample of 200 agencies of the remaining US law enforcement agencies.

[5] The 2003 LEMAS dataset and survey instrument can also be viewed and downloaded at www.icpsr.umich.edu.

agencies surveyed in 2003, 90.6% or 2,859 agencies responded). Finally, although the 2003 LEMAS like the RAND studies also focused on agency preparation, it does ask a few questions about law enforcement actions which engage the community.

The LEMAS questions relevant to counterterrorism are 27(t), 33(a and b), and 36, which are summarized in Tables 5.1–5.3. When agencies were asked about their use of personnel to address homeland security tasks (Table 5.1), interestingly, a majority of agencies that participated in the 2003 LEMAS simply did not respond to this question (69%), reflected in the almost complete nonresponse (98%) of small agencies. Additionally, for those agencies that did respond, the vast majority indicated that they addressed the problem without creating or using a specialized unit. This may indicate that even for larger US agencies, counterterrorism is not prioritized over other functions that do require specialized resource allocation.

The LEMAS also asked whether an agency had a written plan of action for terrorism events or whether mutual aid or cooperative agreements existed between the surveyed agency and other municipal or state agencies (Table 5.2). While we tried to only report upon LEMAS questions that directly asked about terrorism-specific policies, it should be noted that the way Questions 33a and b are written does not specifically exclude nonterrorism efforts. Because of this, percentages shown here

Table 5.1 Personnel allocation for terrorism-related tasks (Question 27t)

Activity	Total ($n = 2,859$)	Large ($n = 891$)	Small ($n = 1,968$)
Specialized unit with full-time personnel	9.1%	28.6%	0.3%
Dedicated personnel, but no specialized unit with full-time personnel	11.4%	34.8%	0.8%
Addresses the problem but without any dedicated personnel	10.3%	31.3%	0.8%
Does not address problem	0.8%	2.1%	0.2%
No response given	68.5%	3.1%	98.0%

Table 5.2 Whether agencies have written plans and mutual aid/cooperative agreements for terrorism (Questions 33a and b)

	Total ($n = 2,859$)	Large ($n = 891$)	Small ($n = 1,968$)
Question 33a: Does your agency have a written plan that specifies actions to be taken in the event of terrorist attacks? (Include emergency operation plans that would be applicable to such an attack.)	57.2%	81.6%	46.2%
Question 33b: Does your agency's plan include mutual aid or cooperative agreements between city, county, transit, public works, and/or other agencies?	25.7%	79.1%	1.5%

Table 5.3 Other activities that police engaged in related to terrorism (Question 36)

	Total (n = 2,859)	Large (n = 891)	Small[a] (n = 1,968)
Partnership with culturally diverse communities	7.2%	22.6%	0.3%
Public antifear campaigns	4.7%	14.7%	0.1%
Dissemination of information to increase citizen preparedness	15.0%	46.2%	0.9%
Community meetings on homeland security/preparedness	12.9%	40.0%	0.7%
Increased sworn officer presence at critical areas	23.7%	73.8%	1.0%
None of the above	3.6%	10.5%	0.5%

[a] These percentages are low, as almost all small agencies did not answer these questions

may be inflated. For example, it appears that the vast majority of large agencies (82%) and almost half (46%) of smaller agencies have written plans of action for emergencies. Yet, the almost nonexistence of cooperative agreements of smaller agencies (1.5%) is notable and surprising. Because of their size, we would expect that they would be more likely to have such agreements with other agencies.

Finally, the 2003 LEMAS asked agencies a series of questions that focused on what can best be described as "community-oriented" counterterrorism responses which are not found in the RAND studies (Table 5.3). While larger agencies are more likely to engage in community partnerships, antifear campaigns, educating the public, and community meetings, these are still less emphasized compared to the one tactic that could be argued as the least community-oriented – increasing presence at critical areas. Thus, not only does it appear that police are more comfortable responding to terrorism in ways involving planning or interagency agreements, but if using "community-oriented" tactics, are more likely to favor traditional approaches (like increased police presence) over other types of community-based approaches (such as partnerships or antifear campaigns).

Overall, the RAND, CSG/EKU, and LEMAS surveys provide an important foundation for gaining a sense of the tendencies of the nature of the American law enforcement response, especially since September 11th. In particular, most police agencies in the United States do not appear to prioritize counterterrorism in their daily work and do not specifically dedicate large amounts of resources or personnel to such activities (strategic or tactical). For those that do (usually larger and multi-jurisdiction agencies), their activities tend to fall under the more general categories of planning, interagency cooperation, mutual aid agreements, and information sharing (or at least developing plans to share information). These findings are interesting, especially given the overall increase in the financing of law enforcement activities by the Department of Homeland Security.

Explanations for why local, state, and even federal agencies tend towards these types of general activities, or in many cases, inaction, may include lack of resources, little interest in counterterrorism activity due to a low-risk perception, a belief that other agencies are or should be responsible, an uncertainty about how to respond, or perhaps an uncertainty about whether certain responses are appropriate, legal, or even harmful. Further, federal homeland security allocations tend to be biased toward state and larger metropolitan jurisdictions, and may drive the belief by smaller agencies that they are at lower risk or that other state or federal agencies are more responsible or are acting. These tendencies might also be the result of the surveys themselves, whose questions are focused more on preparedness activities rather than on-the-ground street level tactics, physical movement of resources, alternative/community-based approaches (with the exception of the LEMAS survey), surveillance, prevention, or deterrence activities.

Aside from these studies, there is little known about the extent to which law enforcement agencies are engaging in counterterrorism activities. Nor are there rigorous evaluations of existing practices. Recently, Lum et al. (2006a,b), undertook a Campbell systematic review and meta-analysis of counterterrorism tactics to search for at least moderately methodologically rigorous evaluations of counterterrorism interventions. After examining over 20,000 pieces of literature that mentioned terrorism, they found only a total of 112 articles from peer-reviewed sources which discussed as "law enforcement responses to terrorism," *none* of which satisfied moderate methodological thresholds to be included in the Campbell systematic review. The seven qualifying studies that were located did not address police efforts, but focused on such interventions as metal detectors in airports, fortifying embassies, military strikes, U.N. resolutions, or increased punishment for offenders.

A New Assessment of US Police Counterterrorism Efforts

Given the scant research systematically documenting police counterterrorism efforts, Lum and Fachner carried out a new survey to build a broader understanding of police counterterrorism efforts. Since previous studies focused on preparedness and planning, this survey also asked agencies about their more tactical or on-the-ground operations.

The Study and Survey Instrument

Lum and Fachner surveyed agencies as to whether they engaged in 63 counterterrorism activities which ranged from long-term planning to on-the-ground tactics.[6]

To do this, they categorized these activities into seven broad areas: interagency cooperation and coordination, strategic planning, training, information and intelligence, technologies, deterrence, and surveillance. The sources of information that Lum and Fachner used to derive these general categories and the specific activities

---

[6] The full survey instrument can be accessed at http://gunston.gmu.edu/clum/Resources/USDOJ-MOPSSurvey.pdf.

included the RAND, LEMAS, and CSG/EKU studies as well as the law enforcement-related research Lum, Kennedy and Sherley found in the course of conducting their Campbell review (see Table 5.1, Lum et al., 2006a:8). The authors also consulted with experts and open-source information, especially with regard to law enforcement technologies.[7] The seven response areas were:

Interagency Cooperation and Coordination. Police agencies may be engaged in interagency cooperation, exercises, or cooperative agreements across local, regional, state, national, and international jurisdictions. These may include joint emergency response drills and exercises, the sharing of information and data, coordination of case management and planning, joint investigations through inter-jurisdictional task forces, or the development and/or use of centers which employ representatives from multiple police agencies and other governmental and non-governmental entities.

Strategic Planning. Strategic planning includes those activities which are preparatory in nature or have long-run characteristics. Such activities might involve developing standard operating procedures that detail unit deployment and mobilization prior to and during attacks, including coordination with other agencies and individuals or engaging in simulations and drills. Strategic preparation may incorporate risk assessments of places, people, and groups, which can range from basic and informal anticipations (for example, command staff suggesting places that are high risk based on their experience or hunches) to the use of more advanced calculations and predictive formulas (see, for example, US Department of Homeland Security, 2003b).

Training. While training activities may overlap with strategic planning and preparedness, we highlighted them separately. Training sessions may provide personnel with skills that are believed to support counterterrorism activities, help officers respond more efficiently or effectively to events, or provide analysts with tools to better develop prevention programs. Such training might also include instructions on how to use equipment and technologies such as hazmat suits, bomb detection devices, or global positioning software; interpersonal skills training (e.g., language, cultural or sensitivity workshops); or on how to respond to mass casualties, riots, or biological weapons.

Information Collection and Analysis. These activities can include the use of tip lines or watch lists, or the creation of specialized research and intelligence units to find, store, analyze, and disseminate information that may be used to detect terrorism-related activity. The improvement of information technology systems, databases, and processes to facilitate these goals may also be included in this category.

Technologies. Technologies (other than information systems) that might be relevant to law enforcement efforts to counter terrorism can be generally grouped into surveillance,

---

[7] The survey was sent to numerous individuals for comments, additions, and deletions. Additionally, Dr. Allan Turner, a program manager for the Department of Homeland Security who specializes in knowledge related to law enforcement counterterrorism technologies, was also consulted.

detection, analytic, and communication devices and can include a wide array of items such as night vision and thermal imaging equipment, container scanners, biological detection devices, risk assessment software, or search and rescue tools. Because of the variety of such technologies, Lum and Fachner only focused on asking agencies about some well-known technologies, such as protective gear, biological and chemical weapon detection equipment, communication devices, metal detectors, or biometric equipment, but will provide other examples in the discussion.

General Deterrence. As opposed to surveillance activities which are used to detect unlawful actions by suspected individuals or groups, general deterrence responses are those which use preventative measures to target entire populations or places believed to be vulnerable. For example, a counterterrorism intervention that has been evaluated – metal detectors in airports – would be considered a general deterrence tactic (Lum et al., 2006a). Other activities might include placing concrete barriers around buildings (or entire jurisdictions, such as the separation barrier in Israel), limiting access to places, randomly searching individuals in subway stations, using closed-circuit television (CCTV) monitors, increasing police presence at risky places, increasing the certainty of punishment, or creating international resolutions against the use of violence.

Surveillance. Surveillance can include actions which attempt to monitor and detect clandestine activities with the goal of building cases, investigating incidents, identifying key individuals, or uprooting terrorist cells or networks. Traditional investigative techniques such as undercover operations, wiretapping, monitoring financial or internet activity, or other case building approaches may be included in this category. Surveillance may also employ CCTV monitors placed at strategic locations (for example, in subway stations or on busy streets) to capture events as they unfold.

It should be emphasized that these activities were not chosen because they are effective. Indeed, we do not know whether they are. Rather, these 63 activities listed in the following tables and the seven categories in which they fit were chosen because they are believed to represent a range of potential police activities related to countering terrorism. Agencies were also allowed to add other activities that were not listed.

To administer the survey, Lum and Fachner randomly sampled 200 agencies from the 2003 LEMAS, 100 of which had 100 or greater sworn officers ("large agencies") and 100 agencies that had less than 100 sworn officers ("small agencies"). They contacted the chief executive officer (chief, commissioner, superintendent, etc.) of each agency to solicit their participation (methods available to administer the survey included mail, fax, email, telephone, or an online survey interface). On the survey and letter of instruction, agencies were specifically asked to only answer affirmatively if they were currently using the activity "specifically counter, respond to, manage, deter, detect or prevent terrorism or terror-related threats."

The survey was first administered in March 2007, with six follow-ups between March and December 2007. As of December 2007, 85 agencies have responded. A number of agencies refused to officially respond, arguing that answering the survey could lead to compromising national security. Many other agencies who did respond simply stated that they did not engage in any counterterrorism activities. In those cases, we recorded those agencies as having responded, but answering "no" for all activities we asked about. Given our persistent and repeated efforts to obtain information from these agencies, and given the researchers prior experience with surveying police agencies, we suspect that the low response rate in this particular survey was due to these two reasons – secrecy and suspicion (unnecessary, in our view, given the nature of the survey questions) or simply that the agency was not conducting the on-the-ground counterterrorism activities of which we asked.

Results

Results within each of the seven categories are provided as follows, using the proportion of responding agencies who answered "yes" in engaging in a particular activity within each category. We report results for each activity first across the total sample ($n = 85$) and then separated into large ($n = 46$) and small ($n = 39$) agencies. Again, it should be noted that results may be inflated if there is a correlation between willingness to respond and activity engagement.

Interagency Cooperation and Coordination

Interagency cooperation and coordination was the category in which the most consistent and affirmative answers were provided by respondents (Table 5.4). Most of the activities in Table 5.4 are being practiced by at least half of the

Table 5.4 Interagency cooperation and coordination

Activity	Total ($n = 85$)	Large ($n = 46$)	Small ($n = 39$)
Regular, formalized basis with other state or local law enforcement	67.1%	78.3%	53.9%
Met with state, local, or federal law enforcement for coordination efforts	64.7%	76.1%	51.3%
Command staff attended conferences	63.5%	67.4%	59.0%
Interagency response drills	63.5%	76.1%	48.7%
Received training from department of homeland security (DHS)	61.2%	71.7%	48.7%
Regular, formalized basis with federal law enforcement	56.5%	69.6%	41.0%
Must report to federal, state, or other local agencies	54.1%	60.9%	46.2%
Interagency or regional taskforce or fusion center	47.1%	60.9%	30.8%
Use of homeland security information network (HSIN)	25.9%	37.0%	12.8%
Worked with local universities or think tanks	11.8%	17.4%	5.1%

responding agencies. These primarily focused on meeting and interacting with other agencies or even some regularity in meeting with or receiving training from federal agencies. These findings are consistent with the RAND survey and can be best characterized as less resource intensive and more focused on general coordination efforts.

The high level of activity in this category is interesting because of underlying tendencies of which it may represent. Coordination activities and rhetoric in any bureaucratic system could reflect not only purposeful planning, real public demands, or a belief that such activities work best, but can also reflect the shifting of responsibility and misperceptions about responsibility and leadership. Operating within the realm of cooperation and coordination could also result in little substantive action actually occurring, because of the often general and vague nature of such activities as well as a lack of a clear action or leadership infrastructure. Further, as with other activities used to counter terrorism, it is uncertain to what extent these activities are carried out specifically for terrorism or whether they were "co-opted" from existing activities and assumed to be applicable to terrorism.

Strategic Planning

Although not as regularly engaged in as interagency cooperation, strategic planning was the category of activities of which police agencies were also likely to be involved (Table 5.5). Over half of all responding agencies conduct terrorism-specific emergency response drills (58%) followed by indications of the existence of formal plans within their broader jurisdictions (42%) and within their agencies (35%). Like interagency cooperation, "strategic planning" can be specific to terrorism, or co-opted and applied more generally to all hazards.

Table 5.5 Strategic planning

Activity	Total ($n = 85$)	Large ($n = 46$)	Small ($n = 39$)
Terrorism-specific emergency response drills	57.6%	69.6%	43.6%
Formal intrajurisdictional response plan	42.4%	54.3%	28.2%
Formal within agency response plan	35.3%	45.7%	23.1%
Formal process for risk assessment	34.1%	45.7%	20.5%
Formal protocol for national threat levels	25.9%	34.8%	15.4%
Formal response plan with federal government	24.7%	37.0%	10.3%
Specialized unit specifically assigned to terrorism issues	24.7%	41.3%	5.1%
Specific written policies in SOP related to terrorism	23.5%	30.4%	15.4%
Regular command-staff meetings	20.0%	21.7%	17.9%
Formal response plan with community groups or leaders	10.6%	13.0%	7.7%
Formal response plan with local business/private security	5.9%	10.9%	0.0%

Overall, like interagency cooperation, higher responses here indicate that US agencies tend to focus on more general, long-term strategies. As planning activities become more specific, more action-oriented, or involve entities outside of law enforcement, agencies are much less likely to participate. For example, notice the least likely planning activities in which agencies participate. These include having formalized response plans with community groups, businesses, or private security firms, regular meetings with command staff, specific written policies within the formal standardized operating procedures manual, or specialized units specifically assigned to terrorism.

Training

Another more long-term activity that police seem likely to engage in to counter terrorism is training (Table 5.6), especially for response to hazardous materials ("hazmat"). The problem with asking about hazmat training activity on surveys is that this type of training is not rare; it is often provided to officers during academy training to address a wide variety of hazardous spills to which the police respond. Thus, it is unknown, despite our instructions to responding agencies to only answer affirmatively as applied to terrorism, whether such training was developed for purposes of countering new threats like terrorism, or if that type of training is now being co-opted into a counterterrorism response.

Training on how to gather intelligence also received high affirmative responses. The high proportion of agencies that answered "yes" to this activity possibly reflects more general training in investigations or a general belief that much police training is about gathering intelligence. The larger percentage of "cultural training" should also be viewed with caution, as the quality and nature of such training in police agencies is not only unknown, but anecdotally believed to be of poor quality.

Information Collection and Analysis

The fourth type of activity we inquired about was whether agencies engaged in information and intelligence activities. Under this category, we asked departments

Table 5.6 Training

Activity	Total ($n = 85$)	Large ($n = 46$)	Small ($n = 39$)
Conducted/received hazmat training (chemical or biological hazards)	68.2%	80.4%	53.8%
Conducted/received training in intelligence gathering	49.4%	56.5%	41.0%
Training session in academy	40.0%	47.8%	30.8%
Conducted/received cultural training	37.6%	47.8%	25.6%
Increased recruitment diversity	5.9%	6.5%	5.1%
Conducted/received foreign language training	1.2%	2.2%	0.0%

5 Police Activities to Counter Terrorism

Table 5.7 Information collection and analysis

Activity	Total (n = 85)	Large (n = 46)	Small (n = 39)
Receiving information, tips, updates, from federal government	58.8%	65.2%	51.3%
Use of federal watchlists or databases	35.3%	39.1%	30.8%
Intelligence unit which can be mobilized for terrorism	27.1%	39.1%	12.8%
Process for building relationships with local community members	24.7%	34.8%	12.8%
Process for collecting information from local businesses	22.4%	26.1%	17.9%
Checking residency/immigration status of arrestees	14.1%	21.7%	5.1%
Existing database for terrorism information	12.9%	15.2%	10.3%
Specialized intelligence analysts	8.2%	15.2%	0.0%
Intelligence unit for terrorism	4.7%	8.7%	0.0%
Existence/use of a tip line	3.5%	6.5%	0.0%

about their collection, use, and analysis of information, as well as their development of information systems. Interestingly, the most common activity of which agencies engaged was in passively *receiving* information, tips, and updates from the federal government (see Table 5.7), reflecting both the reactive nature of American policing and related to this trait, a possible belief that counterterrorism is a federal, not local concern. Again, there are less affirmative responses when agencies are asked about their intelligence outreach to non-law enforcement entities, or in the actual development of units, analysts, or tip lines for terrorism data collection. In fact, the activity least engaged in was tip lines. This is consistent with previous research by Lum (2005) who found that not only is tip line use rare in the United States (despite its seemingly high use reflected in reality-television shows), but that the tip lines that are used are usually manual and archaic, where tips are written down on pieces of paper and filed.

These findings are especially telling. Despite widespread rhetoric in the law enforcement community that information and intelligence are key to countering terrorism and supporting interagency cooperation, there appears to be much less activity in this area than one might expect. The activities that US agencies are most likely to engage are passive, not proactive, and include receiving information rather than generating it. Furthermore, such activities such as "building relationships with community" or "using federal databases" could potentially be co-opted from already existing systems (for example, like the use of the FBI's National Crime Information Center (NCIC) database system).

Technologies

When we asked agencies about their use of other technologies, affirmative responses dramatically declined (Table 5.8). Except for the activity of "purchasing

Table 5.8 Technologies

Activity	Total (n = 85)	Large (n = 46)	Small (n = 39)
Purchased protective gear/clothing	65.9%	76.1%	53.8%
Ready access to biological and radiation detection equipment	35.3%	52.2%	15.4%
Ready access to explosives detection devices	32.9%	43.5%	20.5%
Purchased transportation equipment	18.8%	28.3%	7.7%
Specific radio frequency channels	12.9%	19.6%	5.1%
Installing/using metal detectors in public places	10.6%	15.2%	5.1%
Geographic information software	9.4%	15.2%	2.6%
Vehicle-mounted or portable computers for counterterrorism	7.1%	10.9%	2.6%
Contingency plan for network failure	5.9%	6.5%	5.1%
Cyberterrorism unit	3.6%	6.5%	0.0%
Biometric technology for identification purposes	2.4%	2.2%	2.6%
Other (not specified)	3.5%	4.3%	2.6%

protective gear/clothing" which could have been done for more general purposes or a co-opted technology, activities engaging terrorism-related technologies were low. Furthermore, the technologies with the lowest affirmative responses seem more terrorism specific or proactive. When we discussed this finding with homeland security "insiders," they confirmed this generally low interest by local police agencies in acquiring such terrorism-specific technologies.

General Deterrence

The most common deterrence tactics used by the responding agencies (although used by less than a majority) include increasing security at high-risk targets and also public areas and events (Table 5.9). This finding was consistent with the LEMAS survey, specifically in the finding that the most likely "community-oriented" counterterrorism deterrence tactic used was "increasing security at critical areas." The use of other tactics is minimal, including undercover operations, use of immigration laws, random searches, and traffic checkpoints. The low use of these tactics may be connected to the fact that many of these interventions and enforcement activities also are highly controversial in the United States in terms of their use and legality, and therefore agencies may be less likely to use them or report their use.

Surveillance

And finally, like deterrence activities, US police agencies do not regularly employ surveillance interventions for the specific purpose of countering terrorism (Table 5.10). CCTV systems are rarely used in the United States, and even less used are

5 Police Activities to Counter Terrorism

Table 5.9 Deterrence

Activity	Total (n = 85)	Large (n = 46)	Small (n = 39)
Increased security in high-risk targets (government, utilities, military)	37.6%	41.3%	33.3%
Increased security in public areas (shopping centers, parks, schools)	24.7%	30.4%	17.9%
Increased security checkpoints at public events	15.3%	21.7%	7.7%
Increased use of canine units	14.1%	19.6%	7.7%
Increased undercover operations	5.9%	8.7%	2.6%
Increased amount of personnel	5.9%	10.9%	0.0%
Increased enforcement on illegal immigration laws	7.1%	8.7%	5.1%
Random searches in public places	3.5%	6.5%	0.0%
Random traffic check points	3.5%	4.3%	2.6%

Table 5.10 Surveillance

Activity	Total (n = 85)	Large (n = 46)	Small (n = 39)
Video cameras in public places	14.1%	17.4%	10.3%
Monitoring internet activity	7.1%	13.0%	0.0%
Increased electronic surveillance in specific locations	4.7%	6.5%	2.6%
Wire taps on phone lines	2.4%	4.3%	0.0%
Monitoring banking records	2.4%	4.3%	0.0%

the monitoring of records, data mining, or wiretaps, at least among state and local police departments. Again, controversies surrounding the use of these technologies may explain their minimal use and/or reporting.

Emerging Themes and Tendencies

From these data, three themes and/or tendencies of law enforcement counterterrorism responses in the US emerge. In this section we discuss these three themes and then follow with comparisons with Haberfeld et al.'s (forthcoming) international observations.

Theme 1: The focus of US law enforcement's counterterrorism efforts is on Interagency coordination and general preparedness planning.

Consistent with the RAND, LEMAS, and CSG/EKU surveys, the Lum and Fachner survey indicates that American law enforcement agencies, if they engage in counterterrorism activities at all, tend to emphasize interagency coordination and general preparation for emergencies than more specifically allocating resources to tactics such as deterrence/surveillance activities, tip lines, or specialized units. This is reflected in the more consistent affirmative responses to questions about interagency discussions, training, drills, and information reception, rather than information generation. A closer examination of the questions within more general categories such as interagency cooperation, strategic planning and training also shows that those activities which had higher response rates are marked by less immediate action or on-the-ground tactics, and more discussing, talking, meeting, or planning.

Some examples of these more general coordination and planning efforts include the JTTFs, Fusion Centers, and "TOPOFF" exercises. The JTTFs are units coordinated by the FBI's National JTTF and combine federal, state, and local law enforcement agency representatives and resources to work on investigations or intelligence gathering. These units have been in existence well before September 11th and have focused on a wide range of activities, some which are not necessarily terrorism specific. Recently, states have also developed Fusion Centers (see US Department of Justice, Bureau of Justice Assistance, 2006), which coordinate information gathering, analysis, and sharing across state and federal jurisdictions, and also facilitate partnerships with other public and private organizations toward this goal. Another example that has included interagency response drills has been the TOPOFF series (short for "Top Officials"), a Congressionally mandated simulation exercise which was used to reveal vulnerabilities in terrorism responses for the purposes of improving preparation (see Arnold et al., 2000; US Department of Homeland Security, 2003a). Such drills can also include interagency and multijurisdictional components to test for the efficacy of responses across a region or state.

We surmise the emphasis on developing these more general coordination and preparedness activities reflects a few factors. First, after September 11th and the 9–11 Commission Report (National Commission on Terrorist Attacks, 2004), for reasons of both liability and public demands, police agencies have increased their attempt to cooperate with each other, even if only to develop memorandums of understanding. This type of approach reflects the relationship between local, state, and federal agencies in the United States, especially in matters such as terrorism and other major disasters, which are often dependent upon each other. Failures in coordination, therefore, are often seen as the reason behind poor government responses to major disasters. This dependency may factor into calculations by agencies as to whether they should engage in more specific activities and incur associated costs. Often, organizations lower on the federal-state-regional-metropolitan-municipal hierarchy see agencies above them as responsible for countering terrorism (see Donnermeyer, 2002). Even smaller jurisdictions that have risky places (airports, border points, ports) may believe that the larger jurisdiction in which they are housed are "taking care of the problem," which may simultaneously explain both their own inactivity, yet greater involvement in interagency cooperation.

The idea of "co-opting" or adapting already existing agreements, training modules, technologies, and equipment into the counterterrorism enterprise also reflects the general and often ambiguous nature of these activities. Agencies may engage in co-optation because they believe this may be the most cost-effective approach to countering terrorism in light of what they may perceive to be a low threat or the responsibility of another agency. Overall, it is difficult to determine to what extent the actions indicated by agencies are specific to responding to counterterrorism, what types of training were modified for counterterrorism and what training was simply renamed, and further, the types of training now renamed. Nonetheless, it appears from the data collected thus far that these types of long-term, planning, and interagency strategic activities are the preference of US law enforcement agencies.

However, while interagency coordination and strategic planning activities like JTTFs, Fusion Centers, TOPOFF, or co-opted standard procedures or memos of understanding are the norm, they remain unevaluated, despite their seemingly logical and asserted benefits. We therefore do not know, for example, whether these types of interagency coordination in fact increase information sharing, and in turn, whether that coordination facilitates the prevention of and response to terrorism. However, a recent nonevaluative review of such task forces by the Office of the Inspector General (2005) indicates some promising aspects of these interagency approaches at least in their implementation (although the outcomes are still uncertain). We also know more generally that multijurisdiction information sharing and collaboration has been viewed as a promising crime reduction strategy (see, e.g., Taxman et al., 2002) and may be useful in improving the ability to coordinate separate and distinctive information systems (Lum, 2005; Taxman and McEwen, 1997). Nonetheless, the fact that these activities are the most used and demanded but remain almost completely unevaluated as to their outcome effectiveness is a ripe area for research.

Theme 2: Agencies are much less likely to use "on-the-ground" tactics, technologies and actions that require allocation of physical resources or immediate action.

The significantly lower responses by agencies on questions probing more specific and "on-the-ground" tactics (deterrence, surveillance, community planning, information collection and analysis, and other prevention activities) not only reflects the flip side of Theme 1, but also gives further insight into the nature of US law enforcement counterterrorism. Items in which less than 10% of responding agencies answering affirmatively were often those activities that require some form of immediate action, resource allocation, tactical deployment, use of a technology, or engaging non-law enforcement entities such as community groups or businesses.

For example, both large and small police agencies do not normally engage in either surveillance or general deterrence activities, the use of CCTVs in public places, internet, phone or banking monitoring, or other types of electronic surveillance. There could be a number of hypotheses as to why this is the case, including a sensitivity to using highly debated techniques and laws that may infringe on privacy (e.g., the Patriot Act[8]), or lack of funding or knowledge in using technologies. While financial burden or lack of knowledge may explain the lack of surveillance, the low use of general deterrence activities may further reflect worries

---

[8] See Uniting and Strengthening America by Providing Appropriate Tools Required to Intercept and Obstruct Terrorism (USA Patriot Act) Act of 2001, H. R. 3,162, 107th Congress. Retrieved May 1, 2007 from http://frwebgate.access.gpo.gov/cgi-bin/getdoc.cgi?dbname = 107_cong_public_lawsanddocid = f:publ056.107.pdf.

over civil rights violations of counterterrorism enforcement approaches. General deterrence activities usually require police agents to engage in preventative approaches across groups of individuals, the vast majority of whom are not suspect. This could lead to racial, ethnic, or religious profiling, as it has in the past. Police agencies were more likely to respond affirmatively to the use of increased security at high-risk targets and public places, but are less likely to use security checkpoints at public events, increase undercover operations, use anti-immigration laws, or conduct random searches or checks of the pedestrian or driving public.

Further indications of an aversion to engaging in these types of on-the-ground, tangible action and tactics can be found in questions under the category of "Information Collection and Analysis." Notice, while the majority of agencies have passively received information, tips, and updates from the national government regarding terrorism, they are less likely to carry out more proactive information gathering and analytic activities. Less than 10% of agencies responded that they have specialized intelligence units or analysts to deal with terrorism and only a minute percentage of agencies have tip lines for terrorism (see also Lum, 2005). While 35% of agencies claimed to use federal watchlists and databases (which could simply mean the use of FBI's NCIC system), fewer agencies had developed processes to collect information from the community or build their own databases regarding terrorism. These findings support our earlier guess regarding intelligence gathering training. Lum and Fachner suspected that the higher affirmative responses to intelligence gathering training but the much lower corresponding use of intelligence gathering may together indicate that intelligence training is more broadly defined (or perhaps co-opted) for counterterrorism efforts, or that the application of that training has yet to be fully realized.

Finally, the low use of technologies further reflects this theme. Of the technologies of which Lum and Fachner inquired, technologies more likely to be used were those that were also more likely to have existed prior to September 11th and have broader applications (e.g., access to hazardous material gear, clothing, and equipment, as well as access to explosive detection devices or communications technologies). Agencies may make cost-benefit calculations in deciding whether to purchase technologies to specifically counter terrorism based on whether other agencies with whom they cooperate have those technologies, their own perception of their jurisdiction's risk levels, or perhaps the uncertainty as to the effectiveness of certain technologies.

Perhaps the low use of specific technologies and equipment by agencies is but one reason why the Departments of Homeland Security and Justice have made recent efforts to increase the use of technologies by police agencies for counterterrorism purposes. For example, the Department of Homeland Security's Commercial Equipment Direct Assistance Program, or CEDAP (see US Department of Homeland Security, 2006, 2007), encourages agencies to apply to the DHS for different types of surveillance, detection, communications, and analytic technologies (some examples of these technologies are listed in Table 5.11). We suggest that if governments wish to increase the use of technologies in law enforcement efforts against terrorism, not only must they be willing to fund such efforts, but technologies

5 Police Activities to Counter Terrorism   121

Table 5.11 Examples of law-enforcement counterterrorism technologies from CEDAP (Adapted from: http://www.ojp.usdoj.gov/odp/equipment_cedap.htm)

Technology type	Functions
Surveillance	
TacSight SE35 thermal imager	Shows heat signature of objects, including through smoke and fog; ×2 and ×4 zoom
GYRO stabilized binoculars w/night vision	Compact and lightweight night vision binoculars; ×10, ×12, ×14, or ×16 magnification
Portable video surveillance system	Manned or unmanned system; can manage up to 4 cameras; motion detection
Tactical Lincoln system	Electronic surveillance hardware and software; GIS analytic functions; information sharing functions; interoperable; populations of 100,000+ and 100+ sworn officers
Armornet overt camera/transmitter digital wireless	Camera system for night and day; remote control; rapid deployment; cameras are dome style; one camera takes approx. 7 min to install
Communications	
Incident commander's radio interface (ICRI)	Compatible with old and new, commercial and military, land and mobile radios, satellite, cell phones, and landline phones; supports up to 5 radios; populations of 25,000 or more and 25 or more personnel
Radio interoperability system (RIOS)	Allows communication across dissimilar radios or telephones
Analytic	
StarWitness video pro	Reconstructs video evidence; population of 50,000+ and agency of 50+ sworn officers
MobileSynch records Management software	Records management, mobile data, data sharing for within and outside agency; provides data about people, places, and things for fixed and mobile environments; populations of 100,000+ and 100+ officers
Homeland security Comprehensive assessment model	Tools to perform a comprehensive assessment; identifies critical infrastructure and vulnerability; gives an "all hazards" assessment
Countermeasures risk analysis software	Addresses and pinpoints trouble spots in a computer system, building, or project; system calculates level of risk based on 30-min survey of the user
Advanced vehicle tracking system	Small, lightweight GPS-based tracking system; data storage for over 10,000 locations
Analyst's notebook 6 software	Visual investigative analysis; reveals patterns and hidden connections
Chemical, biological, radiological, or nuclear detection and mitigation	
CDEAP PPE kit	Full-body coverage garment including boots and gloves; inhalation and dermal protection; mandatory requirements for use include written plan, annual questionnaire, and fit testing
LCD-3 Lightweight chemical detector	Wearable chemical detector constantly samples air; provides detail of agent type, concentration, and dosage; strongly recommended for hazmat certified agencies only
Berkley nucleonic 951 PRD	Palm-sized gamma radiation detector for nontechnical personnel

must also be shown, through evaluation, to be effective, cost effective, and easy to use and operate.

Theme 3. Community-based activities and interactions with nongovernmental agents are rarely used to counter terrorism, despite rhetoric to the contrary.

The final theme which emerged from Lum and Fachner's survey was that "community-based" interventions, activities, and strategies remain elusive and rarely operationalized. This is an interesting finding, as among law enforcement practitioners and the Department of Homeland Security, there has been much interest in, and rhetoric about, using tenets of community policing to create strategies to counter terrorism (see Davies and Murphy, 2004; Innes, 2006; Loyka et al., 2005). In theory, community-oriented counterterrorism law enforcement could include programs which establish better relationships with community groups to obtain information about potential perpetrators (or victims) and improve the legitimacy more generally of the police among groups affected by both terrorism and counter-terrorism efforts.

When dividing community-based questions from the survey into those that specifically addressed terrorism and those that were more general and likely already in place, the lack of terrorism-specific community oriented applications becomes even more noticeable, as less than 10% of agencies responded affirmatively to these questions. In other words, law enforcement agencies are not regularly devising specific community-oriented response plans with community groups, leaders, local businesses, or private security, nor do they use tip lines to receive terrorism information from the public. However, for questions that were more general in nature, there were more affirmative responses. These included whether agencies had conducted cultural diversity training, or had general processes for building relationships with local community members.

What might explain this disconnect between rhetoric and reality? While more exploration is needed, there are a number of hypotheses that are possible. For instance, police may feel more comfortable, or may even feel more benefited, when engaging other law enforcement agencies in interagency cooperation, as opposed to interacting with the community. Or, perhaps the implementation of such vague and general approaches eludes the police, which is not only consistent with the 2003 LEMAS questions pertaining to community responses, but also the well-known problems in implementing community policing more generally (Mastrofski, 2006; Mastrofski and Ritti, 2000). These results are not surprising, as even traditional law enforcement responses to everyday crime often do not include community-based alternative strategies, despite the widespread rhetoric of community policing that permeates American police discourse.

However, the underuse of a community-oriented strategy does not suggest lack of need. Police executives have expressed fears of losing legitimacy and public trust in the post-September 11th era given the changing nature of their relationship with the community during this moral panic (International Association of Chiefs of Police, 2005). Such alternative, community-based approaches may yield important gains in improving the legitimacy of the police while they engage in counterterrorism tactics (National Research Council, 2004; Sherman et al.,

2002; Tyler, 1990). In turn, such strategies may be an important part of the counterterrorism equation itself, as the Northern Ireland experience has shown how changes in the community-orientation of a police service can reduce law-enforcement provoked terrorism (see Independent Commission on Policing in Northern Ireland, 1999). However, while there have been a few scattered examples of community-based counterterrorism tactics (e.g., Philadelphia Police Department's terrorism information hotline,[9] or New York City Police Department's NYPD SHIELD program[10]), the nature, extent, effectiveness, or quality of these practices remains unclear and needs further evaluation. Perhaps utilizing existing relationships and agreements with the community is a good place to begin a counterterrorism dialog, given that police are less likely to engage in community-based programs that are more counterterrorism specific.

Further, the contradictions in a community-based counterterrorism response render such tactics difficult to consider and implement. While seemingly positive from a rhetorical standpoint, community policing might have detrimental effects when used for counterterrorism, as one ethnic group may wield the police against another or incorporating one community's priorities into a strategic plan may lead to crackdowns on others. For example, tip lines may be used to report "suspicious" behavior that may simply be a cultural practice (for example, praying). Strategies may be "effective" in obtaining information, but also may worsen police-community relations. Or, community concerns regarding illegal immigration may lead to the use of terrorism panics to address nonterrorism concerns and groups not traditionally associated with terrorism.

A final note regarding the low use of community-oriented policing strategies: Lum and Fachner found, much to their expectations, that the interaction with the research community remains low (11%). This finding reflects a longstanding, cultural suspicion by police agencies in working with this particular community group regarding many types of issues, as well as a gap between the outputs of research and the needs of practitioners. The problem with this lack of community-based interaction, however, is that researchers may be able to contribute to police efforts by providing evaluations of interventions, offering a broader view of available alternatives, aiding in more scientifically rigorous approaches to risk assessments, and assisting agencies in applying for federal funds for further research and development in this area. As seen earlier, knowledge about what interventions are effective and why police use or do not use technologies, equipment, strategies, and tactics provides an important evidence base for their response.

---

[9] See http://www.ppdonline.org/hq_terrorism.php. This hotline provides information to the public in both English and Arabic.

[10] See http://www.nypdshield.org/public/about.aspx. This program provides private businesses and security with information regarding terrorism risk and alerts and also to receive information from this sector.

Counterterrorism by Police in Europe and Israel

The tendencies and themes discovered of US law enforcement efforts may be specific to both the relatively rare American experience with terrorism and the federal, multitier system of law enforcement in the US. In this next section, to provide a broader international perspective, we reflect on two existing projects, one conducted for the National Institute of Justice by Haberfeld and her colleagues in six European nations (reported here by Haberfeld and Lieberman) and the second by Weisburd and his colleagues regarding Israel.

Europe

Between January 2005 and June 2006, Haberfeld and her team (Joseph King and Heath Grant) traveled to six European nations – the United Kingdom (including Northern Ireland), Ireland, the Netherlands, Sweden, Spain, and Turkey – to examine counterterrorism activities by police agencies. Their research goals included collecting information about the level and scope of the existing counterterrorism training implemented by local law enforcement agencies, discerning how September 11th had affected these agencies at both local and global levels, and gauging community perceptions and feelings about the level and quality of law enforcement responses in light of pressures to deal with terrorism problems.

To accomplish these goals in often sensitive environments, Haberfeld et al. (forthcoming) conducted semi-informal meetings with the upper echelon of the various forces, as well as leaders of specialized units whose primary responsibility was in counterterrorism response or training, either at the headquarters or local level. They also arranged to meet with law enforcement officers at lower ranks who were either assigned directly to the special units in charge of counterterrorism activities and/or other relevant units such as those focused on improving community relationships for purposes of addressing terrorism concerns. Such focus group discussions included as few as two officers to as many as 12, depending on the location, timing, and the level of their cooperation. Participants were informed about the protocol and IRB requirements of their data collection, and Haberfeld's team took written notes and sometimes received written material during these discussions.

The research team was also able to conduct focus groups with various community groups in Ireland, the UK, Spain, and Turkey using samples of convenience. These groups ranged in size from two to ten participants of various backgrounds. For example, in Turkey they spoke with representatives of the Ankara Bar Association, religious leaders of various minority groups, journalists, and media representatives such as television and movie directors. In Spain they interacted with journalists, students, and lawyers. In the U.K. and Ireland, Haberfeld's team had the opportunity to meet representatives of various business ventures, community activists, former IRA members, and Muslim Rights activists. Although the focus groups represented a convenience sample, Haberfeld aimed at maintaining the same protocols when familiarizing study subjects with the goals and aims of the research, informing them about consent options, and in the nature and form of questioning. Due to the sensitivity of the topics discussed in focus groups, the researchers took notes but did not tape record interactions.

What follows are brief summaries of some of their findings for each country examined. Although it is impossible, given the scope of this study, to present a systematic and comprehensive overview of each nation's police response with regard to terrorism, this exercise lends an international perspective to some of these themes and also hints at other potential tendencies that warrant more research. However, this section differs in its structure from a thematic approach given the different nature of police organizations in the countries visited by the team – indeed, the situation in European countries is quite different from the US and from each other. The majority of the countries that were visited have national police forces, or at least decentralized forces that are still subject to centralized training and operational guidelines. Furthermore, the history of terrorism, the nature of the present threat, and the alienation and polarization of the communities in different countries renders a theme comparison impractical and artificial, when the local contextual variable are lost and undervalued in terms of their contribution and influence on the specific strategies and tactics. As with the activities reported in the United States, one theme remains consistent – we are still uncertain whether any of these strategies are effective and to what extent they have been adopted. More detailed accounts of Haberfeld's team findings can be found in their forthcoming NIJ final research report.

The United Kingdom (Great Britain and Northern Ireland)

In Haberfeld's visits to Northern Ireland, her team found the counterterrorism response was geared toward the IRA and its splinter groups rather than a more general terrorist threat. For example, after speaking with the officers responsible for confidential informant training, Haberfeld felt activities did not seem to translate beyond local problems into a fight against any other threats, such as Al Qaeda. While training focused on confidential informant legislation, risk assessment and management, as well as targeting, recruiting, handling, and termination of sources, agents were not given special cultural training to recruit members of the Muslim population nor were agents with Arabic skills sought. Additionally, while coordination with England's national security agency, MI5, was rhetorically emphasized, in practice the local enforcement appeared to be a stand-alone enterprise, also indicating the very local aspects of their efforts.

With regard to the Metropolitan Police Service (MPS) in London, the observers interviewed a number of relevant counterterrorism units in the MPS, including the Specialist Operations 13 (SO13) Branch[11] and the Muslim Contact Unit (MCU).

---

[11] In 2006, SO15 took over the responsibilities of the Anti-Terrorist Branch (SO13) and the Special Branch (SO12).

Of particular interest to the team were the activities of the MCU. The MCU, modeled after the Police Service's community policing outreach units, was established to enhance communication between the London Police and the Muslim communities to support and improve counterterrorism efforts. For example, the MCU engaged in discussions and frequent interactions with local Muslim community leaders and youth groups. They did not participate in police raids on the Muslim communities but would be present in the aftermath to explain police actions in an effort to reduce tensions. Additionally, some of the members of the Muslim Unit were of the Muslim religion. Despite these efforts, interestingly, a commanding officer from one of the MPS stations informed the researchers that a steady communication flow between Muslim communities and the police had not been effectively established.

The observers also found indications of jurisdictional overlaps between the local police and the MI5 security services in street-level intelligence gathering. In particular, the local police seemed under the impression that it was the main concern and responsibility of MI5 to gather terrorism intelligence. Furthermore, there appeared to be a very limited exchange of information about potential threats, between the MI5, SO13, and the rest of the local law enforcement units. An attempt to remedy this was made through the formation of the Rainbow Unit. The Rainbow Unit attempts to improve information sharing by moderating an intranet connection that updates the relevant parties about all criminal activities, including terrorism-related offenses.

One on-the-ground counterterrorism tactic of law enforcement agencies in the United Kingdom that was found to be widely used is CCTV technology, which has been traditionally employed to fight "everyday" crime (see Norris and Armstrong, 1999; Welsh and Farrington, 2003). Haberfeld and her colleagues received access to the MPS communication center which revealed over 2,400 CCTV cameras located throughout London, constantly monitored by MPS personnel. However, there appeared to be no systematic preventative approach or assessment logarithm in which video feeds are monitored with regard to terrorism, and CCTV has been used more as a response tool in the aftermath of incidents.

Ireland

Haberfeld's team found that law enforcement responses in Ireland focused on gathering intelligence about IRA connections between Ireland and Northern Ireland. At the same time, there was much reluctance to merge the efforts directed against IRA-related activities with the efforts directed against the global terrorist threat, and the researchers were confronted with strong resistance when referring to the IRA and its factions as terrorists groups. Further, they found there was no counterterrorism training provided to patrol officers and a lack of interest in doing so by interviewed academy officials. With regard to new threats from Al Qaeda, the Guarda's Intelligence Unit of Dublin did not employ any Arabic-speaking officers.

The Netherlands

Haberfeld's team interviewed officers in the Aliens Police Unit of the National Police Service (KLPD) which is charged to "supervise foreign nationals, with a focus on criminal activity, anti-social behavior, illegal aliens, and the prevention of abuse and exploitation of immigrants" (Ministry of the Interior and Kingdom Relations, 2004:20–21). This unit primarily views its role as processing illegal aliens and maintaining a database about them (although it appeared that they did not conduct analysis on that information) and do not necessarily perceive themselves to be strictly a counterterrorism unit. The research team found, however, that there was a feeling among those officers of a lack of preparedness for what was believed to be a real and growing problem of illegal immigrants who are released to the public, after an initial detention, some of whom displayed extremist orientations while incarcerated. Researchers were told that there were no mechanisms in place that could familiarize local police officers with current terrorism-related issues and that the legal system was not effective in preventing illegal intrusion into the country. Additionally, they found no intelligence gathering efforts at the local level, or counterterrorism training for beat officers or for the Alien Police.

Sweden

The researchers found counterterrorism law enforcement efforts a new venture in Sweden. Although Sweden has not been the victim of terrorist attacks in the past few decades, some have argued that individuals actively associated with terrorist organizations are believed to have immigrated to Sweden (Norell, 2005). Haberfeld's team found that the Swedish Police treats counterterrorism as the responsibility of the street officer. However, this philosophy does not appear to be supported by a particular plan or proactive strategy. Her team noted that a "nontraditional" approach was espoused in responding to crime incidents within immigrant communities, but the meaning and connection with this to counterterrorism was unclear. The researchers also found that the need to establish counterterrorism units was not of immediate concern, and the perception was that the Security Service has a good grasp of the terrorism situation and should be responsible in providing the relevant information to the National Police. Indeed, the Swedish Security Services did not appear to have much contact with the local, neighborhood police forces, despite the belief of the role of the street officer in preventing and responding to incidents.

Spain

In their interactions with this law enforcement apparatus, Haberfeld and her colleagues discovered that like Northern Ireland, decades of enforcement against local threats were not necessarily translated into preparedness against the more recent Islamic threat. For example, participation in the European Task Forces against terrorism was minimal and did not result in specialized training or the creation of an intelligence sharing system. In larger cities the local law enforcement also played a role; however, from what was learned from interviews with the police in Madrid, this role was more supportive than proactive. For example, activities that the local police engaged are directed toward community group outreach through a well-developed Community Policing Unit, in which the officers reach out to communities to provide reassurance about police performance rather than collecting intelligence. It appears that this unit has a one-way orientation, more to reassure the public rather than collect information.

The lack of training and preparedness at the local level also seemed to suggest a culture of ignoring the role of the local police in countering terrorism. Informal interviews of the Policia National, in charge of their Community Policing Units, led to the conclusion by researchers that the outreach performed by these units was geared toward other, nonterrorism, criminal activities and little interaction was taken with local municipal police forces with regard to the main terrorist threat – activities by the Basque national separatist organization *Euskadi Ta Askatasuna*. This despite findings by the researchers, from conversations with the Madrid Municipal police force, that local beat officers were very much aware of the extreme sentiments against the Spanish government and the "West" harbored by local Muslims. However, there are no mechanisms in place to channel this information to the National Police or the Civil Guard.

Turkey

Similar to their counterparts in Europe, the Turkish National Police's primary focus is on countering domestically generated terrorism. In conversations with the TNP's counterterrorism and intelligence chiefs, Haberfeld's team found that the approach to terrorist suspects differed from the approach to other criminals. For example, the main goal is to maintain surveillance on core leaders and active supporters, who according to their estimates constitute a rather small number that can be easily contained by law enforcement. The TNP also attempts to prevent what they estimate are hundreds of thousands of passive supporters from becoming involved with more of the core's activities. The TNP also asserted, which the researchers could not confirm, that its most effective tool to achieve this goal was that it conducted investigations and interrogations of terrorist suspects with a "velvet gloves" approach[12] to reduce the possibility of an interactive effect between police counterterrorism actions and the spread of terrorism.

---

[12] The "velvet glove" approach refers to a politically sensitive interrogation technique used on suspects of terrorist activities, where the guiding principle is not necessarily to elicit confessions or intelligence, but rather a larger concern for how the method of the interrogation and the investigative techniques will be perceived by the larger group of passive supporters in the community from which the suspect was apprehended. The TNP counterterrorism unit appeared concerned about alienating passive supporters who may turn into active supporters.

Haberfeld found limited cooperation between the TNP and the Gendermarie, the country's national security agency, who are also involved in counterterrorism activities. When speaking anonymously the researchers, ranking members of the Gendermarie shared feelings of a lack of cooperation and exchange of intelligence with the TNP, which they felt was critical to countering terrorism. The researchers also found that patrol officers did not receive specialized training in the area of counterterrorism and were told by the TNP that their everyday knowledge of the problem was enough for patrol officers to respond. Based on conversations with patrol officers in Istanbul, the researchers found, however, that officers lacked knowledge about the problem and response. Unless officers were designated to serve in specialized units, no special training was provided either to officers or supervisors.

Comparisons

Some general conclusions and comparisons can be drawn in light of the three themes found in US policing, but unique tendencies also emerged from Haberfeld et al.'s (in press) research, based on the specific nature of the counterterrorist response in each of the visited countries. In Northern Ireland, it was observed that there is very little coordination between the PSNI and other law enforcement agencies. Although there is some cooperation with some of the EU national police forces, it appears that this is more based on the initiative of the other nations and their respect for the professionalism of the PSNI. The community-based activities are rather nonexistent in any formal format, other than the overall commitment of the PSNI upper leadership to diversify the force as much as possible. No specific involvement of the local community in counterterrorist activities was mentioned. Given the social context of the problem and the relaxation of the tensions between the Catholic and Protestant population, which was followed by almost complete demise of the militant terrorist groups, Haberfeld and her team felt that the PSNI should be focusing more on the "new threat" of the militant Muslim terrorism and make some attempt, at least pro forma, to involve the local community in the fight against the global threat.

The potential of the information sharing between the United Kingdom forces through Operation Rainbow (and more recently Project Delphinus, which emphasizes seven points of tactical approach: policing plan, ownership, community, partnership, intelligence, briefing, and response) remains to be seen through formal evaluation. The key component to the successful implementation of such a tactical approach will be the level of cooperation on the part of the public, a challenging mission. As seen in many of the countries that Haberfeld observed, there appeared to be little effort by police forces to either improve their own legitimacy within communities which may be connected to a terrorist risk or threat, or to establish means of information gathering within these communities. Haberfeld's observations of UK's Muslim Community Units indicated that despite rhetoric to the contrary, such units were vastly underutilized. Additionally, her discussions with the Aliens Police in the Netherlands also suggested that police may not know how to engage the community and, in some cases, may broadly associate Muslim or other immigrant communities with terrorism. The complicated nature of a community-oriented counterterrorism response has also been documented in other countries as well (see Chalk and Rosenau, 2004; Fair, 2005; Weisburd et al., 2002; Whitlock, 2007).

The difficulties of establishing interagency coordination were evident in other nations, although again, showing glimpses of promise. In Ireland, the lack of interagency cooperation with other law enforcement forces in the EU might see future change, given the increasing importance that Europol and the Council of Europe place on the exchange of intelligence and other pertinent information between its member countries. However, this will not replace the dire need for the involvement of the local communities in an attempt to gather more real-time information about the changes in demographics, trends, and attitudes toward militant groups in other countries and in Ireland itself. In the Netherlands, while interagency cooperation exists between the law enforcement agencies that deal with the tactical end of the counterterrorist response, the cooperation between the different units that do not have tactical responsibilities is practically nonexistent. Again, it is the lack of involvement with the local communities that appears to be the most dangerous omission in the fight against terrorism in Holland. Given the high number of immigrants there, most of them of Muslim origin, it is imperative for law enforcement organizations to open the doors into communities that embrace and socialize the newcomers.

In Spain, there are no outreach units dedicated to forming partnerships with the local communities and the alienation between the immigrants (including second and third generation) appears to be the "ticking bomb" problem for the Spanish law enforcement. Such disconnect may be further exacerbated by the ignoring of the local police, who have the most potential of outreach to these communities. Similarly, the overall response of the Turkish National Police to the terrorism problem seems to be militaristic in nature, with no real involvement or partnerships with non-governmental organizations that may be capable of channeling information and sentiments within various groups of the society. This approach might be a costly one, in the more distant future, if the polarization between the secular government and the religious Muslim opposition shapes itself into a violent conflict.

The possible common thread between the countries visited by the Haberfeld et al. (forthcoming) is a "looking the other way" approach with regard to the importance that communities can bring to a counterterrorism response. With the exception of the most recent developments in the United Kingdom, it appears that the realization that partnerships with the local communities (especially polarized and alienated ones) are a key component to countering both home grown and global terrorist threats is dangerously missing from the strategies incorporated by various law enforcement agencies surveyed in this study.

Israel

Because of frequent attacks, the Israeli police have developed a number of approaches to countering terrorism, the subject of a current study by David Weisburd, Tal Jonathan, and Simon Perry. Like Haberfeld and her colleagues,

Weisburd et al. use a qualitative approach, interviewing high-ranking Israeli police officials as well as representatives from the Ministry of Public Security in Israel which oversees the national police service to describe an "Israeli Model" of police counterterrorism efforts. From their initial discussions, they found that the Israeli police tend to engage in three types of counterterrorism activities of which they propose to study:

Proactive Initiatives

These activities involve developing intelligence and conducting proactive investigations to root out and arrest individuals who plan to use terrorism, as well as coordination activities between the police and intelligence agencies. The Israeli Police and the army also cooperate in providing information to the Israeli Internal Security Service (SHABAK). In addition to intelligence gathering and coordination, Weisburd et al. also found that the Israeli police focus on undermining the infrastructures that support terrorism, including identifying and prosecuting funding sources (i.e., charities) and focusing on drug enforcement, a believed source of terrorist financing.

Response Activities Once an Attack Is Launched

Weisburd et al. also describe numerous "obstacle and delay" tactics which attempt to respond to terrorism once an attack has been launched, either by slowing or capturing terrorists in the act, or by educating the public for everyday preparedness. These may include setting up obstacles in the path of terrorists traveling to a target or to disarm suicide bombers. With regard to education, the researchers indicate that terrorism education takes place early, in elementary schools, and also through the use of public mediums.

Response Activities Post Attack

The Israeli police also engage in activities to respond to attacks which have already occurred, by attempting to control or reduce damage and injury. In addition to first response, such procedures might include limiting access to facilities to reduce further bombings by working with private security personnel of high-risk places.

It should be noted that these qualitative observations of both Haberfeld's and Weisburd's teams are not intended to assert the effectiveness of such tactics, just as the listing of US tactics also does not imply effectiveness. Rather, their examinations emphasize that such strategies need to and can be evaluated for effectiveness through scientific evaluation. In the case of Israel, evaluations of effectiveness may prove fruitful, given what appears to be regular on-the-ground, observable police activity and a larger number of incidents in which to study. This stands in contrast to countries like the United States where there are fewer events to analyze.

Where Do We Go from Here? An Agenda for Future Action and Research

Given prior and the current research, the answer to our initial inquiry into what local and national police agencies are doing to counter terrorism is telling. It appears that police organizations try to respond to terrorism rationally, carrying out those activities which can address perceived risk levels and satisfy public demands for safety, while at the same time do not overburden resources normally allocated to "everyday" crime prevention. Such resources are not only financial or physical (e.g., time, money, personnel, equipment), but also intangible (e.g., the level of legitimacy the agency is given by the community, jurisdictional reputation among law enforcement peers, ability to maintain the rule of law). In the Lum and Fachner survey of American police agencies, this rationality manifests as the paradoxical approach taken by agencies of simultaneously engaging in interagency agreements, co-opting existing technologies, and carrying out training and strategic planning, while at the same time, exhibiting caution about extending efforts into resource-intensive activities and on-the-ground tactics. In some cases, agencies choose not to engage in counterterrorism at all. In Haberfeld's research, indications of responsibility avoidance, shifting, denying, and/or hoarding of counterterrorism functions across units, regions, and ranks also suggest the agencies may be trying to minimize cost and burden, while at the same time, do what they believe is necessary and beneficial.

While such organizational rationality is often limited by financial, legal, and practical constraints beyond an agency's control, there are also factors which distort and limit decision making and policy that the police can control. In particular, the lack of information and its use obstructs decision-making rationality and reflects a reactive police culture that is suspicious of research, analysis, assessment, and information technologies that facilitate information and evidence-based policing. The lack of information impedes an agency's ability to accurately assess risk, evaluate the effectiveness of interventions, determine the actual costs and benefits of engaging in activities, and also accurately gauge the extent to which other agencies or units are responding to a shared problem. In other words, the evidence base for the rational decision making of which agencies appear to be engaged when deciding what to do about terrorism and counterterrorism is weak..

Where, then, does all of this leave us? We are not suggesting that certain counterterrorism activities should be used by all police agencies or even that certain tendencies of the police are problematic. What we are asserting is that there may be ways to improve decision making and the evidence base of law enforcement counterterrorism activities by addressing three needs. Specifically, a more detailed, concrete, and precise understanding of police counterterrorism responses is needed; second, more evaluations of counterterrorism interventions are required to know whether such activities are effective; and third, a research infrastructure for counterterrorism interventions must be developed to support the first two needs. If this evidence-base is left unaddressed, we will continue to not know whether the current approach that police agencies appear to be taking is effective. Each of these needs warrant some discussion.

A Detailed, Concrete, and Precise Understanding of Police Counterterrorism Activities is Needed

Police counterterrorism activities are often shrouded in rhetoric and ambiguity, resulting in a gap between what police claim they are doing and what they are actually doing. Both contributing to, and a product of, this ambiguity and confusion is the shifting, co-opting, denying, or hoarding of responsibilities across jurisdictions and within police units as well as presumptions and assumptions about activities by others. Examples might include a state highway patrol agency that trains its recruits about the use of hazmat suits for accidental chemical spills on freeways claiming that because it has conducted this training, it is prepared to respond to biological terrorism (such as a release of Anthrax). Or, an agency may claim that it is involved in interagency preparedness activities regarding a future terrorism event because it already has a memorandum of understanding with another agency for responding to a natural disaster such as an earthquake or flood. A community policing unit may claim that it is actively engaging the community in a counterterrorism response simply because it meets once a month with citizens in town hall meetings and happens to mention terrorism in passing. In other words, not only do we not know what police are doing more generally, but the *exact* nature of strategies and tactics is also unknown.

This ambiguity is a problem of which police managers should be very concerned. Even if the risk of a terror attack is low, agencies that wish to be prepared cannot be certain that the infrastructure they have in place actually addresses terrorism or if it is simply an "empty shell." And, contrary to perhaps the mythology that surrounds the police, such ambiguity does not arise simply because police are trying to remain confidential or secretive about clandestine investigative activities. Rather, the reasons are probably much less romantic or exciting; limited knowledge, resources, lack of clear objectives and goals, and conflicting demands are the most likely causes of such vagueness. While the goal may be a balanced expenditure which gauges risk and capabilities, such rationality requires information and an evidence-base that is currently almost nonexistent.

In addition to understanding the substantive, exact nature of police counterterrorism responses, explaining *why* agencies differ in their responses is imperative in unpacking police counterterrorism tactics. Multiple factors may influence an agency's response, and an understanding of these factors is crucial, especially in joint country ventures where one country is providing counterterrorism training to another. The overall counterterrorism tendencies found in US policing, for example, may not be appropriate for countries with highly centralized national policing structures. Community-oriented approaches may be disastrous in locales which already suffer from high levels of ethnic conflict. Or, the opposite may be true, all the more emphasizing the need to evaluate this approach in multiple arenas.

Furthermore, some countries may engage in responses that may be completely unacceptable in other places due to the political or social climate of those places. In Lum's democracy studies, she has found statistically significant variations between police preferences for the style of crime control explained by the extent to which countries had democratized (Lum, 2007). Countries under governance structures that are highly sensitive to concerns of civil liberties, privacy, human rights, and due process may be more restricted by what they can do to prevent terrorism from occurring and may be more concerned about the collateral effects of interventions. Haberfeld and Gideon (2008) have also discussed how effective policing of terrorist incidents can take a toll on democratic policing. Many of the chapters in this volume also deal with this concern.

Some factors which should be considered in deciphering the nature of country's law enforcement response might include:

- *The nature of the terrorism problem itself*, including the frequency, risk, perceptions of risk, origins, and/or history of the terrorism problem, and the relationship of justice and enforcement agencies to that problem
- *The political context*, including the type of governance system of that nation (and therefore the laws, legal norms, political culture, and political systems that emerge from that governance structure), the relationship between the police and other government agencies, or the relationship between that nation and the international arena
- *The social context*, including a nation's social structure, nature and levels of ethnic, religious, or racial conflict, level of heterogeneity of society, social isolation of minority groups, public pressures, history of conflict, existence of factions, levels of other types of crime, or other aspects of a jurisdiction, including poverty, unemployment, education, or quality of life
- *The relationship between law enforcement agencies and citizens*, including the level of legitimacy that the police have, how connected police are to communities, and their ability to gain information from civilians; and/or
- *Other factors*, including the geographic proximity of that agency to a high-risk location, and aspects of the police organization itself, including its administrative competency, culture, resources, ideology, or the extent to which other problems dominate that agency's agenda (for example, crime, drugs, weapons, trafficking).

Rigorous evaluations that assess both the effectiveness and collateral effects of counterterrorism interventions must be conducted

In addition, and naturally following the determination of the nature of law enforcement counterterrorism activities and responses, such responses must be evaluated. Specifically, this means determining, through scientifically rigorous methods, whether interventions are causally connected to outcomes and goals of the intervention. Such evaluations also must include determining whether interventions cause harm or have unintended collateral effects. Building such an evidence base for counterterrorism activities can improve the limited rationality of decision making that police agencies currently operate.

To date, there has not been a single evaluation which rigorously tests the effectiveness of law enforcement counterterrorism interventions. In the recent Campbell systematic review and meta-analysis of counterterrorism strategies, Lum et al. (2006a) examined over 20,000 pieces of literature that mentioned terrorism and found only a miniscule percentage (2.5%) of articles from peer-reviewed sources which even mentioned law enforcement responses. None of these satisfied even a moderate level of rigor to be included in the Campbell systematic review. What this means is that we do not know if information sharing between police agencies reduces the risk of a future terrorist attack, whether guarding a water or power plant deters sabotage, or whether having an interagency mutual aid agreement or written plan makes responding to terrorism more effective. We do not know if JTTFs improve the investigation of terrorism suspects, whether community-based responses decrease citizen fear, or whether increased crackdowns on illegal immigration lower the overall risk of attacks or simply alienate immigrant communities. We are unsure if an increase in the perceived legitimacy of law enforcement in communities will reduce the risk of local youth from these communities joining terrorist cells, nor do we know if sensory, biochemical, or weapons-based technology can be effective in preventing terrorism.

Yet, there are many claims that police strategies, technologies, and interagency agreements are "effective" simply because they are used, and that during their use, terrorism does not occur. However, police use of counterterrorism tactics and strategies alone does not imply effectiveness, nor do claims of effectiveness made by politicians, police practitioners, and policy makers. And, just because an activity is implemented exactly in accordance to a budgeted plan (and passes financial audits), this also does not prove effectiveness (e.g., US House of Representatives, 2004). Only rigorous scientific evaluation of counterterrorism interventions by the police can reveal effectiveness (Sherman et al., 2002) and also collateral effects.[13]

---

[13] Determining what the term "effectiveness" means regarding terrorism is fraught with difficulties in and of itself (Lum et al., 2006b; Spencer, 2006), especially given the complex nature and "delicate balances" of policing in democracies (Amir and Einstein, 2001; Crelinsten, 2007). Effective tactics may also have costly collateral effects, which must also be included in evaluations (and cost-benefit analyses) of the use of counterterrorism interventions.

What is disturbing is that there is little indication that police agencies are interested in knowing whether the counterterrorism policies they use, or are considering to employ, are effective. In recent surveys of police administrators on what they viewed as priorities in long-term strategizing about counterterrorism, evaluating the effectiveness, efficiency, legality, ethicality, and costs and benefits of counterterrorism approaches was not even mentioned (see, e.g., Donnermeyer, 2002; International Association of Chiefs of Police, 2005). This is also reflected in the lack of interaction with research and evaluation communities in Lum and Fachner's survey.

Creating a research infrastructure for police counterterrorism activities

The absence of understanding and evaluations of police activities to counter terrorism combined with public pressures to "do something" leads to the same conclusion that Lum et al. (2006b) have made about understanding counterterrorism more generally. A research infrastructure, to support evidence-based decision making, is needed to improve this state of limited rationality decision making, just as research infrastructures have been developed in other public policy intervention areas (policing, education, etc.). As Lum et al. (2006b) describe, there are numerous aspects to creating a research infrastructure which not only include actually evaluating interventions, but also changing the focus and spending of government agencies toward rigorous evaluations, exploring alternative methods for evaluation, creating access for researchers to study interventions, improving dialog and interaction between researchers and practitioners, mandating evaluations through law, and also developing delivery mechanisms for research into policy and practice. With regard to countering terrorism, there are a few more specific suggestions to highlight.

First, police might consider what is already known to be effective in policing more generally to hypothesize about what policing efforts might work against terrorism. Lum and Koper (forthcoming) suggest categorizing other types of effective crime prevention activities whose outcome effectiveness is known (for example, those cataloged in Sherman et al., 2002) along shared dimensions or characteristics within a "prevention matrix" (see also Weisburd and Eck, 2004), in order to find general mechanisms of prevention within these dimensions that prove the most fruitful. Fitting counterterrorism activities within this matrix may prove more promising in determining what might work, as opposed to simply guessing.

The recent examination of police practices by the National Academy of Science National Research Council (2004) and the updated University of Maryland Report to Congress (Sherman et al., 2002; Sherman et al., 1997) provides such a base for agencies to work with and has deemed certain police tactics more evidence based than others (for example, place-based targeting approaches, such as hot spots policing). Clarke and Newman (2006) have also pointed out that applying a routine activity and situational crime prevention approach to countering terrorism may be useful (something already seen in places like Israel). Such an approach has been shown to be useful in blocking opportunities and situations of crime (see Clarke, 1983, 1992; Clarke and Cornish, 1983) and so too might such interventions work with terrorism. Indeed, as Lum et al. (2006a) show, there already exists evaluations of one type of situational counterterrorism approach – metal detectors at airports – which have shown promising effects in reducing airplane hijackings (see Cauley and Im, 1988; Enders et al., 1990; Enders and Sandler, 1993). There is also some evidence that given the right context, the use of CCTV and other situational crime prevention measures may be useful (see Eck, 2002; Welsh and Farrington, 2003).

Second, researcher, police practitioners, and government funding agencies must be open to cooperation to generate more evaluations of police counterterrorism activities. The challenges, however, that come with the general call for "more evaluations" are not minor, especially with terrorism, where outcomes measured are often small, data are confidential, and access to information is often denied. Creating a research infrastructure to support the call for increased evaluations is one way of improving this situation. Additionally, researchers, the police, and policy makers need to overcome myths, fears, and uncertainties about the intentions and capabilities of each other. Furthermore, government agencies should take the lead in encouraging and building into public policies and laws requirements for evaluation of those policies, and developing mechanisms of funding, delivery, and interpretation of research evaluation results to practitioners and policy makers.

Of course, the effectiveness of police counterterrorism efforts can be relative to other nonpolice strategies. It is unclear whether law enforcement agencies can impact terrorism more than other types of tactics or whether a criminal justice perspective is the most appropriate way to frame the problem of terrorism and subsequently its response (McCauley, 2007).[14] As Crelinsten (2007) points out, the topics of terrorism and efforts to counter it are complex and interwoven, spanning broader social and political realms (see also Jongman, 2007). Such efforts may be so far removed from a law enforcement approach (for example, finding ways to reduce the economic, social, and political isolation of immigrant and refugee communities) and, in some parts of the world, could potentially have a greater impact than law enforcement strategies. As Wilkinson (2007) also has argued, winning the war on terrorism may have just as much to do with ideological battles as it does with police efforts to crack down on terrorist finances, for example. Telhami (2002) has also emphasized delegitimizing the idea of terrorism, suggesting that such an approach is important in reducing both the supply and the demand for terrorism.

Yet, all these hypotheses require testing and evaluation; without which, decision making will continue to be distorted and limited. There is no doubt that police have multiple and reasonable concerns about engaging in counterterrorism activities, including whether their efforts will match risk, increase *or* decrease their legitimacy with the public, effectively stop terrorism, and place the cost and

---

[14] This was the subject of a discussion between Martha Crenshaw, Clark McCauley, Jerrold Post, and Jeff Victoroff in a special panel hosted by the National Consortium for the Study of Terrorism and Responses to Terrorism (START) of the University of Maryland at the National Press Club in Washington, DC (November 28, 2006).

benefit responsibility onto the right agency. In this chapter, we advocate that at least part of the answers to these very difficult questions lies in establishing an evidence base for such decision making, and creating a research infrastructure for counterterrorism interventions.

References

M.Amir and S. Einstein (eds). 2001. *Policing, Security and Democracy: Theory and Practice*. Huntsville, TX: Office of International Criminal Justice.
A.G. Arnold, G. R. DiPietro, C.W. Mucha, A.M. Sadwski, C.W. Schaffer, R.S. Sigamoney, C.H. Sinex, and W.F. Smith. 2000. *Analysis of Communications Effectiveness for First Responders during TOPOFF 2000. Technical Report*. Washington, DC: US Department of Justice, National Institute of Justice.
J-P. Brodeur. 1983. High and low policing: Remarks about the policing of political activities. *Social Problems* 30(5): 507–520.
J. Cauley and E.I. Im. 1988. Intervention policy analysis of skyjackings and other terrorist incidents. *The American Economic Review* 78(2): 27–31.
P. Chalk and W. Rosenau. 2004. *Confronting the Enemy Within: Security Intelligence, the Police, and Counterterrorism in Four Democracies*. Santa Monica, CA: RAND Corporation.
R.V.G. Clarke. 1983. Situational crime prevention: Its theoretical basis and practical scope. In: M. Tonry and N. Morris (eds). Crime and Justice: An Annual Review of Research (Vol. 4). Chicago, IL: University of Chicago Press.
R.V.G. Clarke. 1992. *Situational Crime Prevention: Successful Case Studies*. Albany, NY: Harrow and Heston.
R.V.G. Clarke and D.B. Cornish. 1983. *Crime Control in Britain: A Review of Policy Research*. Albany, NY: State University of Albany Press.
R.V.G. Clarke and G.R. Newman. 2006. *Outsmarting the Terrorists*. Westport, CT: Praeger.
Council of State Governments and Eastern Kentucky University. 2006. *The Impact of Terrorism on State Law Enforcement: Adjusting to New Roles and Changing Conditions*. US: National Institute of Justice. http://www.ncjrs.gov/pdffiles1/nij/grants/216643.pdf
R.D. Crelinsten. 2007. Counterterrorism as global governance: A research inventory. In: M. Ranstorp (ed). *Mapping Terrorism Research: State of the Art, Gaps and Future Direction*. Abingdon, UK: Routledge.
H.J. Davies and G.R. Murphy. 2004. *Protecting Your Community from Terrorism: Strategies for Local Law Enforcement Series (Vol. 2). Working With Diverse Communities*. Washington, DC: US Department of Justice, Office of Community Oriented Policing Services and Police Executive Research Forum.
L.M. Davis, J.K. Riley, G. Ridgeway, J.E. Pace, S.K. Cotton, P. Steinberg, K. Damphousse, and B.L. Smith. 2004. *When Terrorism Hits Home: How Prepared are State and Local Law Enforcement?* Santa Monica, CA: RAND Corporation.
J.F. Donnermeyer. 2002. Local preparedness for terrorism: A view from law enforcement. *Police Practice and Research* 3(4): 347–360.
J.E. Eck. 2002. Preventing crime at places. In: L.W Sherman, D.P . Farrington, B.C. Welsh, and D.L. MacKenzie (eds). *Evidence-Based Crime Prevention*. London, UK: Routledge.
W. Enders and T. Sandler. 1993. The effectiveness of antiterrorism policies: A vector-autoregression-intervention analysis. *The American Political Science Review* 87(4): 829–844.
W. Enders, T. Sandler, and J. Cauley. 1990. UN conventions, terrorism, and retaliation in the fight against terrorism: An econometric evaluation. *Terrorism and Political Violence* 2(1): 83.
C.C. Fair. 2005. *Urban Battle Fields of South Asia: Lessons Learned From Sri Lanka, India, and Pakistan*. Santa Monica, CA: RAND Corporation.

M.R. Haberfeld and L. Gideon. 2008. Policing is hard on democracy or democracy is hard on policing? In: M.R. Haberfeld and I. Cerrah (eds). *Comparative Policing: The Struggle for Democratization*. Thousand Oaks, CA: Sage.

M.R. Haberfeld, J. King, and C.A. Lieberman. (in press, 2009). *Counter-terrorism response around the world: a comparative perspective*. NIJ Final Report.

Independent Commission on Policing in Northern Ireland. 1999. *A New Beginning: Policing in Northern Ireland*. The report of the independent commission of policing for Northern Ireland. Norwich, UK: Her Majesty's Stationary Office.

M. Innes. 2006. Policing uncertainty: Countering terror through community intelligence and democratic policing. *The Annals of the American Academy of Political and Social Science* 605(1): 222–241.

International Association of Chiefs of Police. 2005. *Post 9–11 Policing: The Crime Control – Homeland Security Paradigm*. US: US Department of Justice. http://www.theiacp.org/pubinfo/finalpost911policing.pdf.

B. Jongman. 2007. Research desiderata in the field of terrorism. In: M. Ranstorp(ed). *Mapping Terrorism Research: State of the Art, Gaps and Future Direction*. Abingdon, UK: Routledge

S.A. Loyka, D.A. Faggiani, and C. Karchmer. 2005. *Protecting Your Community from Terrorism: Strategies for Local Law Enforcement (Vol. 4): The Production and Sharing of Intelligence*. Washington, DC: US Department of Justice, Office of Community Oriented Policing Services and the Police Executive Research Forum.

C. Lum. 2005. *Tip Line Technologies: Intelligence Gathering and Analysis Systems. Phase I Final Report and Executive Summary*. SPAWAR (Department of the Navy)/National Institute of Justice Grant. http://www.ncjrs.gov/pdffiles1/nij/grants/211677.pdf.

C Lum. 2007. *Preferences of police supervisors from twenty-two democratizing countries: Community-oriented policing or zero tolerance?* Unpublished manuscript.

C. Lum, L.W. Kennedy, and A. Sherley. 2006a. *The Effectiveness of Counterterrorism Strategies: A Campbell Systematic Review*, Campbell Collaboration System Reviews. http://www.campbellcollaboration.org/doc-pdf/Lum_Terrorism_Review.pdf

C. Lum, L.W. Kennedy, and A. Sherley. 2006b. Are counter-terrorism strategies effective? The results of the Campbell systematic review on counter-terrorism evaluation research. *Journal of Experimental Criminology* 2(4): 489–516.

C. Lum and C. Koper. (Forthcoming). Is crime prevention relevant to counter-terrorism? In: B. Forst, J. Greene, and J. Lynch (eds). *Security and Justice in the Homeland: Criminologists on Terrorism*.

S.D. Mastrofski. 2006. Community policing: A sceptical view. In: Police Innovation: Contrasting *Perspectives*. In: D. Weisburd and A. Braga (eds). Cambridge: Cambridge University Press.

S.D. Mastrofski and R.R. Ritti. 2000. Making sense of community policing: A theoretical perspective. *Police Practice and Research* 1: 183–210.

C. McCauley. 2007. War versus justice in response to terrorist attacks: Competing frames and their implications. In: B. Bonger, L.M. Brown, L.E. Beutler, J.N. Brekenridge, and P.C. Zimbardo (eds). *Psychology of Terrorism*. Oxford, UK: Oxford University Press.

Ministry of the Interior and Kingdom Relations. 2004. *Policing in the Netherlands*. The Hague, Netherlands. http://www.politie.nl/Overige/Images/33_85725.pdf.

National Commission on Terrorist Attacks. 2004. *The 9/11 Commission Report: Final Report of the National Commission on Terrorist Attacks Upon the United States*. Washington, DC: Government Printing Office. [Authorized Paperback Edition published by W.W. Norton and Company].

National Research Council. 2004. *Fairness and Effectiveness in Policing: The Evidence*. In: W. Skogan and K. Frydl (eds). Washington, DC: The National Academies Press.

M. Norell. 2005. *Swedish National Counter Terrorism Policy after 'Nine-Eleven': Problems and Challenges*. Stockholm, Sweden: Swedish Defense Research Agency (Report No: FOI-R-1618-SE). http://www.foa.se/upload/pdf/foi-norell-r-1618.pdf.

C. Norris and G. Armstrong. 1999. *The Maximum Surveillance Society: The Rise of CCTV*. Oxford, UK: Berg.

J.K. Riley and B. Hoffman. 1995. *Domestic Terrorism: A National Assessment of State and Local Preparedness*. Santa Monica, CA: RAND Corporation. http://www.rand.org/pubs/monograph_reports/2005/MR505.pdf.

L.W. Sherman, D. Gottfredson, D.L. MacKenzie, J.E. Eck, P. Reuter, and S. Bushway. 1997. *Preventing Crime: What Works, What Doesn't, What's Promising: A Report to the United States Congress*. Washington, DC: National Institute of Justice.

L.W. Sherman, D.P. Farrington, B.C. Welsh, and D.L. MacKenzie (eds). 2002. *Evidence-Based Crime Prevention*. London, UK:Routledge.

A. Spencer. 2006. *The Problems of Evaluating Counter-Terrorism*. Madrid: University of Madrid (UNISCI), Research Unit on International Security and Cooperation; Discussion Papers, No: 12.

F.S Taxman and T. McEwen. 1997. Using geographical tools with interagency work groups to develop and implement crime control strategies. In: D. Weisburd and T. McEwen (eds). *Crime Mapping and Crime Prevention: Crime Prevention Studies* (Vol. 8). Monsey, NY: Criminal Justice Press.

F.S. Taxman, J.M. Byrne, and M.H. Thanner. 2002. *Evaluating the Implementation and Impact of a Seamless System of Care for Substance Abusing Offenders: The HIDTA Model*. Maryland: University of Maryland Centre for Applied Policy Studies Bureau of Governmental Research.

S. Telhami. 2002. *The Stakes: America and the Middle East*. Boulder, CO: Westview.

T.R. Tyler. 1990. *Why People Obey the Law*. New Haven, CT: Yale University Press.

US Department of Homeland Security. 2003a. *Top Officials (TOPOFF) Exercise Series (TOPOFF 2) After Action Summary Report*. Washington, DC: US Department of Homeland Security. http://www.dhs.gov/xlibrary/assets/T2_Report_Final_Public.doc.

US Department of Homeland Security. 2003b. *Vulnerability Assessment Methodologies Report*. Washington, DC: Office of Domestic Preparedness, Department of Homeland Security. http://www.ojp.usdoj.gov/odp/docs/vamreport.pdf.

US Department of Homeland Security. 2006. *Commercial Equipment Direct Assistance Program Equipment Catalogue (CEDAP Catalogue)*. Washington, DC: US Department of Homeland Security.

US Department of Homeland Security. 2007. *Fiscal Year 2007 Commercial Equipment Direct Assistance Program guidance*. Washington, DC: US Department of Homeland Security. http://www.ojp.usdoj.gov/odp/docs/FY07_CEDAP_GUIDANCE.pdf.

US Department of Justice, Bureau of Justice Assistance. 2006. *Fusion Centre Guidelines: Developing and Sharing Information and Intelligence in a New Era*. Washington, DC: US Department of Justice. http://www.iir.com/global/products/fusion_center_guidelines_law_enforcement.pdf.

US Department of Justice, Bureau of Justice Statistics. 2006. *Law Enforcement Management and Administrative Statistics (LEMAS): 2003 Sample Survey of Law Enforcement Agencies* [Computer file, ICPSR04411-v1, Ann Arbor, MI: Inter-university Consortium for Political and Social Research [producer and distributor]. Washington, DC: US Department of Justice.

US Department of Justice, Federal Bureau of Investigation. 2004. *Report to the National Commission on Terrorist Attacks upon the United States: The FBI's Counterterrorism Program since September 2001*. Washington, DC: US Department of Justice. http://www.fbi.gov/publications/commission/9-11commissionrep.pdf.

US Department of Justice, Office of the Inspector General. 2005. *The Department of Justice's Terrorism Task Forces*. Washington, DC: US Department of Justice. http://www.usdoj.gov/oig/reports/plus/e0507/final.pdf.

US House of Representatives. 2004. *Effective Strategies against Terrorism: Hearing before the Subcommittee on National Security, Emerging Threats and International Relations of the Committee on Government Reform*. 108th Congress, 2nd SessionFebruary 3http://www.mipt.org/pdf/Effective-Strategies-Against-Terrorism.pdf

D. Weisburd and J.E. Eck. 2004. What can police do to reduce crime, disorder, and fear? *Annals of the American Academy of Political and Social Science* 593: 42–65.

D. Weisburd, O. Shalev, and M. Amir. 2002. Community policing in Israel: Resistance and change. *Policing: An International Journal of Police Strategies and Management* 25(1): 80–109.

D.Weisburd, T. Jonathan, S. Perry. (Forthcoming). The Israeli model for policing terrorism: Goals, strategies and open questions. *Criminal Justice and behavior*

B.C. Welsh and D.P. Farrington. 2003. Effects of closed-circuit television on crime. *The Annals of the American Academy of Political and Social Science* 587: 110–135.

C.Whitlock. 2004. French push limits in fight on terrorism: Wide prosecutorial powers draw scant public dissent. *The Washington Post*, 2 November. http://www.washingtonpost.com/ac2/wp-dyn/A17082–2004Nov1?language = printer (accessed July 12, 2007)

P. Wilkinson. 2007. Research into terrorism studies: Achievements and failures. In: M. Ranstorp (ed). *Mapping Terrorism Research: State of the Art, Gaps and Future Direction*. Abingdon, UK: Routledge.

Chapter 6
The Implications of Terrorism on the Formal and Social Organization of Policing in the US and Israel: Some Concerns and Opportunities

Jack R. Greene and Sergio Herzog

Abstract Policing around the world is organized at different levels of government, often with overlapping jurisdiction, function, and structure. As one surveys police systems across the world, the roles and functions of the police have similar overlapping, and at times, competing characteristics. Given complexity in the roles, functions, strategies, structures, and cultures of the police, modern-day policing has become even more complicated, being simultaneously focused on preventing and responding to "ordinary crime," and now to responding to domestic and international terrorism. In the new millennium, policing throughout the world has increasingly taken on an expanded national security role, such that it might be expected that policing should be rapidly changing to meet its new challenges. This chapter considers the nature of such change in two very different countries – the United States and Israel, with particular concern with the evolving roles of each in the face of international and, at times, domestic terrorism. The chapter seeks to outline the structural, analytic, and personnel contours of policing in the two countries with the view that police entry into terrorism prevention, response, and mitigation roles is linked to, and has important implications for, the formal and social organization of the police.

Current structures and functions of the police are easily tied to the historic development of the police as agents of social control, and in some countries, such as Israel, more closely tied to issues of national security. As the roles and functions of the police have changed over time, organizational premises of policing have been challenged, police culture strengthened or weakened, and acceptance of the police by the larger community repeatedly tested. In democratic societies, this continual "testing" of the boundaries of social control is perhaps inevitable, owing to inherent tensions between social control and individual freedoms.

Pressures to reshape policing also come from local and international events, and public reaction to police responses to these events. In this case, the changing roles,

J.R. Greene (✉) and S. Herzog
College of Criminal Justice, Northeastern University, Boston, MA, USA
e-mail: j.greene@neu.edu

functions, and structures of the police often come at the police, rather than from the police (Greene, 2000). That is to say, change in policing has often been externally motivated, while internally resisted. Like most social institutions, change in policing is often glacial, owing to social, political, financial, and emotional investments in historic policing models that inevitably temper the rate and depth of institutional change. Police organizations, like other bureaucracies, are often slow to change, even in the face of environmental pressures to do so.

Guyot (1979) likened change in policing to "bending granite," attesting to the stability of police structures over time, including rank systems, and their ability to resist change. Bayley (1994:88), examining the claims made of decentralized policing, suggested "the reality falls short of the rhetoric." Skolnick and Fyfe (1993:92) find that "the fundamental culture of policing is everywhere similar." The stability of this culture, according to Skolnick and Fyfe (1993:92), is rooted in the idea that "the same features of the police role – danger, authority and the mandate to use coercive force – are everywhere present" whether the police are, in the US, Israel, Europe, or elsewhere. Most recently trends and "reforms" of the police associated with team, community, and problem-oriented policing in the US, Israel, and elsewhere, have met similar internal police resistance (see Greene, 2004:30–53; Maguire, 1997:547–576; Weisburd et al., 2002).

The underlying structures and cultures of policing have often yielded to change begrudgingly – if at all, as policing across the world has been historically inward looking and fiercely protective of its institutional boundaries (see Chan, 1997; Maguire, 1997). At these boundaries, there have been, and continue to be, observable tensions between the police and those policed, whether the issue is about domestic crime or matters of international security (Sunshine and Tyler, 2003). These tensions are often revealed in the face of police practices, leading to concerns about police legitimacy (Greene, 2007).

Even within countries where policing is more centrally organized (nationally or regionally), the "on the ground" behavior of the police is still shaped, in part, by local customs, traditions, and problem sets, as well as public reaction to actions taken by the police. This is the case whether the policing action is taken in South Central Los Angeles, Miami, Tel Aviv, or Jerusalem.

In some ways policing at the local level is also inevitably tied to police/minority group relations (Chan, 1997). Ultimately, the police, whether they are federal, state, or local, need to win the "hearts and minds," as well as the confidence of the local body politic, if they are to be seen as legitimate as well as effective. Illegitimate policing on its face is undemocratic, likely opposed by the body politic. Moreover, policing which is undemocratic relies most heavily on the public's fear of the police rather than on compliance with a law supported by social consensus (see Manning, 2003). In democratic societies, policing for terrorism must be cognizant of the tensions between police use of authority and the legitimacy that the police derive from those policed.

Changes in police organizational structures, cultures, and strategies are now being further stressed by increasing environmental pressures to address terrorism as well as crime. As a practical matter, like politics, all terrorism is local, at least in terms of impact and consequence. Recognizing the local consequences of terrorism, police throughout the world are more attuned to civic concern about terrorism. Police attempts to address terrorism locally have involved strategies seeking to link crime responses to those of terrorism (see Carter, 2004), thereby extending the current "technology" of the police to matters of national security and terrorism. However, while all terrorism is likely criminal, the processes, structures, networks, and analytics associated with crime prevention and detection are not clear in their application to terrorism (see Greene, forthcoming; Morselli, 2005). In all likelihood, policing terrorism is different than policing crime, although the two occasionally overlap.

This chapter focuses on the formal and social organization of policing in two different democratic countries, the United States and Israel, with particular concern with the evolving roles of each in the face of international and, at times, domestic terrorism. The chapter seeks to outline the structural, analytic, and personnel contours of policing in the two countries with the view that police entry into terrorism prevention, response, and mitigation roles is linked to, and has important implications for, the formal and social organization of the police.

First, we consider the underlying "models" of policing for counter-terrorism that define and structure police strategies and on-the ground actions in the US and Israel. These "models" are rooted in considerations of the police role in a democratic society, the rule of law, and the need for extraordinary measures that may be necessary to effectively address terrorism. Here our concern is with understanding the underling philosophical basis for terrorism interventions and how those philosophies shape police actions and responses.

Next we briefly consider the historical and modern differences in policing in the US and Israel, and the implications of such differences for both crime and terrorism prevention and responses. Here we argue that the historic development of each country's policing service has conditioned the responses that the police can make in the crime and terrorism arenas. By understanding the institutional, organizational, and cultural contours of policing in the US and Israel, we can examine how each respective police system has evolved, and how each focuses on matters of terrorism.

Finally, we discuss issues associated with strategy and structural change in policing in the US and Israel, with particular concern for several important change areas that need to be addressed. This is followed by a consideration of what research may be needed to fill in our gaps in knowledge about policing strategies, organizations, cultures, and on-the-ground operations that contribute or detract from effective terrorism responses.

Underlying Counter-Terrorist Philosophies and Strategies

One way of thinking about the underlying philosophies and strategies that provide a rationale for counter-terrorism is to look at the different models presently available – as either being "soft" or "hard" in their approach and consequences (see Clutterbuck, 2004). The first ("soft") category includes conciliatory models aiming to prevent terrorist attacks by means of compromise and negotiation. Such philosophies are revealed in attempts to manage negotiations with terrorists, or political reforms that decrease motivation to engage in violent acts of terrorism (Perliger, 2006; Sederberg, 1989). In many democracies, such approaches were originally adopted, and elements of them remain today. In the police world this has often taken the form of hostage negotiation strategies.

Harder or more forceful models tend to focus on different aspects of violent confrontations with terrorism, both by military means, and through the regular components of criminal justice systems (Clutterbuck, 2004; Crelinsten, 1987, 1998; Crelinsten and Schmid, 1992; Hocking, 2003; Pedahzur and Ranstorp, 2001; Perliger, 2006). These models emphasize the differences in approaching the problems in terrorism from a military as opposed to a justice system perspective. Three models emerge from this discussion, the War, Criminal Justice, and Widened Criminal Justice Models. These models are detailed as follows.

The War Model

Due to the increasing strength, danger, and level of violence applied by terrorists, and the widening number of countries thought to be supporting such behavior, terrorist threats have come to be viewed as existential threats, threatening political systems, their citizens, and even the sovereignty of nation states. Consequently, an increasing way of thinking about terrorism responses by some democratic governments is that because the army and other military (and not police) bodies are the only formal organizations trained to act against high levels of violence, especially coming from external actors, they should be seen as the most capable and made largely responsible for fighting terrorism. Although not completely overlapping we see this approach in the rhetoric of the "war on terrorism."

According to Dunlap (1999), the adoption of this perspective results in an increasing "police-ization" of the military, that is, a growing tendency to look at the armed forces to perform tasks that are essentially law enforcement in nature. Here the objective appears to insert a military for a civil policing presence. The US military presence in Iraq illustrates this approach quite clearly. Similarly, the longstanding British military presence in Northern Ireland, and the Israeli military and police presence in the Palestinian territories illustrate the War Model in operation.

Because the War Model tends to provide justification for the use of extreme force normally not allowed in democratic settings such approaches are also often seen as infringing on the basic liberal-democratic principles of the countries taking such actions. Consequently, the main challenge that democratic regimes are forced to deal with in the application of the War Model is the need to develop ways for applying counter-terrorist means successfully, while simultaneously avoiding damaging civil and human rights (Chalk, 1995, 1998; Clutterbuck, 2004; Crelinsten and Schmid, 1992; Pedahzur and Ranstorp, 2001; Perliger, 2006; Sederberg, 1989).

The Criminal Justice Model

Unlike the War Model, the Criminal Justice Model for combating terrorism, applied by several democratic regimes since the 1970s, stems from a view of terrorism as criminal violence in a civilian context. Based on this perspective terrorist events should be treated as any other criminal offense by the regular mechanisms of law enforcement – the court system, and especially by the police who are seen as formally sanctioned by the state with the tasks of order maintenance and crime control (Clutterbuck, 2004; Crelinsten and Schmid, 1992; Deflem, 2004; Pedahzur and Ranstorp, 2001). This perspective does not attribute relevance to the motive behind the violent act or to instrumental objectives, but to the act itself. Operationally viewing terror as a criminal event provides much more flexibility to the state in determining its goals and ways of acting against terrorism (Deflem, 2004).

One of the central characteristics of the Criminal Justice Model is the exclusivity of police forces in fighting terrorism (Pedahzur and Ranstorp, 2001; Schmid, 1992). However, it should be noted that when the Criminal Justice Model has been applied it has had relatively low effectiveness in addressing terrorism. As a result there are almost no countries today adopting the Criminal Justice Model as a central means for addressing terrorism. Based on its potential to balance use of force and democratic lawfulness, some have widened the model by broadening the range and agents who use forcible means (Pedahzur and Ranstorp, 2001; Reinares, 1998). Consequently, an extended or Widened Criminal Justice Model has emerged and has been adopted by most Western governments.

The Widened Criminal Justice Model

The increasing strength, complexity, and frequency of terror attacks in the democratic world have resulted in the combination of components from the War and Criminal Justice Models. In most cases this is expressed by expanding the boundaries of the Criminal Justice Model and more specifically by adapting police organizations to the use of means that deviate from traditional police enforcement practices. These changes include developing new forms of police work such as creating specialized units to address terrorism and intelligence issues, widening the training of police officers to include terrorism and appropriate responses to these events, expanding the use of protection devices and technology designated to confront exceptional violence, broadening cooperation between police and intelligence bodies, and finally, recruiting personnel with appropriate skills from the military (see Perliger, 2006; Shultz and Sloan, 1980). This process has grown over the last decades to become a dominant approach to responding to terrorism (Pedahzur and Ranstorp, 2001) and may be seen in different countries, such as in Greece (Kassimeris, 1993), Italy (Della Porta, 1992; Stortoni-Wortmann, 2000), the Netherlands (Schmid, 1992), and Spain (Reinares, 1998).

As this model continues to evolve it seems that the main operational change has been the creation of special units working inside police organizations to cope with terrorism. In most cases these units are trained for special tasks such as the rescue of hostages and those kidnapped, and responding to terrorists that are located in fortified areas (Wardlaw, 1989). These unique capabilities allow police forces to bridge the existing gap between their established abilities in the treatment of civilians and the need for new abilities to address high levels of violence with paramilitary tactics (Chalk, 1995; Perliger, 2006).

The pressures of responding to terrorism have resulted in the creation of specialized units in the US; many local police agencies across the country have created special counter-terrorist divisions (most notably New York and Los Angeles, see later), complemented by coordinating offices at the state and federal levels (Deflem, 2002). All these units have a military structure and include unique training and command hierarchy, sometimes even disconnected from the rest of the police organization (Chalk, 1995). Such units are also found in the Israeli police, who are trained to enter towns or villages where terrorist acts are being planned.

Presently, some of these police units (US and Israeli) engage in a variety of international activities, encouraging international cooperative structures and organizations that aim to foster collaboration in the fight against international crime. Obviously, increased concerns over the threat of international terrorism since the terror attacks on September 11, 2001 have sharply accelerated these developments. Consequently, police institutions across the globe have accelerated and broadened their counter-terrorism strategies both domestically and abroad (Deflem, 2006).

While in the US and in some European countries terrorist attacks have been previously experienced, they have generally been sporadic and broadly distributed across the world. Of course Israel has faced the most numerous and severe terrorist attacks persistently over the course of its statehood. (Weisburd et al., forthcoming).

In Israel it may be argued that there is somewhat a blurring of the War and Criminal Justice Models, which is qualitatively different than in the US. That is to say, in Israel the very close association between the military and the Israeli National Police (INP) actively blurs the lines between military and civil responses to terrorism. Whereas in the US such police responses may "model" aspects of the military (see Kraska, 1993, 2001), in Israel these functions are intentionally integrated.

Most recently the INP appear to be moving toward a Widened Criminal Justice Model. This shift in focus was preceded by vocal public concern that the Israeli police had abandoned their crime and public safety focus, rather concentrating almost exclusively on terrorism. In response to such public concern the recently appointed chief of the INP stated that the Israeli police will now balance the handling of serious crime with broadened public service activities (see Weisburd et al., forthcoming).

The Widened Criminal Justice Model, while most prevalent in the Western world, has been criticized on two levels. First, it has been argued that the main problem of this model is the blurring of the limits between police and military organizations (see Bowden, 1978; Chalk, 1995; Kraska, 2001; Perliger, 2006). Second, the merged War/Criminal Justice Model raises concerns about the conditions under which these special police units are activated and sustained. Although they are oriented to activity in what may be considered "war situations in civilian arenas," the danger is that the government may use them in borderline situations, such as mass order disturbances, demonstrations, and crime prevention activities (for example arrests in dangerous places), among others (Perliger, 2006).

So, each model of response to terrorism by local police has strengths and weaknesses. We believe how those models have been chosen is largely a function of the history of terrorism in a particular country, as well as the customs and practices of the police in providing public safety to the civil population.

Policing for the Twenty-First Century and Beyond: Some Important Comparisons

Counter-terrorism can be viewed as the sum of policies, programs, and operations that governments undertake to meet the challenge of terrorism (Falkenrath, 2001). In this regard, note that differences in experience with terrorism, both across and within nations, also shape differences in their systems of legislation, so that national laws and international conventions may often differ, making enforcement and cooperation at an international level very complex (Deflem and Maybin, 2005). Such complexities are clearly revealed in a review of policing in the US and Israel.

By way of shorthand, it can be stated that Israel has experienced concerns with terrorism and national security consistently from its inception in 1948 to the present, whereas the US has been relatively unaffected by international terrorism until the latter half of the twentieth century. The roads taken by the United States and Israel relative to developing counter-terrorism strategies are, in part, associated with the substantial differences in the histories of each country.

A comparison of the US and Israeli policing systems is necessarily conditioned by differences in the historical trajectories of each country. The US system of policing is highly decentralized revealing a policing quilt work of some 18,000 local, county, and state policing agencies, overlapped with several specialized federal policing agencies, and one more generalized federal police agency, the FBI. The historical roots of such a fragmented system stem largely from an American distrust of centralized power and authority, the expansive land mass represented by the US and its territories, and localized cultures wanting oversight of local police.

Moreover, after the US War of Independence, with few exceptions but including the US Civil War, policing in the US has not encountered what for Israel has been a persistent existential-strategic threat, that is, threat to the ongoing existence of the Israeli state. Largely speaking, from mid-nineteenth century to September 11, 2001, the US enjoyed a largely benign environment relative to external terrorism aimed at the US government.

At the same time US policing, because its local imprint has largely been focused on "curbstone to curbstone justice", typically public crime and disorder in cities and towns. Due largely to the local nature of policing in the US terrorism responses became the guarded province of the federal government, until the World Trade Center and related incidents in 2001. The post-September 11, 2001 period of policing for terrorism in the US can be characterized as a search for appropriate and complementary roles for local and federal police in a newly emerged security or counter-terrorism agenda (see later).

In contrast to the US, Israel's approach has been to centralize its policing functions from their inception, while focusing them most directly on terrorism and national security. While other countries, such as those in Scandinavia, also have centralized police forces, the connection of these forces to matters of international terrorism is less pronounced suggesting that Israel's centralization processes have been motivated differently in comparison to other centralized policing systems. Moreover, the governmental structure of Israeli policing significantly differs from the structure and function of policing in the United States.

Whereas US policing is highly fragmented, and at best loosely coupled (see Maguire, 2003; Manning, 2003), policing in Israel is highly centralized and coordinated. Structural and operational differences in policing between the US and Israel are also likely a function of the size and complexity of each country.

In the US crime and the maintenance of social order are seen as local matters, often fiercely guarded by those in political power (Fogelson, 1977). From their onset the police in the US have been more locally than federally affiliated. Federal police did not formally emerge until the 1930s in the US, while local police were more formally constructed mid-nineteenth century.

In the 1970s US federal policing did expand, but not on the scale of local policing. Even the federal initiative to put more "community policing officers" on the street under the COPS programs of the Clinton Administration in the 1990s (Roth, 2000), largely ignored federal policing. It was not until the events of September 11, 2001 that US federal policing received more attention and financing. Through the US Department of Homeland Security (DHS), federal policing including customs services and border patrols have been significantly increased.

Since the early 1970s the responsibilities of the INP have included preventing and investigating crime, securing prisoners, and maintaining the social order and public safety. In 1974, however, after a series of Palestinian terrorist attacks in Israel, culminating with the targeting of a school in the northern city of Maalot, the Israeli government expanded the police mandate to include responsibility for internal security. As suggested in the 1974 *Police Annual Report*, for the first time the government "… had turned the INP from a single mission force to a dual mission force" (INP Annual Report, 1974:7). Following this decision, the INP made major changes, focusing mainly on conceptual, organizational, doctrinal, and budgetary revisions.

Among other decisions taken at this time was the idea that in order to prevent terrorist and criminal activity in residential areas a Civil Guard was necessary. This Civil Guard now includes tens of thousands of civilians, and maintains a network of neighborhood Civil Guard Bases (about 400 in 2008), which are tasked to recruit and operate armed mobile and foot patrols comprising volunteer citizens. The Civil Guard also conducts training programs and organizes rapid response teams for emergency situations, hopefully increasing both general prevention and public awareness (Gideon et al., 2008). Despite its various tasks, one of the main goals of the Civil Guard has been to assist the INP in counter-terrorism, thus revealing a prime reason for its creation.

In addition to the creation of the Civil Guard, in 1975 a new department was established (the Operational Department of the INP) aimed at coordinating the activities of various police operational units including patrol, traffic, and bomb disposal among others. The creation of this department was focused on increasing the effectiveness of all police units, particularly as they respond to terrorist events. Finally, two special units, the Police Antiterrorist Unit (Ya'mam) and the Bomb-Disposal unit, were established for exclusively combating terrorism (Weisburd et al., forthcoming).

Being a dual mission force (security and crime) characterizes the INP to this day. In this regard it is important to note that although the INP still maintains this dual function, a more appropriate balance between the two functions is being sought with the "classical" roles of the police receiving higher priority (Vilk, 1999).

In this regard it should be stressed here that today most of the Israeli public and its political leaders do not consider conventional terrorism as an existential-strategic threat. This shift in public and political opinion is related to a greater willingness among Palestinian and Israeli leaders to pursue a diplomatic solution in their relationships with one another. This is reflected in the 1993 peace accord signed by the then prime minister of Israel Itzhak Rabin, Israel's formal recognition of the Palestinian Liberation Organization as the political representative of the Palestinian people, and progress in the negotiations between the two peoples that have eased tensions. Moreover, signed agreements and hopes for a permanent peace and the gradual transfer of territories to the recently established and elected Palestinian Authority represent a shift in Israeli policy toward the Palestinians. Accordingly, in our times the Iranian nuclear threat has replaced concern with Palestinian terrorism in Israel (see Weisburd et al., forthcoming).

Figure 6.1 was constructed to depict several institutional, organizational, and operational dimensions of policing in the US and in Israel thought to facilitate or hinder terrorism and domestic policing responses. Also presented in Fig. 6.1 is a brief consideration of the implications of such organizational and institutional arrangements for broadening the security role for US policing, as well as the need to broaden the civil police role toward domestic law enforcement and social control in Israel.

At the institutional level, the differences between the US and Israel are important to understand because they provide the context for how governmental services are organized throughout the two countries, and how those governmental services impact policing. As shown in Fig. 6.1, the US is a very large and complex society, with a decentralized governmental structure. Both these factors add considerable governance and ultimately policing complexity. At the same time, Israel is a small, rather homogeneous country, with strong national and religious identities. The population of Israel and the US State of Massachusetts is comparable, as are their land areas. In 2005, the State of Massachusetts employed 16,286 police officers,

Focus	Dimension	US Government and its Police	Implications for Security Role	Israeli Government and its Police	Implications for Public Safety Role
Institutional	Country Size and Complexity	Extremely large 300M, highly complex, diffuse regional and local identities	Diffuse problems and risks, many actors at the federal level; very difficult to coordinate	Coherent, small 6M, strong national and religious identities	Should be strong, but police are not particularly part of civil or community process
	Political/Administrative Structure of Government	Decentralized, strict separation between domestic and military policing actions	Separation of governmental powers inhibits attachment, identity and practice of security roles	Centralized, inclined toward militarism	Reduces identity with local problems unless they are terrorism problems
	Persistence and Depth of Experience with Terrorism	Episodic with limited impact on daily life at local level, except for a few major events	Limited understanding of effective roles to be played at all levels of government, considerable competition	Continuous since statehood, seen as part of daily life	Understanding of effective roles for domestic public safety may be eclipsed by security issues
	Integration of state security apparatus	Intentionally weak, often by legislation and different organizational cultures	Difficult to establish, new trust must be built, but on what has been a conflict oriented foundation	Intentionally very strong, as a matter of national legislation and necessity	May exclude out groups, e.g., Arab Israelis, leading to internal problems

Fig. 6.1 Comparison of US and Israeli Police Forces on selected elements

6 Implications of Terrorism on the Formal and Social Organization Policies   153

Focus	Dimension	US Government and its Police	Implications for Security Role	Israeli Government and its Police	Implications for Public Safety Role
	Financing of Law Enforcement and Security	Considerably complicated, local financing most focused on traditional policing	Financing for security has been exclusively federal with "incentives" and "controls" that are complex	Considerably less complicated, financing from the central government	Less local "voice" in how the police spend their time
	Institutional Complexity	Highly fragmented	Difficulty in establishing a uniform structure	Highly Centralized	More difficulty in establishing local identity
Organizational	Police Organizational Focus	Crime and Order Maintenance; new security role being adopted	May be difficult to link civil order to security concerns as a matter of organizational design	Security Role, attention to crime and disorder but often through a security lens	May be difficult to link security matters with other civil order matters to find an appropriate balance
	Size and complexity	Large, complex number of police agencies with considerable variation in complexity	Difficulty in seeing a clear local police role in "security" which exceeds local jurisdiction	Small and integrated across many groups focused on security	May miss opportunities for broadening police legitimacy in domestic matters
	Intelligence role for police (specialization)	Intentionally restricted. Some specialization but mostly generalized	Legally restricted, historically not trusted, therefore poor structure	Highly developed, started as part of police role	Can inhibit community (minority) communication with police

Fig. 6.1 (continued)

Focus	Dimension	US Government and its Police	Implications for Security Role	Israeli Government and its Police	Implications for Public Safety Role
Operational	Source of recruits/ attachment to military	Historical recruitment from military, now civilly focused	Lack of experience in centralized organizations, strong unionism	Very strong, active involvement with military, transposition of roles and personnel	Shift crime and order problems to last priority
	Attitudes Toward Out Groups	Mixed, racially based	Polarizing at times	Us versus them, conflict based	Mostly polarizing
	Attachment to local community	Reinforced by hiring and assignment policies	Strengthens local attachment to policing, enhancing legitimacy	Little, highly mobile police force, national, not local attachment	May detract from the social legitimacy of the police or their surrogates
	Style of Policing	Mixed, some passive, socially facilitating and aggressive	Can be used for building effective communications strategies	Aggressive/Militaristic	Likely to have negative impact for civil policing matters

Fig. 6.1 (continued)

roughly 50% of the officers in Israel.[1] The near doubling of police personnel between Massachusetts and Israel attests to the significant investments Israel has made especially in matters of combating terrorism. Moreover, such figures do not count the presence of a very large Civil Guard, comprising civilian volunteers (see earlier).

As evidenced in Fig. 6.1, the decoupled, loosely connected, and fragmented nature of US policing has the potential to greatly inhibit coordinated terrorism responses across the country or even within regions. Searching for common ground among the various agencies of the US policing system is a central need if coordination is to proceed. While "risk" also varies across the US, the scale of the country, and the decentralized nature of policing within it, creates obstacles to building an effective and coordinated terrorism response system.

In the US, the relative absence of experience with terrorism has also been a considerable limitation in crafting an effective counter-terrorism response, especially by the local police. Police in the US have been almost exclusively focused on matters of local crime and social order, in the domestic context, and as a result have had little exposure with or understanding of terrorism.

As a highly localized governmental service, policing takes on considerable variation across the US and is politically and financially grounded in local customs, tradition, folkways, and laws. Additionally, policing in the US is highly fragmented with wide variation in institutional capacity to address issues of terrorism, while having a strict separation between military and civil policing. These two factors contribute to difficulty in making terrorism a local focus (absent capacity or responsibility to address terrorism), as well as creating effective links between the federal government and local communities. Moreover, the international and domestic intelligence apparatus of the US is largely centralized in the federal government, creating a disjuncture between intelligence gathering at the federal level, and actions taken on the basis of that intelligence at the local level.

While the local populace in the US is generally concerned about terrorism, for many small police agencies the responses to such problems are, first, rather unclear and, second, often beyond their financial and tactical grasp. Moreover, in many of these places risk is very low, but public concern is high, creating yet other tensions.

The cumulative pattern that emerges in Fig. 6.1 for US policing explains the adoption of a Criminal Justice, and at times a Widened Criminal Justice Model (at least in the large cities) for addressing terrorism. To be clear, however, the Widened Criminal Justice Model in the US has faced challenges, even to federal processes where "enemy combatants" were housed at military facilities, such as those in Guantanamo Bay, Cuba. Such challenges suggest that the Criminal Justice Model, at least in philosophy, is most desired in the US.

By contrast, as shown in Fig. 6.1, in Israel the size and complexity of the society, the centralized and somewhat militaristic orientation of both its citizens and institutions

---

[1] Reported in the Uniform Crime Reports, Federal Bureau of Investigation (2005).

toward governmental affairs, the sense of being continually under siege, the generally seamless integration between policing and military affairs, and the more centralized and relatively lower level of institutional complexity, all favor a security response that is closely allied with national security actions, and highly centralized. And, of course, a national police service suits such integration as well. This is, of course, further reinforced by the general adoption of a War Model, wherein the distinction between police and military responses is obscure.

Interestingly, the institutional factors that favor a security response in Israel may actually undermine its domestic policing practice, as the unity of the security focus may have overshadowed important public safety needs from the populace. Such approach may undermine the legitimacy that minorities in Israel give to the police. This is especially the case for both Jews of Arabic decent and Arabs residing in Israel. Even so, it is not clear that Israeli citizens would trade security for more domestic policing, but a review of the official website of the Israeli police gives relative short discussion about civil policing and community contact, and is more generally focused on matters of security. However, as previously discussed such a disjuncture between civil policing and national security interests has led Israel to begin to embrace a broader dual role for its police (public safety and security). How Israel pursues this dual role for its police remains an open question.

From an organizational perspective, the US and Israel also differ considerably. In the US, police organizations are not particularly organized for security, rather having followed a generalist approach in patrol for nearly a century; they are more focused on crime and disorder than on security, and have been historically restrained from intelligence gathering. By contrast, in Israel the police security role is highly developed with considerable specialization; police organizations are clearly integrated and linked under a unified command structure; and the intelligence role of the police has historical roots and contemporary stems.

Operationally, police recruitment in the US has shifted toward civilian populations (rather than military), and the breadth of experience in what are typically highly structured organizations (other than the military) is often lacking in the US. And while the federal government has organized considerable apparatus for addressing terrorism in the US, most police in the US are barely trained adequately as first responders. Of course in Israel, these circumstances are less poignant for security, but the over reliance on a more internal security model of policing may continue to separate the police in Israel from those policed.

Absent what can be considered a pressing need (imminent threat of terrorism), local policing in the US is likely consigned to a supportive role when it comes to detecting and preventing terrorism, but a major role in mitigating the impact and consequences of terrorism events (see Greene, forthcoming). The clarity in roles for local police in the US, unlike roles specified for policing in Israel, remains an important obstacle for both the development of integrated governmental strategies for addressing terrorism in the US, and in preparing police at all levels of government for their changing roles vis-à-vis terrorism.

There are other issues that impinge on the US police response to terrorism, particularly at the local level. Crime remains a major public issue in the US, and with rising crime rates (particularly for violent crime), it is unclear if the local police can indeed refocus their efforts more explicitly, or rather in a larger way, on terrorism given fixed resources. Moreover, local communities, while stressed with the moral panic accompanying discussions about terrorism in the US, still demand much from their local police, and as local policing is funded locally, satisfying such demands has immediate implications for the police.

Finally, in some ways the police in the US have lost their primary attachment to military perspectives, although military emphases in certain parts of larger police agencies are clearly evident. While historically recruits often came from the military, this is less the case today. So preparing the civil population for "frontline" work on terrorism (the case in the US) is likely more complex than having those with some military experience adapt to a civil application, which appears to be the case in Israel.

Unlike in the US, the Israeli civil population has been conditioned to be more wary and watchful in respect to the "signs of terrorism," such as small cases or valises left unattended in public spaces, or other "suspicious" behavior that has been associated with terrorist tragedies within Israel. This level of civic awareness regarding terrorism is not particularly evident in the US.

Strengths of the US system that have yet to be exploited in addressing terrorism include their close attachments to the general populace, their "mixed" policing styles, which include mobilizing local communities, and reassurance policing, and their ability to reflect in some significant ways the social mores of the local areas they police. These positive developments in US policing may be a central way of thinking about a local police response to terrorism, which underscores aspects of the Criminal Justice Model, previously discussed, as well as removing some of the tensions between intelligence gathering and civil rights.

At the same time, the centralized style of policing in Israel potentially detracts from its police becoming more community and crime focused, given resource constraints, and assuming that this is a demand of the general populace, which is evident. The synergies between civil and military operations in Israel, including the adoption of such models by the civil populace, may make it difficult to broaden policing in Israel beyond its central focus on security, although the Israeli police are clearly attempting to balance these competing roles.

Strategy, Then Structure: Refocusing Policing on Terrorism

Organizational structure follows strategy according to Chandler (1962). Strategy determines the long-term goals and objectives of the enterprise, whether it is private or public, the adoption of courses of action and the allocation of resources necessary for carrying out goals specified in the strategy. Structure, on the other hand, refers to the design of the organization that implements and administers the strategy. This includes specifying the roles and functions of the organization and its agents, the lines of authority and communication between different offices within the organization, the information and data that flow through these lines of communication, and authority helping to direct and correct the organization's course as it pursues individual or multiple strategies. Structure, then, includes how work is organized to achieve a stated goal or strategy. According to Chandler, and others (see for example Mintzberg, 1979, 1981, 1991; Snow and Hrebiniak, 1980), structure always follows strategy in successful organizations.

Comparing the strategies and structures of police in the US and the INP reveals that the latter may evidence more congruence between strategy and structure than the former (primarily local US policing) when it comes to matters of preventing or responding to terrorism. That is to say, in Israel the primary focus on security has resulted in an organizational system with centralized command and control, a strict focus on matters of security, the linking of national intelligence with local police actions, and the recruitment of police officers from the military, thereby making their orientation and experience consistent with the central strategy of providing security. In the US with its federative policing system, local police have been organized around a different set of strategies, and are only now coming to accept and adopt a security role, albeit on often vague, uncertain and limited terms. It might be said that strategy and structure are misaligned in US policing on matters of terrorism and security at least at the local level of government where the most police resources in the US are situated.

The strategies of US policing at the local level have rarely been focused on matters of security, until most recently. Shifting structures from an "ordinary crime and order maintenance" agenda to one embracing terrorism and security first requires that terrorism and security strategies are clearly specified and adopted, so that structures are implemented that are focused on these new and emerging strategies. In some respects, this is slowly emerging in the face of specialized, military-like units in police agencies in the US, and the adoption of intelligence and military jargon by these units (Kraska, 2001). However, in terms of terrorism responses the gaps between strategy and structure at the local level of policing in the US remain rather wide, and how they are to be closed is yet unclear.

As might be expected, at the federal level in the US a security and terrorism response orientation is more consistent with national strategies and likely more easily adapted into new and more security focused organizational structures. The uneven adoption of a security role across policing at different levels of government in the US reflects the underlying strategies at each level, and the congruence or incongruence of security with those strategies.

Organizations change strategies for many reasons, chief among them are shifts in the external environment (for a review, see Maguire and Uchida, 2000:535–538). In the US such changes have shifted police agencies from their political roots, through administrative reform, into community and problem-oriented perspectives, and now toward security arrangements (Greene and Decker, unpublished). Nonetheless, there is likely a lag in the change toward a different organizational arrangement, as police departments must renegotiate their historic roles and functions with the public, while maintaining institutional legitimacy (see Crank and Langworthy, 1992:348–363). As a consequence, in public sector organizations like the police change is often slow to emerge and take root. The history of US policing attests to the slow adoption of external pressures for change. This has obvious implications for how the police in the US will adopt new and challenging roles focused on security and terrorism.

In Israel the imminent threat of terrorism, coupled with a long-standing history of terrorism events occurring throughout the country, has aligned strategy and structure toward security. Such alignment has had 60 years of reinforcement. In the face of such pressures, it may indeed be as problematic to realign Israel's policing response toward the Criminal Justice or even Widened Criminal Justice Model as it is for the US police to adopt a terrorism focus locally. Such is Israel's challenge.

Given our discussion the questions "how will the strategies of the police ultimately reshape their structures?" and "how will current structures of the police facilitate or prevent certain strategies of the police, particularly those focused on terrorism, from emerging and being effective?" can be posed, perhaps more directly toward changes in the US rather than Israel, given the general congruence between strategy and structure in the Israeli police system.

Such questions are difficult to answer directly, as policing is itself in transition, particularly in the US, and the strategies, structures and cultures of the twenty-first century still evolving. Perhaps more importantly, policing in the US has witnessed only modest changes in strategy and structure over the past century (see Greene, 2000; Maguire, 1997:701–730), even in the face of considerable environmental pressure to change.

What can be examined here are the needs for changes posed in the US by a rapidly changing international environment, and in Israel in a changing internal domestic environment, and the concomitant tendency of policing to resist any and all outside forces for change. Moreover, some trends have emerged in recent years, and given this comparison between US and Israeli policing, we can comment on how each system's perspective (the US and Israel) can offer change options for the other.

Admittedly, much of what follows attempts to interpret general trends, most often happening in the US, given the size and complexity differences, as compared to the Israeli system. Nonetheless, such changes may be important to understand how police services in very different countries are coping with change in the face of terrorism.

Five areas are briefly considered here: (1) the institutional focus on terrorism, and other police functions, (2) the need for new analytics in building a terrorism response, (3) intelligence gathering, (4) the need to create matrix and loosely coupled organizational arrangements, and (5) staffing for terrorism responses by the police. Each is briefly considered below. This discussion is then followed by a consideration of needed research to better understand responses to terrorism in both the US and Israel.

Institutional Focus on Terrorism and Other Police Functions

The strategies of the police, as applied to terrorism and domestic policing include the prevention, interdiction (response to) or amelioration (mitigation) of crime, disorder and now terrorism (see Greene, forthcoming). In the US, police efforts have largely involved secondary responses (interdiction and response to events). Some specialized units dealing with gangs (and organized crime), drugs, and guns, for example, have roles that are more primary in terms of their interventions. In this regard, note that in recent years law enforcement agencies across the world have begun to focus on the ways terrorists have engaged in some illegal activities, such as drug smuggling or cooperation with organized crime, to gain financial support ultimately to be used for terrorist actions (see Weisburd et al., forthcoming). This intelligence approach is very new and whether it shapes policing on the ground in the US or Israel is yet determined. Suffice it to say that currently much of policing occurs "after the fact."

While this has its parallel in Israel, there is considerably more intelligence gathering and local surveillance on matters of terrorism, and in Israel the police function in a preemptive rather than a preventive mode, that is to say preempting events rather than addressing the underlying causes of those events. Such roles are indeed consistent with the underlying security model of the Israeli police.

The INP have evolved to a highly centralized level of organization, with clear ties and functions across police, military and civilian forces charged with terrorism, crime and public order. Israel has only one, national, police force, the INP, which provides police services within the borders of Israel, as well as in the West Bank, where it functions under the authority of the Israel Defense Forces (IDF). Such arrangements afford cooperation between the two forces (INP and IDF). In Israel the IDF is not legally empowered to engage in ordinary police functions within the borders of Israel, but has primary responsibilities for antiterrorist activities in the Palestinian administered areas or in the West Bank.

Organizationally, the INP includes two main components, the regular police force, often termed the "blue" police and the Border Guard, often termed the "green" police. The Border Guard functions as an operational and professional unit of the INP, helping the INP specifically in the area of internal security and the war against terrorism. It works specifically among the Arab population within Israel and also in the Palestinian territories that Israel annexed in 1967. It can be compared, as far as its internal structure, to what is known in other countries as Gendarmerie. Basically, the Border Guard officers have the same authority as regular police officers – they make up about one third of the estimated 28,000 sworn officers in the INP. However, tactically they are deployed in a semi-military manner. Their function is unique and complex, and they fight, protect, and also secure peace and serve the public in various civilian service capacities. In addition, they also play a role in traditional police activities, such as combating crime specifically among the Arab and Palestinian populations (Haberfeld and Herzog, 2000; Weisburd et al., forthcoming).

Unlike other police forces in Western countries the organizational mode of the INP was and largely continues to be militaristic, hierarchical, and centralized, with a distinct combat-security orientation (e.g., Brewer et al., 1996; Gamson and Yuchtman, 1977; Haberfeld and Herzog, 2000; Weisburd et al., forthcoming). This combat-focus is expressed in its highly centralized command hierarchy, sharp divisions of authority and responsibility, clear definitions of the organizational position of each police rank and/or level, strict authoritative leadership, a high degree of written regulations, orders, and norms of behavior; rigid discipline, close internal control over police officer action, manifest distance between commander and rank-and-file level, and many military symbols and ceremonies (see Herzog, 2001).

It should be noted that the military characteristics of the INP have lessened over the past several years. Criticism against the military model led to a demand for the development of alternative models of policing emphasizing a more "civilian" rather than "military" approach to policing. This shift in institutional role was directed principally to renew a balance among police roles and ultimately has led to the development of a "community policing" philosophy, which now has become the most popular approach in Israel (see Weisburd et al., 2002).

The creation of the INP in 1948 occurred during severe wartime conditions (the War of Independence). Consequently, the INP was first established as an integral part of the young Israeli army. This resulted in police affairs having low priority in Israel's first government, in contrast to priorities such as the army, the labor shortage (able-bodied youth were sent to fight the war), and the very limited budget, which took precedence during the formative years of the Israeli government. In these rather difficult times the new police administration chose to adopt the existing military police model of the British Mandatory Police (BMP) operating under the British Mandate for Palestine between 1922 and 1948 – prior to the establishment of Israel – for its primary organizational, administrative, and operational structure (Weisburd et al., forthcoming). Apart from being the most convenient model to adopt at that time the choice was also based on the knowledge that British rule had introduced advanced police-work patterns and professional standards in several areas including administration, discipline, and organization (Herzog, 2001).

Following the war the two institutions (INP and the military) became separate entities, under different ministries. However, the newly created INP was founded at that time primarily by those who had served in the BMP and by army recruits. The INP then adopted, and later redesigned from the British police, its legal basis (the British Mandate Legal Act of 1926), a militaristic style of policing, conventional policing techniques, police structures, civilian ranks, doctrines, inter alia, and most particularly its centralized administration and structure. Moreover, Israel's entire external and internal security apparatus were also based on the British model. The similarity to the British Police was obvious even in visual elements, such as uniforms and ranks, and is still visible today in the Israeli police-work procedures. As a colonial police force, the main role of the BMP was to assist the British government to rule the colony, with its Jewish and Arab residents, by means of a paramilitary centralized force. This included a high combat-security orientation primarily focused on addressing serious mass disturbances, riots, and terrorism (Herzog, 2001).

At the federal level in the US, modeling Israel's more coordinated approach to policing for terrorism is perhaps more evident, with the exception of the direct connection to the military. In the US, the Department of Homeland Security was crafted and has been evolving as a major federal coordinator for terrorism responses, and while the integration of many federal agencies, including the military, is possible, this has been a slow process. Federal policing agencies in the US are themselves often "trapped" by their own particular histories, and by interagency rivalries that have developed over many years. Nonetheless, federal legislation in the form of the PATRIOT Acts provides a legal foundation for more cooperation among federal agencies. Given the fragmented nature of federal policing systems in the US, integration will take considerable time and effort, but links through task forces and other models of flexible or temporary organization appear to be the most adaptable.

At the local level, the problems are more complicated. 18,000 police agencies ranging in size, from the very small to those in New York City, coupled with large variation in the risks to urban, suburban and rural communities, make such interagency linkages difficult. Federal grants-in-aid for terrorism equipment, analytics and communication systems seek to overcome some of this complexity, but it is more likely that linking concentrated areas in the US and building networks in these areas is the most viable option available. While some major cities, like New York or Los Angeles, have sufficient size to forge "stand alone" terrorism responses, in most parts of the country a coordinated or partnership approach is more likely to emerge.

At present, some of the largest cities are indeed engaged in modeling interesting systems of terrorism response. For example, in Los Angeles, Project Archangel seeks to strategically assess vulnerabilities in Los Angeles, and then marshal resources (public and private) to reduce vulnerabilities once discovered. Similarly, in New York City the police have initiated "NYPD Shield" attempting to link private and public sector interests on matters of terrorism.[2] Similar initiatives are underway in many urban cities, but their documentation, types of interventions, and linkages are closely guarded, partly because they are themselves in a developmental state, and partly because they are seen as requiring a "top secret" classification.

In areas that cannot "go it alone," partnerships for terrorism and first response to terrorism incidents are emerging as the course of action. Most visible in this arena is the "pooling" of analytic resources to better understand risk and response (see below). Such partnerships are facilitated in part by agencies prior experiences with task forces in the areas of guns, drugs and gangs.

This process of police orientation toward security matters in Israel is expressed in two important ways. The first is in the establishment of a network of strong national and regional paramilitary units to focus exclusively on internal security. The second is evidenced by the redeployment of the civil police to national security roles (especially dealing with ongoing terrorism). This in turn resulted in a change in recruitment, attracting young men demobilized from elite army units experienced in small-team military operations, highly disciplined, and trained in the use of physical force (e.g. Gilboa, 1998:23–24). These recruitment changes continue to reinforce the security focus of terrorism responses in Israel, even when those responses were from the civil police.

A centralized police force in Israel had other perceived and real benefits as well. Such a force could save scarce resources by concentrating effort and manpower

---

[2] See LAPD and NYPD websites for descriptions of these initiatives.

in centralized specialized units. Operating as a national agency facilitated a deliberate connection with centralized intelligence gathering and investigating processes, and such organizational arrangements make the task of detecting, identifying, deterring, and preventing potential terrorism more efficient.

In the US, linking the many responses of a wide array of police agencies at all levels of government, in a coordinated and effective terrorism response, is a major and continuing challenge. In Israel, moving the police to greater local civic attachment may be equally challenging, given current emphases on a centralized security institutional posture.

Changing Policing Analytics

The history of policing in the US is a history of responding to events, not anticipating them. In the late 1970s, and developing in a more pronounced way to the present, crime mapping, and other forms of temporal and spatial analysis, have come to policing, as have most recently, techniques associated with data mining (see Brantingham and Brantingham, 1991). These improvements have resulted in identifying and addressing "hot spots," and now include measures of community social disorganization that may help police to develop "community-based" responses to crime, disorder, and perhaps even terrorism.

Despite improvements in police analytics occurring over the last 20 years or so, extending these crime and disorder focused analytics to terrorism is not straightforward. In fact, Baker and Faulkner (1993), and Morselli (2005) among others, suggest that extensions of applied network analysis, which "map" out the very different structures of terrorism (as opposed to criminal) enterprises, are necessary if the police or others are to better understand terrorism. Still the analytics of policing in regard to terrorism are improving and are shaping police response to environmental pressures for change.

The possibility of large-scale terrorism threats has broadened the reach of US federal law enforcement agencies in counter-terrorism activities, involving analysis and linking analysis to strategy and structure. In the US, counter-intelligence structures include the DHS, the National Infrastructure Protection Center, the Counter-Terrorism Center of the FBI, and the National Office of Domestic Preparedness. Each of these organizations maintains an intelligence and analysis center, as does the US Secret Service, operating its Threat Analysis Center. Each of these centers brings considerable intelligence resources and analysis to understanding, predicting and then responding to terrorism. The FBI Counter-Terrorism Center also reaches into 18 federal agencies for information, ranging from Health and Human Services to the CIA.

At the federal level, several analytic programs have been initiated, but are yet unassessed. For example, the Homeland Security Advisory System is designed to provide information useful to developing protective responses for terrorism. The general public sees this through the Color-Coded Advisory System, having little practical application, but those in law enforcement receive Homeland Security Threat Advisories and Information Bulletins, that provide information about potential threats and incidents, while also providing information about critical infrastructure. Federal advisories and bulletins are targeted to police at the federal, state, and local level, as well as to private security organizations and targeted international agencies. Additionally, the Homeland Security Information Network (HSIN), a computer-based counter-terrorism communications system, serving all states, five territories, Washington, D.C., and 50 major urban areas, was designed to disseminate information between federal, state, and local agencies involved in combating terrorism. This communication system provides real-time interactive connectivity with the National Operations Center of DHS, creating a collaborative communications environment between the federal government and state and local authorities.[3]

Perhaps one of the newest developments in the "analytics of terrorism" is the creation of fusion centers across the US. While national-level agencies in Israel and the US have the capacity to integrate information and data from several sources, states and cities or regions have less capability for such analysis. Fusion centers have been mobilized in 38 US states over the past several years. These centers were designed to create a data collection and analytic focus within states, to better understand crime and terrorism. These centers are also expected to link up in a national criminal intelligence system that can inform and be informed by such agencies as the DHS and the FBI. Fusion Centers are also expected to conform to the National Incident Management System, a set of information and analytic protocols and data requirements established by DHS.

While early in their development, the fusion center concept has caught on in the US and has been facilitated by federal funding for such efforts. In an evaluation of the US Attorney's Office Use of Intelligence Research Specialists by the Office of the Inspector General, Homeland Security Advisory Council (2005), many of the problems in intelligence gathering and analysis, applicable to the USAO and fusion centers, were discussed. Among the problems confronting these fledgling organizations are: (1) nonstandardized collection of data across sites, (2) difficulty in getting access to selected federal databases, (3) a wide range of analytic tools supporting these efforts, some of which were more difficult to access than others, (4) inconsistent work product definition and structure, (5) the absence of "quality standards for work products," and (6) problems in sharing the work products of analysts (Homeland Security Advisory Council, 2005). Despite the problems in implementing intelligence fusion centers in the US, the national plan is to have a credible process working in each state linked to the DHS and other federal agencies. The Fusion Center idea is modeled after an "all-hazards" approach to terrorism response (Carter, 2004), wherein data on all types of hazards are funneled into an analytic center and re-emerges as intelligence directing police and other first-responder activities. The Fusion Center is meant to integrate data across jurisdictions, thereby smoothing out some of the complexity in police jurisdictions that exist in the US (US Department of Justice, 2005).

---

[3] See DHS website.

In Israel, the intelligence community is composed of a complex organizational set that is responsible for intelligence collection, analysis, and dissemination throughout the country. Three agencies are the major intelligence providers in Israel and they include: the Aman (military), Shabak (domestic), and Mossad (international). The Mossad gathers intelligence outside the country and is not directly involved with internal security. The Aman cannot act, by law, inside the country (except under very special conditions, for instance, in times of war). This is similar to the situation of the CIA in the US. Nonetheless, this is different in comparison to many democratic countries in Western Europe that adopted the Napoleonic legal system where the military police were the major law enforcement entity (such as Gendarmerie, Carabineri, and the like). Internal intelligence is provided by the Internal Security Agency (ISA) or Shabak in Israel. While these agencies (Aman, Shabak, and Mossad) are national-level agencies, like their US counterparts, they too often suffer from overlapping roles and difficulties in sharing and coordinating information. These agencies have been the subject of review and reform introduced to improve their interaction and functioning as the intelligence apparatus of Israel (see for example, Kahana, 2002).

The importance of organizational analytics to institutional reform cannot be overstated. Police agencies, that focus their analytics in differing ways, ultimately shift their structures and responses in the direction of their analytics. We have witnessed such shifts in the use of crime analysis in policing worldwide, wherein police agencies in focusing on the geographic and temporal aspects of crime have also developed interventions that are geographically and temporally specific. Shifts in the analytics in policing can also be expected to have import for police structures and interventions rooted in such analytics.

As important as changes in the underlying analytics of police are for responding to terrorism, sharing information within the police community, and with appropriate external others, is also critical. In both the US and Israel, information sharing has not been commonplace; rather agencies often shield information from others or deny access to information altogether. Opening the communications and analytic processes within the police and other governmental communities seems straightforward, but organizational structures, legal mandates, and closed cultures often inhibit such information exchange altogether. In a rapidly changing arena like terrorism, such delays are consequential.

Police Intelligence Gathering

As previously suggested, some have argued that the police adopt an "all-hazards" approach to their many and varied roles, such that they collect and analyze the volumes of information that they collect, but in differing ways and with different lenses (Carter, 2004). This is one of the underlying assumptions of the Fusion Center Model described earlier. Such an approach has many complications, however.

First, the range of information collected by the police is indeed substantial, ranging from calls for service, crime counts, arrests, and identification of problem locations for crime or social disorder. Using this large and often unanalyzed database, as a source of police "intelligence," may be problematic, as much of this information currently goes unassessed in American and Israeli police agencies.

Second, the quality of that information is unknown at present. Individual police agencies struggle with the reliability of their data systems; linking them across jurisdictions will surely compound these problems, leading perhaps to intelligence that is questionable, and hence of questionable value. Even in unified systems, such as in Israel, variation in data collection, entry, and analysis can and does occur.

Third, and perhaps most important, is the utility of this "information" for understanding behaviors that fall outside the general norms of "ordinary crime." While it might be true that the police may have stopped an identified terrorist or given a traffic ticket in the past, linking traffic stops or citations to terrorism is likely a fruitless exercise. In the DC Sniper case of John Allen Muhammad and Lee Boyd Malvo, the snipers had been stopped and checked by patrol officers several times near shooting locations. The connection between the stops and the sniper incidents was not apparent at the time, and only in hindsight was this information seen as a means of preempting the behavior of these two domestic terrorists.

Simply put, the amount of information that is collected by the police at all levels of government is enormous, often rather spotty, and likely not well used in modeling terrorism. The sheer volume of the data may preclude its usefulness in developing intelligence. Intelligence models that have been associated with other more specialized features of policing, including drugs, guns, organized crime, and the like, are indeed better models for developing police intelligence systems for terrorism, than are the relatively simple "time and space" models of crime mapping. Moreover, linking police agencies in the collection of these data and their interpretation is a likely improvement to such processes, as previously described for Fusion Centers. Such developments can indeed change the information basis of the police, making it less difficult to adopt a clearer terrorism prevention and mitigation strategy.

Designing Matrix and Loosely Coupled Organizational Arrange Arrangements

The new era of police focus on terrorism in the US and elsewhere in the world, including Israel, calls for more flexible design in organizational arrangements. Two such designs are gaining some credibility with the police and are briefly considered here: on the one hand, task forces and similar intermediate organizational structures, and on the other, public and private partnerships. Each is contributing to a "bending" of the "granite" structures identified by Guyot (1979). Much of this review engages issues visible in US policing, although the close connections between the INP and IDF in Israel have also employed task forces in joint operations, and public–private partnerships can both improve police–civic relations and engage "external others" in broadening security responses in Israel as well. Places where we have seen this is in both protecting and then dismantling settlements in Israel.

Task forces came about in the US in the 1970s and 1980s, and gained considerable support as vehicles for bringing disparate police, prosecutorial, and other government agencies together to address a "fixed" problem, such as drug or weapons sales, organized crime, or gangs. Each of these crime types typically exceeds the jurisdiction of individual agencies, and as a result, linking these agencies provides a vehicle for improving police communications, coordinating tactical responses, and ultimately improving police effectiveness in addressing these crime types.

In an assessment of multijurisdictional task forces conducted by Hayslip and Russell-Einhorn (2001), several problems with establishing these task-centered organizations were observed. Most police task forces have confronted several communications and information-sharing barriers including: (1) different orientations about crime, safety, and terrorism, as one moves from the federal to the local level of government; (2) different organizational jargon and cultures; (3) the general absence of a "sharing" ethic among both federal and local agencies; and (4) a concern with the security of information, and hence limitations on sharing information with "unknown" others – including police sharing this information with one another – e.g., federal agencies versus local agencies (see Hayslip and Russell-Einhorn, 2001).

Despite problems in launching and sustaining multijurisdictional task forces in the US, Joint Terrorism Task Forces (JTTFs) have been implemented across the US and have wide participation from law enforcement agencies at all levels of government. There are currently 103 JTTFs operating out of all FBI Field Offices, and some FBI Resident Agency offices throughout the US (see OIG, 2005a,b). Task forces have the initial advantage of being "temporary organizations," and affiliation with them has little direct organizational import for participating agencies, making joining them perhaps easier for a wide range of police agencies. In a way, these forms of temporary organization may be an important form of transition for police organizations in the US that have operated on the basis of unitary and internal authority structures, where authority is solely contained within the agency, to a federative or confederative model, where authority is shared, at least functionally across agencies. Such models, while suffering from the need to "negotiate" language, functions, temporary structures, and even internal cultures, may actually provide some "common ground" for seeing problem-oriented policing move beyond a single jurisdiction on matters of terrorism. Such models have enjoyed some success in addressing drugs, guns, violence, and gangs (see Hayslip and Russell-Einhorn, 2001), and have import for linking police agencies in metropolitan or regional areas (see earlier).

In contrast to task forces, police in the US have begun to understand the value of public/private partnerships in addressing issues of crime and disorder. Such partnerships can indeed be expanded to matters of terrorism as well. In the US and elsewhere, control and oversight for many infrastructure services (telecommunications, rail, energy, and the like) is substantial. In the US it is estimated that 85% of the nation's infrastructure is overseen by private, not public interests (see Department of Homeland Security, 2004).

Community and problem-oriented policing introduced the idea of partnerships for crime prevention, and collective responses to crime and disorder, and now terrorism. This has application both in the US and Israel. Community and problem-oriented policing stress more complex partnerships between police, other government agencies, and the private sector. Such approaches may be useful in revealing terrorism networks and intentions, but to do so will require a collective focus, and the sharing of information about what terrorism is, how to identify it, and what to do with this information once acquired.

Nonetheless, much of the "success" attributed to community and problem solving policing can be associated with building relationships with "external others." And while partnerships still remain complicated for the police, particularly in light of their emerging homeland defense and terrorism response roles, it is the local police who have made the necessary inroads and connections to begin to bridge gaps between the police and other public and private institutions, capable of informing the definition of terrorism as well as forming appropriate strategies for dealing with terrorism.

The choice of the task force and public/private sector approaches is obviously conditioned by the choice of counter-terrorism strategy or model. Whether a War, Criminal Justice, or Widened Criminal Justice Model is selected will condition willingness to enter into such arrangements.

Staffing for Terrorism

The contrast between the US and Israel in their ability to attract personnel to address terrorism is striking. Israel's recruiting model relies on seeking personnel from the military, who already "buy-in" and have training for issues of national security and terrorism, enhancing this as the central mission for the INP.

In the US, recruitment for police officers has been complicated on many levels. First, police agencies across the country have complained that the pool of qualified applicants is shrinking. Competition from the private sector, fewer recruits drawn from the military, and shrinking municipal and state budgets supporting the hiring of police officers have combined to strain US police recruitment and retention efforts.

Moreover, local hiring and evaluation processes, evidencing considerable variation, also complicate recruitment for entry-level police officers at the local level of government in the US. The variation in opinion about what constitutes a good police officer, from the perspective of knowledge, skill and ability, is expansive. As Haberfeld (2007:464) suggests, "In the United States, there is a lack of consensus on what constitutes the most important skills and requirements for police officers to acquire and hone. ... [Consequently] policing is subject to an enormous variety of educational and training requirements." Given the wide array of tasks assigned to local police in the US, coupled with a 20-year emphasis on community and problem-oriented policing that has been mostly focused on dealing with local crime, disorder, and social control, it is not likely that local police can take up a "front line against terrorism response" easily. This is particularly the case in gathering information on possible "terrorism" roles and responses, which remain vague and unclarified.

As first responders, police do have the capacity to mitigate the impact of terrorism incidents. Training and preparation in emergency response, the containment of areas and people, and other similar on-the-ground responses are well within the grasp of local police in the US and elsewhere, and have been heavily emphasized since the 9/11 attacks, when the lack of intelligence coordination has been strongly criticized (Weisburd et al., forthcoming).

At the analytic level, police agencies of any size will need to acquire skills that have not been in the purview of police recruitment and selection systems historically. To some extent, the police have begun such analytic expansion in the hiring of "crime analysts," who are shaping police analytics toward crime from a spatial and temporal perspective. Expanding that perspective to analytics for terrorism is a new frontier for policing at all levels of government in the US and likely in Israel as well.

One important shift in policing in the US and elsewhere is the greater inclusion of "civilians" in police agencies. During the expansion of the COPS programs in the US between 1994 and 2000, nearly $9 billion was spent on programs that moved the US police toward a community-oriented policing model. Under the COPS MORE program, nearly 13,000 civilians were hired for participating in US police agencies, at a total expenditure of some $287 million (see Roth, 2000). While many of these civilian roles were devoted to lower-level clerical, communications, and dispatch functions, the idea of increasing civilian representation in US policing was indeed reinforced and acted upon.

It is anticipated that increased civilianization of policing has several benefits, most important of which for our discussion is attracting people with advanced analytic skills, that may be useful to understanding terrorism and responses to terrorism. Such a potential feeds into our prior discussions about analytics, intelligence gathering, and ultimately to structural changes in policing as well.

Concluding Comments and Research Implications

Terrorism is at once extralocal in its genesis and local in its impact. How policing grapples with terrorism is a local, as well as a national concern. In the US with a history which has been relatively free of terrorism, mobilizing the police and others for a terrorism response has also been quite challenging, but for precisely the opposite reasons. The size and scope of the country, together with a broadly decentralized and fragmented system of governance, has added complexity to creating a national plan for terrorism, which is capable of broad implementation. While in several of the largest cities in the US such arrangements are more advanced, there are considerable areas of the country where responses to terrorism remain fledgling, if they exist at all.

In Israel, the link between national security and the day-to-day functioning of the Israeli society is well established. Since its inception in 1948, Israel has had a continual struggle to maintain the integrity of its State, in the face of what have been and continue to be almost daily terrorism attacks. Such an experience, while mobilizing the country into security operations, may have diverted attention toward other policing functions that are important for civil society. Balancing the "rule of law" interests with the national interests of the Israeli State has been a difficult challenge.

The available vehicles for improving responses to terrorism also differ between the United States and Israel. In the US, personnel recruitment, selection, training, and deployment systems still reflect the local bias for "generalized patrol" activities, and the important local influences that characterize US policing. For US policing, improving the analytics of terrorism, broadening the institutional relationships that the police have with other policing and governmental agencies, as well as with the private sector, are important ways in which the US police can enhance their capacity to address terrorism and ultimately reshape the institutional apparatus of the police more generally. Nonetheless, terrorism responses are most likely to be national in character, as local policing generally lacks the jurisdiction or capacity for such arrangements. Except for the largest US cities, like New York and Los Angeles, where robust programs are in place and international linkages commonplace, much of local policing in the US is defined as crime and order focused, and terrorism responses, while coordinated with others, are often seen as vague, and time and resource consuming.

In Israel, the unitary structure that links policing with national security furthers a coordinated response to terrorism, but perhaps at the expense of potentially isolating internal problems that may lead to loss of institutional legitimacy, at least among some groups. This is not a recruitment or technology problem; rather, it is an engagement problem that has been overshadowed by the need for national security in the face of a hostile region.

Perhaps addressing terrorism from a prevention perspective is always consigned to the national government, and responses to terrorism are shared with local entities. Since in Israel the police are national in character, focusing them on terrorism is less complicated, perhaps, than in the US. Where policing in a country is "nationalized," then such arrangements are more linked. Where policing is "distributed" across many political and administrative jurisdictions, the coordination mechanisms, like joint task forces or fusion centers, are the most likely available (an accepted) vehicles for information exchange and the coordination of joint action by the police. Such circumstances seem to characterize the differences between the approaches to terrorism evidenced in the US and Israel.

Nonetheless, police organizations are a critical element in combating terrorism. They are the instruments through which the public at-large and the governments in particular are organized against terrorism, and they tend to express the ways by which efforts to avoid and to investigate terrorist attacks can be delivered. In many ways, policing is likely to continue in a pattern of change and experimentation to better accommodate community demands for increased security, but not at the expense of freedom and civil rights.

Because the police seek to protect their communities, the roles and functions of police officers are deeply influenced by the communities they serve. Over several years, members of communities have increasingly been involved with the police to identify serious crime and crime-related problems, and to consider various alternative resolutions to these problems (see Bobinsky, 1994; Sherman, 1986; Skolnick and Bayley, 1986). Accordingly, this chapter sought to review the way coping with terrorism in the US and in Israel has been evolving, and the impact of these changes on the future of American and Israeli policing.

Many police problems related to terrorism are associated with the boundaries of the law and the limits it imposes on police practices (Greene, 2007). Generally speaking, we can say that past attempts by the police to combat terrorism have not been successful. More recent attempts, such as those established after September 11th in the US, as well as in Israel, seek to revitalize police organizations by making them more effective and professional in preventing and responding to terrorism.

How the US and Israeli police respond to terrorism and the consequences of such responses remain uncharted. Research focused on first illuminating police strategies, structures, and practices in the terrorism arena and then assessing the manifest and latent consequences of such endeavors is much needed. As was the case in the US in the 1960s, a program of "studying police terrorism strategies and responses" needs to be focused, likely by federal governments. The agenda that can be outlined for such a systematic inquiry has several questions as its central focus. We believe that these questions are as relevant in understanding Israel's response to policing terrorism as they are to such efforts in the US:

- How is the idea of responding to terrorism and domestic security translated by the police at both the central and the local levels of government? What are the similarities and differences, and what factors shape these responses?
- How do these definitions comport with civic demands for safety and security, as well as civil and human rights?
- How do local police reconcile their "law and order" mandate with a terrorism mandate?
- What information do the local police collect that would inform a terrorism response, and how can that information be integrated with data and analysis that come from more centralized agencies?
- How is police information turned into police intelligence?
- What analytic strategies are available to better understand terrorism and can they be adopted on a wider scale among the police?
- What strengthens or inhibits the sharing of information for terrorism responses within the police community, across government agencies, and with selected external others?

- What are the range of skills, knowledge, and ability that are needed in a modern police agency where terrorism prevention and response are strategically emphasized?
- What types of personnel need to be drawn to police agencies in light of an expanding security mandate, and what training needs to be provided to assist the existing workforce in adapting to these new roles?
- What organizational arrangements are necessary to enhance police ability to effectively marshal terrorism prevention, response, and mitigation roles?

Systematic inquiry into these and certainly other questions can provide critical information to better understand how the civil police: take on terrorism-focused roles, how their decisions and actions affect the incidence and prevalence of terrorism, the institutional legitimacy of the police, and as well as democratic commitment to the "rule of law." Without such a thorough investigation, policing will continue to pursue security and terrorism agenda without adequate grounding about the efficacy of such efforts. It might be argued that much of early twentieth century policing in the US and in Israel suffered from an unexamined police service on matters of crime prevention; police entry into preventing and responding to terrorism is equally unexamined. To continue to do so is to unfortunately repeat history.

References

Baker, W. E., and R. R. Faulkner. 1993. The social organization of conspiracy: Illegal networks in the heavy electrical equipment industry. *American Sociological Review* 58(6): 837–860.
Bayley, D. 1994. *Police for the Future*. New York: Oxford University Press.
Bobinsky, R. 1994. Reflections on community oriented policing. *FBI Law Enforcement Bulletin* 63(3): 15–19.
Bowden, T. 1978. Guarding the state: The police response to crisis politics in Europe. *British Journal of Law and Society* 5(1): 69–88.
Brantingham, P. J., and P. L. Brantingham. 1991. *Environmental Criminology*. Prospect Heights, IL: Waveland.
Brewer, J. D., A. Guelke, I. Hume, E. Moxon-Browne, and R. Wilford. 1996. *The Police, Public Order and the State: Policing in Great Britain, Northern Ireland, the Irish Republic, the USA, Israel, South Africa, and China*. New York: St. Martin's.
Carter, D. 2004. *Law Enforcement Intelligence: A Guide for State, Local and Tribal Law Enforcement Agencies*. Washington, DC: Office of Community Oriented Policing Services.
Chalk, P. 1995. The liberal democratic response to terrorism. *Terrorism and Political Violence* 7(4): 10–44.
Chalk, P. 1998. The response to terrorism as a threat to liberal democracy. *Australian Journal of Politics and History* 44(3): 373–388.
Chan, J. B. L. 1997. *Changing Police Culture: Policing in a Multicultural Society*. Cambridge, UK: Cambridge University Press.
Chandler, A. D. 1962. *Strategy and Structure: Chapters in the History of American Industrial Experience*. Cambridge, MA: MIT.
Clutterbuck, L. 2004. The progenitors of terrorism: Russian revolutionaries or extreme Irish republicans? *Terrorism and Political Violence* 16(1): 154–181.
Crank, J. P., and R. Langworthy. 1992. An institutional perspective on policing. *The Journal of Criminal Law and Criminology* 83: 338–363.

Crelinsten, R. D. 1987. Power and meaning. In *Contemporary Research on Terrorism*, eds. P. Wilkinson and A. M. Stewart, Aberdeen, WA: Aberdeen University Press.

Crelinsten, R. D. 1998. The relationship between the controller and the controlled. In *Contemporary Research on Terrorism*, eds. P. Wilkinson, and A. M. Stewart, Aberdeen: Aberdeen University Press.

Crelinsten, R. D., and A. P. Schmid. 1992. Western response to terrorism: A twenty-five year balance sheet. *Terrorism and Political Violence* 4(4): 307–340.

Deflem, M. 2002. *Policing World Society: Clarendon Studies in Criminology*. New York: Oxford University Press.

Deflem, M. 2004. Social control and the policing of terrorism: Foundations for a sociology of counterterrorism. *The American Sociologist* 35(2): 75–92.

Deflem, M. 2006. Global rule of law or global rule of law enforcement? International police cooperation and counter-terrorism. *Annals of the American Academy of Political and Social Science* 603: 240–251.

Deflem, M., and L. C. Maybin. 2005. Interpol and the policing of international terrorism: Developments and dynamics since September 11. In *Terrorism: Research, Readings, and Realities*, eds. L. L. Snowden and B. C. Whitsel, Upper Saddle River, New Jersey: Prentice Hall.

Della Porta, D. 1992. Institutional response to terrorism: The Italian case. *Terrorism and Political Violence* 4(4): 151–170.

Department of Homeland Security, Global Justice Information Sharing Initiative Intelligence Working Group. 2004. *National Criminal Intelligence Sharing Plan, Assessment Summary*. Washington, DC: Department of Homeland Security.

Dunlap, C. C. J., Jr. 1999. The police-ization of the military. *Journal of Political and Military Sociology* 27(2): 217–232.

Falkenrath, R. A. 2001. Analytic models and policy prescription: Understanding recent innovation in US counterterrorism. *Studies in Conflict and Terrorism* 24(3): 159–181.

Fogelson, R. M. 1977. *Big City Police*. Cambridge, MA: Harvard University Press.

Gamson, W. A., and E. Yuchtman. 1977. *Police and society in Israel*. In, Police and Society, ed. D. Bayley, Beverly Hills, CA: Sage.

Gideon, L., R. Geva, and S. Herzog. 2008. Traditional policing in an era of increasing homeland concerns: The case of the Israeli Police. In *Comparative Policing: The Struggle for Democratization*, eds. M. Haberfeld, and I. Cerrah, Los Angeles, CA: Sage.

Gilboa, M. 1998. The Israel police: Between political dependency and situational autonomy. *Journal of Police and Society* 2:5–37 [in Hebrew].

Greene, J. R. 2000. Community policing in America: Changing the nature, structure, and function of the police. In *Criminal Justice 2000, Vol. 3: Policies, Processes and Decisions of the Justice System*, ed. J. Horney, Washington, DC: National Institute of Justice, Office of Justice Programs.

Greene, J. R. 2004. Community policing and organizational change. In *Community Policing: Can it Work?* ed. W. G. Skogan, Belmont, CA: Wadsworth/Thompson.

Greene, J. R. 2007. Human rights and police discretion: Justice served or denied? In *Crime and Human Rights, Sociology of Crime, Law and Deviance*, Vol. 9., eds. S. Parmentier, and E. G. M. Weitekamp, London: Emerald Group.

Greene, J. R. (forthcoming). Community policing and terrorism: Problems and prospects for local community security. In *Security and Justice in the Homeland: Criminologists on Terrorism*, eds. B. V. Frost, J. R. Greene, and J. Lynch, Cambridge, UK: Cambridge University Press.

Greene, J. R., and S. H. Decker. (unpublished). Transforming American law enforcement: From political to administrative to community to terrorism?

Guyot, D. 1979. Bending granite: Attempts to change the rank structure of American police departments. *Journal of Police Science and Administration* 7(3): 253–284.

Haberfeld, M. R. 2007. Education and training. In *Encyclopedia of Police Sciences*, ed. J. R. Greene, New York: Routledge.

Haberfeld, M. R., and S. Herzog. 2000. The criminal justice system in Israel. In *Comparative and International Criminal Justice Systems: Policing, Judiciary and Corrections*, ed. O. Ebbe, New York: Butterworth/Heinemman.

Hayslip, D. W., and M. L. Russell-Einhorn. 2001. *Evaluation of Multi-Jurisdictional Task Forces Project*. Washington, DC: Abt Associates.

Herzog, S. 2001. Militarization and demilitarization processes in the Israeli and American police forces: Organizational and social aspects. *Policing and Society* 11(2): 181–208.

Hocking, J. 2003. Counter-terrorism and the criminalization of politics: Australia's new security powers of detention, proscription and control. *Australian Journal of Politics and History* 49(3): 355–371.

Homeland Security Advisory Council. 2005. *Intelligence and Information Sharing Initiative: Homeland Security Intelligence and Information Fusion*. Washington, DC: United States Department of Homeland Security.

Israel National Police. 1974. *Annual Report*. Jerusalem: Ministry of Police.

Kahana, E. 2002. Reorganizing Israel's intelligence community. *International Journal of Intelligence and Counterintelligence* 15(3): 415–428.

Kassimeris, G. 1993. The Greek state response to terrorism. *Terrorism and Political Violence* 5(4): 288–310.

Kraska, P. B. 1993. Militarizing the drug war: A sign of the times. In: *Altered States of Mind: Critical Observations of the Drug War*, ed. P. B. Kraska, New York: Garland.

Kraska, P. B. 2001. *Militarizing the American Criminal Justice System: The Changing Roles of the Armed Forces and Police*. Boston, MA: Northeastern University Press.

Maguire, E. R. 1997. Structural change in large municipal police departments during the community policing era. *Justice Quarterly* 14: 147–163.

Maguire, E. R. 2003. *Organizational Structure in American Police Agencies: Context, Complexity and Control*. Albany, NY: SUNY.

Maguire, E. R., and C. D. Uchida. 2000. Measurement and explanation in the comparative study of American police departments. In *Criminal Justice 2000, Vol. 4: Measurement and Analysis of Crime and Justice*, ed.J. Horney, Washington, DC: National Institute of Justice, Office of Justice Programs.

Manning, P. K. 2003. *Policing Contingencies*. Chicago, IL: University of Chicago Press.

Mintzberg, H. 1979. *The Structuring of Organizations*. Englewood Cliffs, NJ: Prentice Hall.

Mintzberg, H. 1981. Organization design: Fashion or fit? *Harvard Business Review* 59: 103–116.

Mintzberg, H. 1991. The effective organization: Forces and forms. *Sloan Management Review* (Winter): 54–67.

Morselli, C. 2005. *Opposing Trade-Offs in Covert Networks: Terrorist versus Criminal Enterprise Contexts*. Paper presented at the European Society of Criminology Annual Meeting, August. Krakow, Poland.

Office of the Inspector General – OIG. 2005a. *Evaluations and Inspections Report I – 2005–2007 – The Department of Justice Terrorism Task Forces*. Washington. DC: Office of the Inspector General.

Office of the Inspector General – OIG. 2005b. *Evaluations and Inspections Report I–2006–003 – Review of United States Attorneys' Offices Use of Intelligence Research Specialists*. Washington, DC: Office of the Inspector General.

Pedahzur, A., and M. Ranstorp. 2001. A tertiary model countering terrorism in liberal democracies: The case of Israel. *Terrorism and Political Violence* 13(2): 1–6.

Perliger, A. 2006. The Factors that Design the Handling of the Democratic Government with Terror. PhD thesis. School of Political Science, University of Haifa.

Reinares, F. 1998. Democratic regimes, internal security policy and the threat of terrorism. *Australian Journal of Politics and History* 44(3): 351–371.

Roth, J. A. (ed.). 2000. *National Evaluation of the COPS Program – Title 1 of the 1994 Crime Act*. Washington, DC: National Institute of Justice, US Department of Justice.

Schmid, A. P. 1992. Countering terrorism in the Netherlands. *Terrorism and Political Violence* 4(4): 81–107.

Sederberg, P. C. 1989. *Terrorist Myths: Illusion, Rhetoric, and Reality*. Englewood Cliffs, NJ: Prentice Hall.

Sherman, L. W. 1986. Policing communities: What works? In *Communities and Crime*, eds. A. J. Reiss Jr., and M. Tonry, Chicago, IL: University of Chicago Press.

Shultz, R. H., and S. Sloan (eds.). 1980. *Responding to the Terrorist Threat: Security and Crisis Management*. Elmsford, NY: Pergamon.

Skolnick, J. H., and D. H. Bayley 1986. *The New Blue Line: Police Innovation in Six American Communities*. New York: Free.

Skolnick, J. H., and J. J. Fyfe. 1993. *Above the Law: Police and the Excessive Use of Force*. New York: The Free.

Snow, C. C., and L. G. Hrebiniak. 1980. Strategy, distinctive competence, and organizational performance. *Administrative Science Quarterly* 25(2): 317–335.

Stortoni-Wortmann, L. 2000. *The police response to terrorism in Italy from 1969 to 1983. In European Democracies against Terrorism: Governmental Policies and Intergovernmental Cooperation*. F. Rienares, Dartmouth, NH: Ashgate.

Sunshine, J., and T. R. Tyler. 2003. The role of procedural justice and legitimacy in shaping public support for policing. *Law and Society Review* 37(3): 513–548.

US Department of Justice. 2005. *Fusion Center Guidelines*. Washington, DC: Office of Justice Programs.

Vilk, I. 1999. Interview with the Inspector-General. *Police Views* 171: 3–5 [in Hebrew].

Wardlaw, G. 1989. *Political Terrorism: Theory, Tactics and Counter-Measures*. Cambridge, UK: Cambridge University Press.

Weisburd, D., T. Jonathan, and S. Perry. (forthcoming). The Israeli model for policing terrorism: Goals, strategies, and open questions. *Criminal Justice and Behavior*.

Weisburd, D., O. Shalev, and M. Amir. 2002. Community policing in Israel: Resistance and change. *Policing: An International Journal of Police Strategies and Management* 25(1): 80–109.

Chapter 7
The Impacts of Policing Terrorism on Society: Lessons from Israel and the US

Badi Hasisi, Geoffrey P. Alpert, and Dan Flynn

Abstract The phenomenon of terror became widespread in the last decade, especially after 9-11 events and the attacks in Madred and London, emphasizing the severity of this threat to the western society and the challenge they bring on police-community relations. This chapter tries to address three major questions: first, what kinds of methods do the police use in order to reinforce public feelings of security, safety and legitimacy; second, to what extent do the public and the police work together to co-produce justice and address terrorism; and third, what are the public's priorities in relation to the policing of terrorism?

Introduction

Prior to the events of September 11th, criminologists had conducted only a few studies into terrorism, and even those were quite limited in scope (Black, 2002; Hamm, 2005; Lafree, 2002; Resenfelf and Buchner, 2002) Since terrorist attacks generally target civilians, and the police are the first and principal responders, citizens and the police are brought together as stakeholders and the major actors in the policing of terrorism. Acts of terrorism have created new challenges for police-community relations. In particular, they have changed the very nature of the police-citizen interaction. The purpose of this chapter is to assess the impact of the policing of terrorism on society, with a major focus on the social ramifications for police-community relations in the United States and Israel. Specifically, the chapter discusses the impact of "new terrorism" on public expectations regarding domestic law enforcement, and reactions from the police. We look at how the policing of terrorism feeds back into the community and influences public attitudes on police performance in the two countries. We focus on what happens to police-community relations when the threat of terrorism becomes a major concern for the police, and

---

B. Hasisi (✉), G.P. Alpert, and D. Flynn
Faculty of Law, Institute of Criminology, Hebrew University, Jerusalem, Israel
e-mail: hasisi@mscc.huji.ac.il

examine how public confidence is affected when police resources and strategies are geared extensively toward terrorism.

Both Israel and America have been targeted by terrorists. The United States has a history of terrorism both inside and outside the country's borders: Wall Street was a terrorist target as far back as 1920, when 30 people were killed in an attack. More recently, on April 19, 1995, a terrorist attacked a United States government office complex in downtown Oklahoma City, causing the death of 168 people and injuring more than 800. And on September 11th, 2001, the United States suffered the deadliest act of terrorism ever committed, in which some 3,000 people were killed by Islamic fundamentalists affiliated to Al-Qaeda.

Israel also has a tragic history of terrorism. Since its establishment, the State of Israel has been exposed to widespread terrorism, perpetrated primarily by Palestinians and Arabs from the region. The world was shocked, for instance, when Palestinians killed Israeli athletes during the 1972 Munich Olympics. Some 20 years later, suicide attacks became a common strategy among Palestinian extremists on the West Bank. The phenomenon of Palestinian suicide terrorism emerged in the beginning of the 1990s, and increased significantly during the years 2001–2002, causing the deaths of hundreds of Israeli civilians.

We place our analysis in the context of the social and political aspects of Israel and the United States that are most relevant to relations between police and community at an era when terrorism is a major concern to all. Unfortunately, there is very little published research on which to base our discussion; accordingly, it is our intention to formulate arguments and ideas for others to consider and evaluate. We shall begin by briefly describing old and new terrorism and indicating pertinent differences between Israel and the United States, before turning our attention to the various methods used to fight terrorism in the context of these different cultures.

Before we turn to the core of the article it is important to ask if our observations concerning American and the Israeli cases can be generalized to other democratic societies. Many police agencies in other western countries have increased their activity while policing terror, especially after September 11 events. The police forces worldwide utilize intelligence departments, operate Special Forces, and are active in the defensive thwarting of terrorist attacks. Most of them are also strongly active in the reconstruction of attack sites through their role in coordinating the various rescue forces. As will be shown in the following sections, our conclusions regarding police-community relations while policing terror refer to police work in general and not just to the Israeli and the American cases.

Old and New Terrorism

Terrorism is not a new phenomenon, and has been extensively deployed as a strategy in domestic and regional disputes (Hoffman, 1998; Merari, 1993). Familiar examples include the IRA in Northern Ireland, the Basque separatist movement in Spain, the Palestinians in the Gaza Strip and the West Bank, the Tamil Tigers in Sri Lanka – the list could go on and on. However, during the last decade we have witnessed the emergence of a "new terrorism" that experts argue is targeting less specific targets, exemplified by Bin Laden's campaign against the United States and Western influence in the Middle East. This "new terrorism" is directed at urban centers and causes devastating damage by targeting civilians, making this threat into one of the most salient challenges to the Western way of life.

Over the last decade, "new" terrorism has created an unprecedented rise in the number of victims and has seen the use of highly destructive weapons. In particular, it has been directed at urban centers, causing extensive damage (mass casualties, economic and psychological harm, etc.). Terrorism is designed to increase citizens' fear that they may be caught up in an unpredictable and violent attack, attacks that are usually directed at everyday public settings, where mass civilian casualties are likely to occur. Terrorism seeks to manufacture uncertainty and destabilize the social order by making it seem unsafe in some manner. This threat can change the way citizens think, feel, or act in relation to their own security. Terrorism seeks to make every member of the target population feel unsafe simply by virtue of their association with that community or nation (Cromer, 2006). This fear demonstrates the most prominent impact of terrorism, namely, creating an overwhelming fear of victimization among citizens.

In contrast to "old" terrorism, the location and the timing of "new" terrorist attacks are not usually announced in advance. As a result of this uncertainty, the police have to cover a wide range of "hot spots" where such attacks may occur. These efforts consume police resources, and often have ramifications for the police's interactions with the public and the way traditional crimes are dealt with ("High Policing" vs. "Low Policing"). In particular, when the threat of terrorism increases, police assets across the board are reduced – including resources allocated to fight street crime – as funds are redirected to terrorism prevention activities instead. This might influence the public's attitudes toward police that crime control is their low priority (See: Bayley and Weisburd, this volume).

Policing Terrorism

While Israel's civilian population has been living with the imminent threat of terrorism for many years, America only started to take the threat seriously since the 9/11 attacks. Indeed, the entire American law enforcement community now feels under pressure to better prepare the American public for any potential chemical, radiological, biological, nuclear, explosive, or suicide attacks. To this end, the police have been developing new strategies including, but not limited to: securing air transportation through large-scale security screening, conducting hazard vulnerability assessments of critical infrastructures in order to fortify them, developing Continuation of Government (COG) and Continuation of Operations Plans (COOP) to sustain vital societal functions, developing public alert systems, deploying biological monitoring systems; ramping up public safety communications connectivity, and forming intelligence fusion systems to better process vital counterterrorism intelligence.

However, as sophisticated as the government may become in terms of homeland security, even through to the level of the local police, the best plans and strategies will only be effective if they are carried out in active partnership with the community. Ironically, though, as the police devote more and more time and effort to perfecting counterterrorism strategies and tactics, they tend to spend less time on problem solving and relationship building in the community. Thus, there is a tendency for the public to become increasingly alienated from the police just as the latter are developing plans and strategies that require better police-community relations than ever before.

The two major methods applied by the police in fighting terrorism are "proactive and reactive." Proactive methods are intended to prevent, deter, and disrupt terrorist activities. Defensive methods are aimed at protecting vulnerable places and effectively restoring order in the eventuality of a terrorist attack (See Weisburd et al., forthcoming). We shall look at the impact of policing terrorism on police-community relations through these two main dimensions. Although several studies have been written on the policing of terrorism in recent years, we know little about how the police mobilize communities to cooperate with them in order to prevent acts of terrorism or how they are mobilized after terrorist attacks. Similarly, we know very little about the impacts of policing terrorism on society. In fact, in a recent review of the literature, Lum et al. (2006) identified only one study that had evaluated law enforcement responses to terrorism, and that was a study of airport security. "Thus," Lum et al. (2006:492), argued, "almost all the research on terrorism could be broadly described as thought pieces, theoretical discussions or opinions." As a result of our lack of knowledge, we direct our attention to the following questions:

1. What kinds of methods do the police use in order to reinforce public feelings of security, safety, and legitimacy?
2. To what extent do the public and the police work together to coproduce justice and address terrorism?
3. What are the public's priorities in relation to the policing of terrorism?

Proactive Measures

The shift in the nature of terrorism has had clear ramifications for the police's role in counterterrorism. Over the last three decades, the common strategy for combating terrorism was to harm terrorist organizations' physical, economic, and operational infrastructures in order to reduce their ability to carry out attacks. In the contemporary era of globalization, terrorist organizations tend to be stateless, thus making them a much more elusive target. They exploit open society and advanced communication technologies in order to develop their infrastructures and evade the monitoring of security agencies. Indeed, the events of 9/11 led to a key question: *How could this happen?*

One answer is the lack of accurate intelligence on terrorist activities in the United States. The police – one of the state security agencies responsible for fighting terrorism – face a major challenge in gathering criminal intelligence and deploying resources to combat terrorism while at the same time maintaining the principles of democratic policing and protecting citizens' civil liberties and developing legitimacy, i.e., convincing the public that the police are genuine and sincere in their counter-terrorism mission. This makes public confidence in the police a very important component in fighting terrorism and means that police accountability is a major variable in the public's cooperation with the police.

Police, Community, and Intelligence

Intelligence plays a central role in the struggle against terrorism. Not only is it vital in thwarting terrorist actions, but it also enables counterterrorism forces to undermine the element of surprise that typically allows terrorists to attack locations that are unsecured or undersecured by defense forces. Police intelligence units are very experienced in operating in civilian environments (areas in which terrorist elements may also be active), and they are able to align with important informants in the community and collect information about possible criminal activities. A common example is police work that collects intelligence on crime families or street gangs (Clutterbuck, 2006; Klerks, 1999). This wealth of experience can be drawn upon when trying to track terrorist activities in the community.

However, citizens' willingness to provide information on terrorism to the police can in no way be taken for granted, as such contact between the police and the community demands a significant degree of reciprocal trust (Oliver, 2006:192).[1] Over the last decade, the establishment of relations of confidence and cooperation between the community and the police has been advanced by community policing projects. In addition, the police have recognized that when the public perceives their actions as legitimate and fostering procedural justice, i.e., due process of law and fairness to all, there is an increase in general satisfaction and cooperation (see Skogan and Frydl, 2004; Tyler, 2006). Nonetheless, it is unclear whether members of the relevant communities have developed sufficient trust and confidence in the local police to provide intelligence on extreme offenders such as terrorists (Innes, 2006). As with crime prevention in general, the police are also often frustrated by the public's short attention span. Following a crime spree or a sensational crime, or even a terrorist attack, there is a public outpouring of information, and crime prevention meetings with the police are well attended. However, after a period of time without incident, public apathy tends to set in, and the police struggle to solicit information for their crime and terrorism prevention efforts.

Another concern about the community's ability and willingness to contribute practical intelligence to the police in its battle against terrorism relates to the quality

---

[1] Intelligence is the product of a process that includes collection (of information), evaluation, collation, analysis, and dissemination. Information (which is what we get from the public) should be considered raw data, and it is not considered intelligence until it has gone through the entire process.

of the information. Most community members are not well informed on how to identify terrorist threats or activities. As a consequence, the police are likely to receive many false reports of terrorist activities as a result of which they must investigate well-meaning but erroneous leads. In any case, the "new terrorism" tends to be more sophisticated and is therefore much less likely to appear suspicious to civilians (Chalk and Rosenau, 2004).

In this regard, the police in Israel have chosen to train and educate the civilian population to detect indications of terrorist activity. Accordingly, Israelis are exposed to public service broadcasts and announcements that enhance their ability to identify suspicious objects, vehicles, or persons, and instruct them on how to behave should they do so (see Appendices 1 and 2). The police visit elementary school and meet with children in order to teach them on the threat of terror and how to behave if they met a suspect person or a suspect object. In the notice in Appendix 1, which is titled "We Can Only Stop Terrorism Together," the Israeli police advise the public as to the possible appearance of a suicide bomber. He might be a young man (or woman) dressed inappropriately for the time of year – wearing a heavy jacket on a summer's day in order to conceal explosives, for example – or he may be carrying a bag or suitcase that might contain a bomb. The announcement also instructs the public on how to detect unusual behavior among terrorist suspects, such as nervousness, fidgeting, sweating, and a tendency to avoid contact with security personnel. Appendix 2 displays a list of recommendations to the public on how to behave at the scene of a terrorist attack, for instance, to leave the vicinity of the attack and seek out a more protected place; and to stay away from tall buildings, glass windows, and motor vehicles.

The data in Table 7.1 show that Israeli society is attentive to terror threats and is inclined to report such threats by calling the police emergency number (100). The majority of calls in 2006–2007, about 52%, reported suspect persons, 25% reported suspect objects, and a similar percentage reported suspect cars. These numbers illustrate the substantial cooperation of Israeli citizens with the police in their efforts at policing terror. Although most of these calls do not necessarily lead to the detection of terror events, the police treat each and every call seriously (Weisburd et al., forthcoming). This kind of police responsiveness is meant to encourage the public to persist in their cooperation with the police in preventing terror.

The public's conduct at the scene of an attack is very important. For example, crowding might interfere with rescue efforts; alternatively, the public may be able to report suspicious objects or persons to the police, possibly leading to the arrest of suspects. Although not as widespread in the United States, announcements are made in airport passenger terminals and train stations with instructions on how to identify suspicious objects and how to report them to the appropriate authorities.

Table 7.1 Israeli public emergency calls (100) in reporting terror threats (Source: Ministry of Public Security, Israel, 2007)

Reported event/year	2006	2007
Suspect person	81,039	68,145
Suspect object	37,480	32,091
Suspect car	36,606	29,787
Total	155,125	130,023

Information is also provided on how the public should behave in case of an emergency, such as evacuating a train in the event of a terrorist attack. These different efforts may reflect the fact that Israel has had greater experience with terrorism than the United States, and can serve as a warning to Americans that more needs to be done to help citizens understand their role vis-à-vis the police in the fight against terrorism. Improving procedural justice and its perception within and among the various communities will assist the police in gaining support and cooperation to fight crime and terrorism.

Difficulties may be encountered in the cooperation between the community and the police particularly when referring to minority groups in society. For example, in the year 2002 Israel was plagued by a wave of terrorism attacks, and in several incidents Israelis from the Arab minority were implicated. These members of the minority either were aware of or took part in the planning or actual perpetration of terrorist activities committed by Palestinians residents of the territories against Israeli citizens. Some of the incidents help shed light on the obstacles in the relationship between the police and the Arab minority in Israel. In one event, an Arab taxi driver from Jaffa, by the name of Khaled Ashur, was involved and, according to his account, he was forced under threats to his life to drive two Palestinian suicide bombers to the scene of their planned attack on Neveh Sha'anan Street in Tel Aviv. Ashur explained that he did not call the police after dropping off the terrorists at the designated location or report to the security agencies about an impending terrorist attack because he feared that he might be lynched simply for the reason that he was an Arab (Sobelman, 2002). In a television interview, he added that Arabs in Israel are afraid to turn to the police because of the fear that they will be harmed [by Israelis or by security agencies] because of the very fact that they approached the police (*Mabat Television Newscast*, 2002).

Another example is the terrorism attack on the bus at Mt. Meron in which nine people were killed and dozens were injured (Aas and Bana, 2002). An Arab student from the village of Be'ana in the Galilee, Yasra Bakri, who was on the bus that same morning, was accused of failing to prevent the attack. During the course of the bus trip, Bakri was warned by the suicide bomber to get off before the imminent explosion. She and her friend got off the bus and did not report the possible commitment of a crime to any of the security agencies, including the police. Bakri's father argued in her defense that she was not certain that the man who talked to her was indeed a suicide bomber. In response to the question, why did not his daughter go to the police and report the suspect, he answered: "How can she report to the police in regard to something that she is not 100% sure about? If I am not sure whether something is black or white, I don't report to the police" (Aas and Bana, 2002).

The two cases described indicate a very problematic view of the police as perceived by Arabs in Israel. The Arabs fear the police, are afraid to avail themselves of their service, and fear for their own wellbeing if they approach the police. The taxi driver Ashur did not regard the police as an institution that is also supposed to protect him as a citizen and was afraid of being hurt if he was to approach the police. In the case of the student Bakri, as well, we are aware of a similar perception – she was deterred from going to the police and in this fashion became suspect in failing to prevent a crime. The act of refraining from reporting to the police mostly reflects the Arab citizen's fear of the police and his/her trepidation at making contact with them. These examples show that in the eyes of Arab minority in Israel, the police are not perceived as providing a civil service but more as a threatening, ruling agency, and contact with this agency is made only in emergencies when the certainty of the danger is 100%, as the father maintained. The detachment and alienation of these citizens from law enforcers has important implications on the effectiveness of policing terrorism, and we see that the weak connection between the minority and the police makes it difficult for the police to carry out its duties in preventing and thwarting acts of terrorism. In addition, it may even harm the relations between the police and the minority and aggravate the lack of trust on both sides.

While nonreporting terror incidents such as these have not been recorded in the United States, law enforcement officials stress the importance of citizens serving as their "eyes and ears." If multiple reports were made to the police about suspicious people and places that turned out to be false, and resulted in a drain on resources and threats to innocent citizens, actions about such suspicions may be revisited.

Immigration and Terror

The policing of terrorism impacts differently on different kinds of social groups. For instance, minority groups with an affiliation to the source of the terrorist threat (e.g., Arab-Americans or Israeli Arabs) add international implications to local law enforcement, which are liable to significantly impinge on police-community relations. These minority groups might be profiled by the police as "enemies within," justifying the use of oppressive measures against them, which in turn may harm the relationship between the police and the minority community. This is likely to jeopardize the community's trust and confidence in the police, i.e., not seeing police as legitimate soldiers in the war against terrorism, meaning that community members will not find the police legitimate and will hesitate to call upon their services or collaborate with them in fighting and preventing crime.

It is true that the police often find themselves in the unenviable position of trying to be responsive to a majority group that disdains immigration, or at least illegal immigration, and minority groups whose cooperation the police must earn. Immigrant communities tend to be poor communities; poor communities tend to be heavy consumers of police services, thus as the police are frequently handling domestic problems, youth problems, and disputes in the immigrant community, they get to get a deep sense of the norms of the communities they serve. When there are unusual activities, such as terrorists hiding in the midst of an immigrant community, local police are in a better position to sense, spot, or hear about it before the federal government.

The public and the police must work together to coproduce justice and address terrorism. A potential roadblock is the harm the police may create in minority communities by their intelligence gathering activities. Specifically, the police must earn the confidence and trust of the community in order to develop information about crime and threatening activities (Tyler, 2006). Police must learn about the communities in which they work using the "problem-solving" model to earn the trust and confidence of the community members. By creating positive and trusting relations with the community, the police can earn legitimacy for themselves and the government they represent (see Belieck, 2006).

Following the terrorist attacks of September 11, many Arab Americans were troubled by increased governmental scrutiny of their communities. Indeed, Arab American communities were more concerned about immigration problems, government surveillance, and racial profiling, especially federal law enforcement agencies. Research shows that the main obstacles to improving the relations between police and Arab American communities are: Distrust between Arab American communities and law enforcement; lack of cultural awareness on the part of law enforcement personnel, language barriers, and concerns about immigration status and fear of deportation (Harris, 2002; Henderson et al., 2006).

In Seattle, Washington Police Chief, Gil Kerlikowske (2006) has raised concerns that the combination of the increase in local crime problems and the constant threat of terrorist attacks have created a "perfect storm of danger." He notes that the poorest (and already highly stressed) communities are the ones that must absorb increasing numbers of parolees and ex-prisoners. To add to the chaos, these returning ex-convicts are likely to confront younger gang members who have taken over their old turf and who have armed themselves at a level not experienced by those returning from prison. Inevitably, he notes, conflicts grow into violence that holds the communities hostage. His point is that in order to have a secure homeland, ensuring the safety of "hometowns" must be a part of the national security agenda. Proper planning, support, and resources must be made available to protect citizens from homegrown predators, as well as international terrorists.

In today's world, Western societies are home to increasing numbers of immigrants, meaning that the police must provide services to larger numbers of documented and undocumented people, often as victims, sometimes as criminals. In any case, many immigrants are unfamiliar with the local culture and language. Police officers and their agencies are faced with a multitude of problems in understanding these new residents, deciphering their actions and words, and trying to figure out if they are threatening or appropriate. Officers must make street-level decisions that take into account possible criminal and terrorist behavior as well as honest blunders that can be explained in terms of cultural differences. Again, the emphasis of the police must be on gathering intelligence in ways that foster procedural justice, develop reliable sources in the target communities, and provide law-abiding community members with respect. In the United States, police agencies may need federal assistance in dealing with individuals, and must clear certain hurdles in order to identify and if necessary detain undocumented aliens and those threatening security. Similarly, police may need help in maintaining a positive relationship with citizens while conducting their investigations into various people and places.

New immigrants face various problems as they adjust to the host country; in some cases they become targets of abuse by criminals in the community, which in turn reduces their feelings of security. In addition, they might hesitate to contact the police, since some of them come from countries with a political culture marked by a poor relationship with the police. If the police fail to build a strong relationship with these important groups and earn a reputation of legitimacy, these residents may feel that they are not being treated fairly and genuinely protected. This takes on added importance when we recognize that police relations with these minorities are more critical than ever in an age of "new terrorism," with terrorists tending to use immigrant communities as an infrastructure for their activities, thus helping to create Kerlikowske's "perfect storm."

Police tend to have mixed emotions and reactions toward immigrants. On the one hand, they may view illegal immigrants as criminals. On the other, if they become victims of crime, and especially domestic crime, and their immigration status inhibits them from reporting it, the police have a natural tendency to want to help and defend them. Thus, the police often have ambivalent attitudes toward illegal immigrant populations, and these attitudes are often perceived by the immigrants. When this occurs, the legitimacy of the police suffers as does the cooperative venture between the police and the public.

Traditional law enforcement strategies can be modified to address many of the specific issues involved in antiterrorism efforts (Henderson et al., 2006). For example, although law enforcement agencies have indeed attempted to build partnerships with members of many communities, they could make a special effort to build strong relations with specific immigrant communities, particularly those whose members come from high-threat countries. To do so, however, often requires the police to ignore the illegal immigration status of certain individuals. At the same time, successful efforts at developing trusting relationships with members of these communities could result in a flow of critical information and intelligence.

The fact that a large number of the terrorist networks active today in Western countries have developed in isolated, traditional, and generally immigrant communities indicates that the local police force must play a vital role in combating terrorism. The local police are trained for long-term interactions with the civilian population, and, by virtue of their daily contact with citizens, are able to build up trusting relations while at the same time being able to offer them direct assistance. This interaction creates an effective intelligence infrastructure within the community, and the potential to recruit informants from it (Lyons, 1999). Police officers are familiar with the central "actors" in the community, they can identify foreign elements that are active in the community, and they have a grasp of the historical and cultural codes by which they operate.

The terrorist incidents in London and Madrid, for instance, involved Muslim immigrants resident in those countries, thus underscoring the importance of the relationship between the police and Muslim communities in Europe and the United States. A survey conducted in the United Kingdom among British Muslims (originating mostly from India, Pakistan, Bangladesh, and other Asian countries) on the bombings in London indicated that 25% were not surprised that the suicide bombers were British (Muslims), and 37% suspected that more attacks by British suicide bombers were liable to take place in the United Kingdom (ICM, 2005). This finding shows that the Muslim community had some indication of these terror events, but that police intelligence failed to uncover it.

The same poll shows that only 5% of British Muslims reported that attacks by British suicide bombers in the United Kingdom were justified. About 50% of the British Muslims thought their community was not doing enough to root out extremist elements, and a similar percentage endorsed the statement that British Muslims are not doing enough to prevent extremists from infiltrating the Muslim community. A significant majority of 88% thought that British Muslims should work with the police to identify and eliminate extremists from the Muslim community. These findings indicate the general importance of police intelligence, as well as the specific opportunity to mobilize British Muslims to collect better intelligence on terrorist activities.

Finally, in addition to the lack of trust in the police, one of the most significant problems in policing terrorism among minorities is the high level of complaints of police harassment and violations of citizens' rights, such as racial or ethnic profiling. Both in the United States and Israel, concerns over racial profiling have done extensive damage to the perception of trust and confidence of the police. In the United States, a significant amount of research has shown that members of minority communities believe the police use race and ethnicity to profile them for criminal behavior. In fact, this same body of research shows that race and ethnicity has an impact on police behavior (see Alpert et al., 2007; Smith and Durose, 2006). A survey conducted in Israel in March 2003, for example, showed that 47% of Israeli Arabs endorsed statements asserting that the police treated them as a security threat (Hasisi and Weitzer, 2007). Research shows the public perceptions of social disorder and threats are influenced by prior beliefs informed by racial stigmatization (Sampson and Raudenbusch, 2004). This fear creates a barrier between the police and the Arab community and makes the task of policing terrorism even more complicated. In both countries, the perception of profiling has eroded public confidence and trust in the police, thereby influencing the perceived legitimacy of the police.

Reactive Measures

The police also play a defensive role in policing terror, especially after an attack. In America, it has often been local police officers who have made important apprehensions of terrorist operatives. Thus, the role of the police includes identifying the terrorists who were involved in the attack, ensuring the evacuation of casualties, and coordinating the activities of the rescue teams (Perliger et al., 2005; Weisburd et al., forthcoming). In Israel, the police are expected to clear a terrorist scene in 4 h in order to bring the public back to their daily routine activities. These strategies reinforce the resilience of the Israeli public against terror attacks, especially when terror aims to weaken the resilience of targeted public. There is a clear protocol on reporting events to the media and keep informing the public on vital information about the terror attack (Weisburd et al., forthcoming). This reduces distress and fear among the public and increases their resilience and cooperation with police instruction (i.e., to stay away from crowded places and to be alert).

The trust between the police and the community becomes central in crisis situations, as the police and the community need each other in order to restore order. There are a number of variables that affect the quality of the relations between the police and the community in preparing for and managing emergency events in general, and terrorist incidents in particular. For instance, the degree of public trust in the information issued by official sources in emergency situations is of major importance. Civilians who suspect that the government is not providing them with reliable information about the emergency situation may not comply with the course of action advised by the authorities. Clearly, failure to communicate effectively can lead to confusion and anxiety, whereas effective communication can promote resilience and social bonding.

It is also of considerable importance that the government be able to act efficiently and effectively in emergency situations. The measure of an effective governmental response in a state of emergency is the degree of readiness of other governmental authorities (i.e., the police, medical, and rehabilitative) that follow the central government's instructions. For instance, the response of the United States federal government in the wake of the Katarina disaster, and the Israeli government's actions during and following the Second Lebanon War, weakened citizens' trust in their government's capabilities and ability to protect them in times of emergency.

One critical need for first responders is a clear chain of command among lead and supporting agencies. Both local crime prevention and the prevention of terrorism are most efficient and effective when the various assets work together as a well-organized and unified structure (Connors and Pellegrini, 2005). First responders who have never trained together may have different strategies, policies, and habits. As a unified force, individuals must understand each other's responsibilities, develop common policies and tactics, train together on these commonalities, and have a mutual understanding regarding incident command and control. Further, intelligence plans must be coordinated with plans of action so that agencies are acting on what they know rather than what they assume.

Since the attacks of September 11th, police departments in the US have had to modify their activities to address homeland security issues, such as guarding at-risk public spaces, and identifying and preparing to respond to possible threats. Because this shift in activities drains resources from routine activities, a general increase in crime might be an unintended consequence (Murphy and Plotkin, 2003).

Stuntz (2002) has argued that three major policing tactics and strategies have emerged since September 11th, namely, profiling Middle Eastern men; gathering, sharing, and utilizing information; and crime prevention. The first two are fairly straightforward tactics, and while influenced by the September 11th attacks, have been used in some form for years. Crime prevention, however, has changed dramatically since terrorism became a concern. In most routine criminal investigations, information is obtained from citizens, informants, and undercover officers. When the target of an investigation is terrorism, however, the most likely source of information is the suspects themselves (i.e., informants among the terrorists, or terrorists who voluntarily confess during an investigation).

Unfortunately, we have precious little empirical information concerning changes in policing agencies since September 11th. Surveys conducted by the US Conference of Mayors (*The Cost of Heightened Security*, 2002), the Massachusetts Statistical Analysis Center (*Fact Sheet*, 2002), and the University of South Carolina (Kaminski and Pelfrey, 2005) indicate that terrorist attacks have led to the reorganization of police departments. In Massachusetts, for instance, slightly more than 60% of police agencies have made changes as a result of 9/11. And in South Carolina, 31% of the departments have created a specific policy on terrorism. Overall, agencies are coordinating with each other for intelligence, surveillance, investigations, crime prevention, and disaster planning.

Although the United States and Israel share many similarities regarding the policing of terrorism (especially after 9/11), there are still some differences that impact on police-community relations. In Israel, the police forewarn the public of the danger of potential terrorist events with information provided by the General Security Service (GSS). This information is disseminated to Israeli citizens by means of the media (written, audio, and visual) in the form of a "hot alert," generally directed at a specific geographical region. This information is widely broadcast and is given a central place on the daily agenda. Police alerts regarding terrorist events are generally accompanied by instructions to the Israeli public on how to behave in the eventuality of an attack. For example, citizens are advised to avoid assembling in crowded areas, such as commercial centers or public transportation stations, or they may be recommended to put off nonessential trips to city centers. The police also urge the public to be on the alert for suspicious objects or persons, and to immediately report any suspicions to the police. This type of assistance is well received by the Israeli public and is a factor in reducing civilian casualties from terrorist incidents (Cromer, 2006).

While the Israeli police and their citizenry share a common enemy, i.e., anti-Israeli Middle Easterners, the American police must contend with a plethora of enemies (i.e., criminals) within the citizen population. Therefore, it is difficult for American police to concentrate their full attention against a common enemy – which is a powerful tool for uniting a population.

The Israel Police make extensive and effective use of plain clothes and undercover personnel surreptitiously planted in important public locations throughout the community to monitor for potential terrorist activity. The police in the United States use some undercover police, but by and large Americans prefer police officers who are highly visible in uniforms and marked vehicles. In terms of community trust, if the public does not see or recognize undercover officers, they have to trust that they are there protecting them. Once again, then, the issue of community trust of the police becomes important to security.

In the United States, the Department of Homeland Security maintains a color-coded "Security Advisory System" (SAS) by which the population is alerted to the estimated threat of the possible terrorist action. The colors on the scale are green, blue, yellow, orange, and red, with green representing a low level of threat, and red signifying a very high degree of threat. The different levels of alert trigger specific actions by federal agencies and state and local governments, as well as affecting the level of security at certain airports and other public facilities. When the color changes to high risk, the actions include increasing police and other security presence at landmarks and other high-profile targets and, in some cases, deploying members of the National Guard to assist local law enforcement on security details (DHS – Department of Homeland Security).

Information indicating a change in the state of alert is widely covered in the United States media and reaches large segments of the population. At the same time, the color code system is not accompanied by clear-cut instructions to the populace on how to behave. Indeed, The National Center for Disaster Preparedness (National Centre for Disaster Preparedness, 2004) has shown that only half of the public express trust in the color code system. The survey also demonstrated that Americans do not know how to react when the level of terrorism threat is raised. Neither federal nor local police forces are trained in issuing or promoting guides of conduct to the population, which could increase public security and reduce anxiety. For instance, in a mass-casualty terrorist incident, it may be necessary to evacuate large numbers of people to a safer location. The survey showed that approximately 60% of the American public would not evacuate immediately, even if they were told that it was necessity to do so. This figure is an improvement over 70% in 2003; still, it indicates a large degree of citizen noncooperation with emergency operations in the event of a terrorist attack. The main reason given for the refusal to partake in immediate evacuation is a concern about locating and transporting family members.

The differences in the responses of Israeli and United States citizens can be explained by several factors. The threat of terrorism in Israel is more concrete, and there is information on operational patterns (such as suicide attacks on public transport or in commercial centers) that makes it easier to advise the population and provide rules of behavior. In contrast, the threat of terrorism in the United States is more general and vague, and there are many potential scenarios, from aviation terrorism to terrorism directed at urban centers. Nor is it clear which methods terrorists in the United States might use: suicide aircraft hijackings (as in September 11th), public transportation terrorism, or perhaps even the use of mass-casualty weapons (biological, chemical or nuclear, also known as weapons of mass destruction). The ambiguity of the source of the threat makes it difficult to devise rules of behavior for the general population to follow.

The amount of time that the public is required to maintain a state of emergency preparedness ("red color" or "hot alert") is also very significant. The declaration of a state of emergency for a prolonged period of time might lead to a routinization of the situation, possibly resulting in civilian cynicism regarding the emergency status. This cynicism might also be fueled by the economic impact of precautions such as restricting travel, refraining from attending public gatherings, negative stock market returns, and so forth. For example, between August 1st and November 10th 2004, the DHS declared a high terror risk (orange) for specific financial institutions in northern New Jersey, New York, and Washington, D.C., citing intelligence pointing to the possibility of a car or truck bomb attack, and naming specific buildings as possible targets (DHS-Homeland Security Advisory System).

An additional concern is that after a protracted period of anticipation, the public will become increasingly indifferent to future declarations, and the civilian level of response to emergency announcements may deteriorate. This situation is similar to hurricane warnings, which are routinely ignored by targeted populations. Moreover, it has even been suggested that control over the threat situation has been exploited as a political tool in the hands of the Bush administration during an election year (Kamen, 2004). In Israel, warnings of terrorist attacks are particularly prominent during the Jewish holiday season (lasting for 7–10 days). This is a relatively brief period of time, during which the public can tolerate restrictions on its behavior until the threat passes.

Another significant difference between the two countries is the centrality of control. The Israel Police is organized on a national basis with centralized control, rather than with state and local departments as in the American system. As a result, the national security efforts of the Israeli police are more integrated than those of their American counterparts. When the Israel Police was originally established it adopted the quasimilitary centralized policing model of the British Mandate. Commanders and officers of police stations belong to a nationwide police enforcement system which implements a common organizational policy and has a shared list of priorities. Employees are paid their salaries through this system and are equally accountable to it in all aspects of their work. This centralization, as well as the close connection with the GSS, facilitates the transmission of intelligence and enable uniformity in offensive and defensive counterterrorist operations. In view of these distinctions, the policing model in Israel is undoubtedly optimal for fighting terrorism; however, this type of model is also responsible for the Israel Police's weakness in dealing with crime in general (See Greene and Herzog, this volume).

In 1974, in response to terrorist attacks on civilians, the "Civil Guard" was formed in Israel, with the police deciding to initiate a volunteer corps to help in the management of internal security. The Civil Guard is based on neighborhood headquarters that dispatch foot patrols, man checkpoints, inspect bus stations and markets, engage in traffic control, and carry out guarding duties at schools, and so on. The initial purpose of the patrols was to prevent terrorist attacks in residential areas. Today the Civil Guard has over 70,000 volunteers; about 7,000 of them are Israeli Arabs. The volunteer units assist the Israel Police in providing security and maintaining public order, preventing crime, and tending to weaker and more vulnerable populations, as well as helping to deal with social problems that are the primary responsibility of the police. The advantages of the Civil Guard are twofold: first, it carries out its activities in the community and can immediately assist in the event of a terror attack; and second, it helps the police with routine work (keeping bystanders from crowding after a terrorist attack, securing public transportation by checking bus stops), thus freeing up resources for the fight against terrorism.

In contrast to the Israeli case, American police agencies are political entities. The chief of a municipal agency is usually appointed, and the sheriff of a county is usually elected. This distinction may appear to be irrelevant, but the differences between an appointment and an election are significant. In the type of agency where the chief is appointed, many decisions may have to go through the body politic –

perhaps the city mayor and council. When the administrator is elected, however, many decisions are made in the light of fundraising and electoral processes. In both environments, law enforcement and public safety may come second to appearing to react quickly to criminal behavior.

The political machines that influence policing are powerful and entrenched. However, the machines that were created by the police to respond to public demands, such as rapid response, and calls for 9/11 systems, are just as controlling. Similarly, community-oriented policing and problem solving were created as a response to the detached, "just the facts"-type of policing that had alienated community members. In recent years, these and other styles of policing have taken on a life of their own. Until September 11th 2001, rapid response to calls for service and the use of problem-solving by unassigned officers or during the down time of assigned officers was seen as a revolution in policing. Since 9/11, the emphasis on routine policing, problem solving, and many other activities aimed at policing traditional crimes has been influenced by the threat of terrorism. This omnipresent threat has increased resources for fighting domestic and international terrorism, and has had an influence on the resources needed to battle street crimes.

One of the critical issues facing American society today is the ability of local police organizations to fight street crime and the new proliferation of gang-related crime while also protecting the public against terrorism. This is a tough challenge, as changing risks can lead to shifting organizational priorities, resources, and asset deployment. What used to be acceptable police practices in guarding against terrorism may no longer be adequate. Meanwhile, the increased costs of protecting against terrorism might cause the rate of "ordinary crimes" to rise.

Organizational change in policing is driven by public and political opinion as well as financial considerations. In a survey of professional policing literature following the September 2001 attack, Marks (2005) reports that changes to police agencies, including the creation of a specific counterterrorism unit, are more likely to occur in the large metropolitan and state police agencies than in the smaller municipal and county agencies. He also notes that regional information-sharing networks have been established by the larger agencies, and that smaller agencies are allowed to participate in them. He further reports that all sorts and sizes of police departments have modified the way they maintain, collect, and share information, as well as the way they use public relations techniques to assure citizens that something is being done to fight terrorism.

Finally, Marks concludes that the increased level of funding and reorganization of federal law enforcement agencies has helped increase the involvement of all levels of police in the country in the fight against terrorism. What is missing, though, is an analysis of these efforts. With the creation of task forces, counterterrorism bureaus, and trained response teams, it appears that many of the large metropolitan areas in the United States are safer in 2007 than they were in 2001; however, we have no real evidence of this assumption. There are many considerations that must be addressed, including whether departments have established or joined regional information-sharing networks, and whether these networks are sufficiently sophisticated or funded to detect or track terrorists. Without appropriate evaluation, it appears the many larger police agencies in the United States have improved their ability to deal with terrorism since September 11th 2001, but the smaller agencies may only appear to have.

The heightened risk of a terrorist attack on American soil has had a serious impact on local policing. The federal response against potential terrorist activities is undeniable, and multiagency task forces involving federal, state, and local law enforcement agencies have been created (Joint Terrorism Task Forces). One consequence of these task forces is the tremendous demand now being placed on police agencies to collect information and provide it to a central clearing house in order to develop and coordinate intelligence on terrorist risks throughout the country. The United States does not have a glowing record of cooperation among law enforcement agencies at the local, regional, state, and federal levels. However, an important component of the American homeland security system involves an ongoing "terror watchlist" of suspects maintained by the federal government. State and local police are asked to check suspects they encounter in daily policing activities against the list and to notify the federal government of matches or encounters.

The Case of the Shopping Mall

Shopping malls are places where many citizens spend time and congregate, and they are symbolic of the Western way of life. Together with their free and easy access, they have become an attractive target for terrorists. Indeed, malls have been targeted by terrorists in Israel numerous times. The security of malls in the United States and Israel is mostly handled by private security companies, supported by the differential presence of the local police. There have been many changes in mall security in Israel and the US, both in terms of training and liaison with law enforcement agencies and in the sharing of information. Since 9/11, local malls have expanded closed-circuit television systems, redesigned entrances to block car bombers, and bolstered training for private security personnel. Nonetheless, security experts acknowledge that malls have to balance the risk of terror against the costs of added security and the economic imperative to be welcoming to shoppers. Furthermore, they doubt, for instance, that most Americans would be willing to go through a metal detector and a bag search before entering a mall, as Israel shoppers do (Eisenberg, 2007).

This tolerance or willingness to relinquish customs may be the most important difference between Israeli and American citizens. In an effort to improve security, the Israeli public will tolerate limitations of several freedoms (such as the freedom to walk freely or the right to privacy), whereas the American public is zealously protective of such liberties. Again, we should note that both populations have faced different experiences of terrorist activities. Israeli malls have often been attacked by suicide bombers, while in the United States, malls, like American subways, have not been successfully targeted.

Fear of Terror

The fear of terrorism in Israel is deep seated; the State of Israel was created in a hostile political atmosphere and from the start its right to exist was challenged by many. This opposition has been expressed in various violent military conflicts throughout the course of the State's existence. Concerns of politicide are inherent to Israeli civilian identity, and the fear of terrorism only aggravates these concerns. In comparison, the fear of terrorism in the United States is not as acute, and anxieties regarding political elimination are not central to the social identity of the American public (although the Al-Qaeda ideology has to a large extent evoked a fear of destruction among the people of the United States).

A survey conducted in 2004 by the National Center for Disaster Preparedness at Columbia University indicated that 81% of respondents from the East Coast and 71% in the West Coast were concerned about the possibility of another terrorist attack. Despite the major attack in New York, the corresponding fear of terrorism found both in the Western and Eastern United States is demonstrative of the psychological effect of the fear of terrorism (uncertainty) and how it affects places which did not experience attacks. One might assume that since terrorists usually target big cities, a fear of terrorism would mostly be represented in the big coastal cities and less in rural communities. A surprising finding of the same survey, however, indicates that the fear of terrorism is in fact slightly higher among respondents residing in rural rather than urban areas (80% and 75%, respectively). Similar rates of fear of terrorism are also prevalent throughout Israel. Despite the fact that terrorists have most often targeted Israel's larger cities (Jerusalem, Tel-Aviv, Haifa, and Netanya), all citizens share a concern about terrorism, even those residing in communities far from the big cities (Hoffman, 2003).

Terrorists aim to weaken citizens' trust in their own government and to undermine the public's confidence in the government's ability to protect the homeland (Hoffman, 1998). Citizens' trust in their government's ability to fight terrorism is thus transformed into an important factor. The 2003 survey demonstrated that 62% of the American public displayed confidence in the federal government's ability to protect the country from terrorism, with this number dropping to 53% in the 2004 survey. Contrary to the public's decreasing confidence in federal agencies, however, the American public's trust in airport security rose from 54% in 2002 to 61% in 2004. Still, only one-third of the public felt confident that their mass transit systems (subways and buses) are in fact protected from terrorism, and less than 40% said they were confident in the ability of the health care system to respond to an act of terrorism.

Contrary to the public's limited trust in the ability of federal agencies to protect them from terrorism, 66% agreed that the local police department could effectively respond to terrorist attacks, and 77% expressed confidence in the local fire department. This is an indication of the central role that the public attributes to local agencies, especially the police, in the fight against terrorism. It also helps explain why American local police agencies increasingly find themselves training in the application of hazard vulnerability assessments and conducting assessments for government, business, medical, and industrial infrastructures in their respective communities.

The police in Israel view their function, at least in part, as providing psychological support to the community in their efforts at dealing with terrorism. This is one of the reasons that the police work so hard to repair the damage and restore a sense of routine to the sites of terrorist attacks as quickly as possible. In contrast, in the United States there appears to be a consensus among police agencies that the focus on terrorism detracts from their primary task of dealing with crime and responding to other community needs. Equally, the communities in these two countries have different expectations from the police. In Israel, where daily threats of terrorism arouse fear and concern, it is natural for citizens to demand that the police focus on terrorism. But in the United States, communities are much more affected by crime and disorder than terrorism, and accordingly they want their police force to focus primarily on those issues.

Each year, the Israel Police issues a report of the police's various areas of responsibility. The report focuses on crime and a range of other topics related to community, education, budgets, etc. A comparative review of police reports over the years 1990–2005 indicates several changes, primarily an increase in the significance of homeland security in the agenda of police work in Israel. Thus, between the years 1990 and 1994, homeland security is barely mentioned in the reports; if it is cited, it is always secondary to the key topic of dealing with crime in all its forms. From 1995, however, there is a noticeable change, with much greater emphasis placed on homeland security, and especially the imperatives of managing and foiling terrorist attacks. In the rundown of the Israel Police's duties, dealing with crime – the traditional role of the police – drops to third place. Dealing with terrorism is first on the list, followed by the need for maintaining public order, which is also related to the policing of internal security (e.g., dispersing demonstrations and illegal assemblies) (Fig. 7.1).

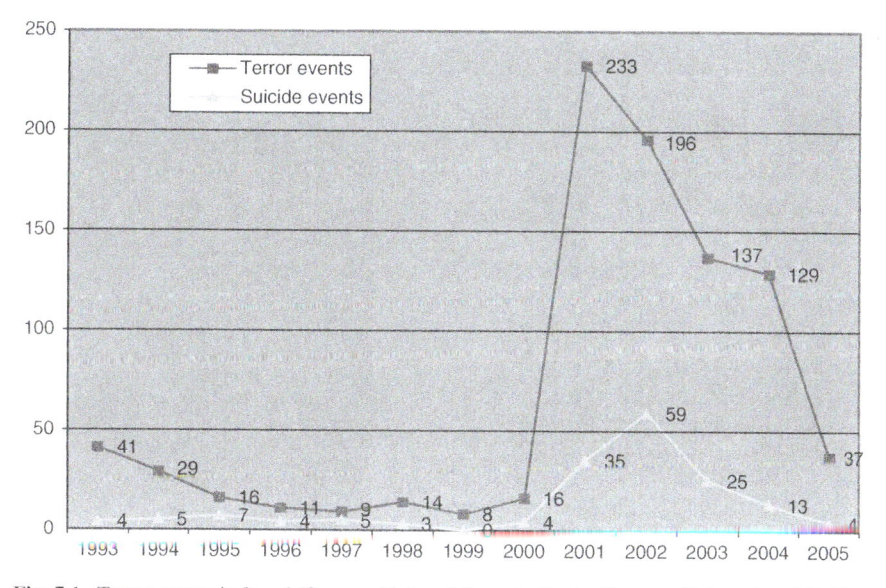

Fig. 7.1 Terror events in Israel (Source: National Security Study Center – University of Haifa)

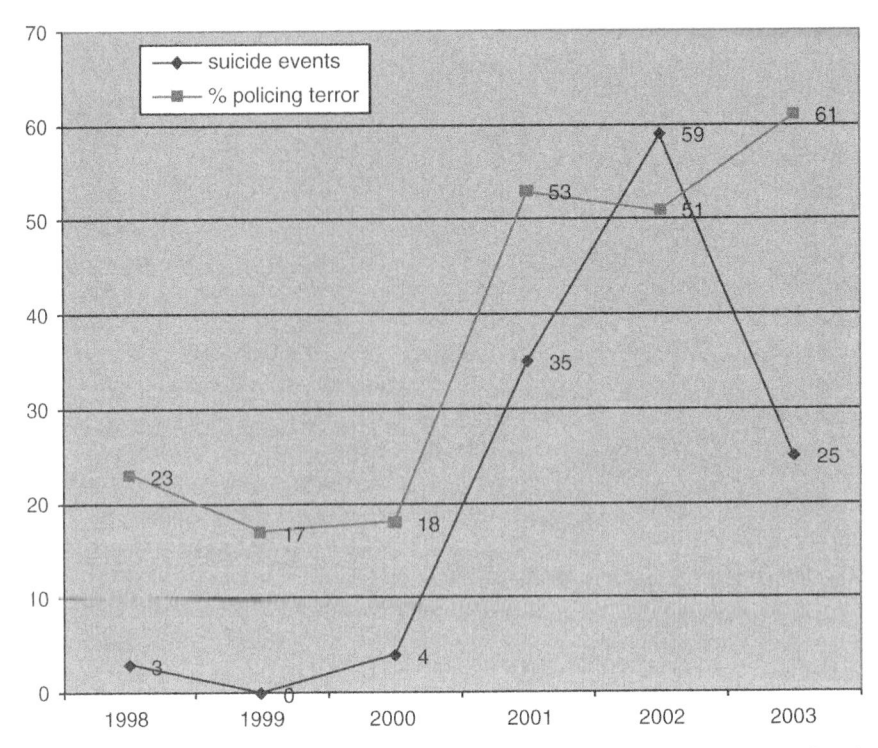

Fig. 7.2 Suicide events and public preference in the policing of terrorism (Source: National Security Study Center – University of Haifa; State of Israel – Ministry of Public Security 1999–2002, Bureau of the Chief Scientist)

This can be clearly seen with data from the Israeli context. Graph 1 shows the frequency of terrorist attacks in Israel from 1993 to 2005, and a subgroup of the numbers of suicide attacks, which had an especially large impact on the public's fear of terrorism. We can see that 2002 was the most violent year in terms of suicide terrorism (Fig. 7.2).

Graph 2 demonstrates the relation between the frequency of suicide terrorist attacks and public-policing priorities. Israeli respondents were asked to rank the priority of policing terror among other police duties (i.e., property crimes, violence, traffic, etc.). The graph shows that in 1999 only 17% of the Israeli public thought the police should be primarily dealing with terror, while this percentage increased sharply to 59% in 2002 and remained high even after the decrease in terrorist attacks.

Proposals for Research

Given that the police are relatively new soldiers in the proactive fight against terrorism and the police are only effective to the extent they garner cooperation from the public, the police need to enhance their police-community team-building skills in the post-9/11 environment. Times have changed and the context in which today's police officers function has changed remarkably from just the last decade. Therefore the police need to update their sociological knowledge bases, most of which were composed and trained years prior to 9/11.

New research designed to develop current insights in the areas of new forms of human diversity, as well as the cultural norms of today's more complex minority groups would be highly beneficial. As the police develop new community relations strategies and even new police officer recruitment strategies, new research-based tactics would ultimately contribute to better public safety in both Israel and the United States.

Summary and Conclusions

In conclusion, we contend that the expansion of terrorism has imposed increased duties and responsibilities on the police. For the most part, however, this has not been accompanied by a corresponding increase in resources with which to handle the additional tasks. As a result, the police are spending less time improving community problem-solving techniques, developing positive police-community relations, and establishing legitimacy. However, in order to successfully execute their new counter-terrorism duties and responsibilities, the police need unprecedented cooperation and involvement from the community. Therefore, it appears that the most effective way for the police to fight terrorism in the long run is to embrace the ideals of improved police-community relations in addition to the defensive policing of terrorism. The police force must accept the responsibility for providing positive leadership in the fight against terrorism by rededicating itself to the principles of community policing, and by uniting the whole community, including ethnic minority groups. This is surely the most effective way for both the police and the public to deal with budding terrorists, who are generally minorities within minority groups.

Inasmuch as the police are a nonrevenue-generating arm of government, they will always struggle for adequate resources. Faced with a plethora of new duties and responsibilities, but lacking corresponding levels of added resources, common sense dictates that something will have to give. Our contention is that it is positive police-community relations that are paying the price, ironically a vital ingredient to the successful discharge of the police's new duties and responsibilities.

The threat of acts of terrorism has created new and technologically complex problems for law enforcement, threats which are not geographically bounded. These threats are aimed at perceived weaknesses resulting from American values and the way of life in the United States. In order to protect American citizens, a smarter solution must be sought than simply increasing patrols or traditional policing. There is much more to do than merely enhancing sea and airport security. This does not mean that policing must totally reinvent itself. Many strategies, techniques, and tactics that have, in the recent past, worked well in domestic crime fighting, such as problem solving, intelligence sharing, public-private partnerships and multiple agency task forces, can be adopted by counterterrorism units. A better-funded police force must embrace these activities as the correct foundation for fighting the newer threat of terrorism.

The Israeli case indicates that there are many areas of cooperation that must be addressed in the US, including the sharing of information among agencies at all levels. While it is important for investigators to receive timely information about potential threats, the levels of security restrictions placed on this information may discourage many from requesting or receiving it. Similarly, many local agencies are not comfortable with the requests and demands made by federal law enforcement concerning the management and control of suspects and persons of interest, especially when civil rights organizations continuously allege that the police profile individuals and violate civil rights in many ways. We are in search of a "perfect balance" among law enforcement agencies and the public so as to avoid the "perfect storm."

Broader Implication

Our chapter has broader implications than the general themes described earlier. Specifically, an important implication of our work involves the challenges of creating a proper balance between preserving and protecting human rights and restricting the liberties of citizens. A general discussion of antiterrorism efforts, civil liberties, and civil rights would be exceedingly broad and not appropriate here. However, discussions of the two most important governmental efforts that have the potential to impose on liberties and protect our welfare are the formal USA Patriot Act (USA PATRIOT Act, Pub. L. No. 107–56, 115 Stat. 272 (2001) and informal use of profiling, whether criminal, racial, or ethnic. Both these topics are addressed to some degree in this and other chapters of this volume. Our brief discussion here is limited to the designed and real impact of safeguarding human rights that may be seen as intrusive ways to limit our treasured liberties. Clearly, balancing freedom and order is a difficult and challenging task, but one that must be achieved to maintain a democracy (Rosenzweig, 2004).

The Patriot Act was seen as a temporary way of achieving that balance. It was a law passed with vast support in Congress soon after the September 11th terrorist attacks. The various provisions of the Act could clearly infringe upon our liberties. The Act is perceived as very broad in scope and has many concerned about abuses (Traynor, 2006). First, the expansions of Executive powers, and second, the fear that advanced technology will be used against citizens, are the general areas of concern.

Perhaps aspects of the Act that impact the daily lives of citizens are the increase in new technologies. These new technologies provide two changes from previous practices: they both expand the domain of information available to federal law enforcement and intelligence agencies, and improve the ability of those agencies to examine and compare information previously collected. Clearly, the enhanced nature and type of information and the enhanced ability to determine its usefulness expands the authority and power of the Executive branch of government.

Criticism of the Patriot Act is more conceptual than empirical (Rosenzweig, 2004). In other words, those who speak out against the Act often do so because of the potential for its use and abuse rather than any facts that have shown its use or harm to citizens. While certain tainted actions have come to light, including the treatment of prisoners, and targeting of groups of people, it is difficult to blame these actions on the passing of the Patriot Act. Additionally, it is impossible to know the impact the Act has had on deterring terrorist activities on US soil. One real criticism of the intent of the Act is that it has gone far beyond its original provisions and must be considered by its longevity. What was originally passed as a temporary law has become continued and a part of our daily lives. These provisions may never be revoked. Just as many air travelers have never experienced boarding an airplane without TSA security checkpoints, it is unlikely that we will ever experience a lower level of security at the national or local level than we do today.

Criminal, racial, or ethnic profiling poses a difficult problem to members of our societies. A reasonable law enforcement tool must balance three separate principles: (1) the level of intrusion or potential harm, (2) the deterrent effect, and (3) the level of specific intelligence linking the suspected activity and the harm that may be averted. As we have noted, the use of profiling is neither efficient nor effective. Advocates of profiling argue that in limited circumstances the use of profiling to prevent terrorism may be reasonable when applied narrowly to national origin information. Unfortunately, a limited use is likely to be expanded, and what once was temporary may become permanent. The slippery slope of profiling needs to be closely watched and used only after the implementation of built-in safeguards.

It may be that effective law enforcement and intelligence gathering activities are necessary to avoid new terrorist acts that involve individuals who are willing to die in an attack. Reactive police work aiming to punish the criminal has no meaning in this type of situation. The old adage that "it is better that ten guilty men go free than that one innocent man be punished" may be modified to note that that it is better to screen or search 10 million innocent people than to have citizens die because the one guilty person was not screened. If citizens acknowledge the need for the government to take intrusive actions to protect them, then policing at the national and local levels will change forever. While we must maintain community policing and problem-solving philosophies and activities, policing will forever include the threat of terrorism.

Suggestions for improvement include the separation of routine police and those assigned to terrorism and other "high" crimes. This suggestion can be seen as a split within agencies or a different focus for local and federal agencies. Other ideas include crosstraining and supervision so all police can serve their citizens in a multifaceted manner. Unfortunately, there is no solid evidence that one approach works better than any other (Lum et al., 2006). In addition, it is difficult to bring all the stakeholders to an agreed upon method to identify, measure, and evaluate outcomes, including deterrence and minimizing damages. We have argued that any emphasis on the policing of terrorism is likely to take assets and resources away

Appendix 1

Appendix 2

from routine policing and the nature and type of criminal behavior that may impact the short- and long-term crime rates. We are without sufficient information to make data-driven decisions, leaving us with the need to look at efforts around the world and to conduct research on different approaches and aspects of policing. Whatever the police, in fact, do, they must protect the public from all threats, including ordinary crimes, routine disorder, and the threat of terrorism.

References

U. Aas and G. Bana. 2002. The accused with not preventing the terror attack in Miron: It wasn't in my hands. *Haaretz Newspaper*, 8 August: p. 1. [In Hebrew].
G.P. Alpert, R.G. Dunham, and M.R. Smith. 2007. Investigating racial profiling by the Miami-Dade police department: A multimethod approach. *Criminology and Public Policy* 6:25–55.
S. Belieck. 2006. Social capital, fear and police legitimacy: Measuring community-based policing in Albania. *Journal of Security Sector Management* 4(3).
D. Black. 2002. Violent Structures. In: *The Workshop on Theories of Violence*, 2002, 10 December. Washington, DC: National Institute of Justice.
P. Chalk and W. Rosenau. 2004. *Confronting the "Enemy within": Security Intelligence, the Police, and Counterterrorism in Four Democracies*. Santa Monica, CA: RAND Corporation.
L. Clutterbuck. 2006. Countering Irish republican terrorism in Britain, its origin as a police function. Terrorism and Political Violence 18:95–118.
T.P. Connors and G. Pellegrini (eds). 2005. *Hard Lessons Learned: Policing Terrorism in the United States*. New York, NY: The Manhattan Institute for Policy Research
G. Cromer. 2006. Analogies to terror: The construction of social problems in Israel during the Al-Aqsa intifada. *Terrorism and Political* Violence 18(3):389–398.
C. Eisenberg. 2007. Shopping malls another target of terrorism? *Newsday.com*, 13 Feb 13. www.newsday.com (accessed April 17, 2007).
Fact Sheet, the Massachusetts Local Law Enforcement Administrative Survey. Terrorism. 2002. Boston: Massachusetts Statistical Analysis Center.
M. Hamm. 2005. After September 11: Terrorism research and the crisis in criminology. *Theoretical Criminology* 9:237–251.
D. Harris. 2002. *Profiles in Injustice: Why Racial Profiling Can't Work*. New York: The New Press.
B. Hasisi and R. Weitzer. 2007. Police relations with Arabs and Jews in Israel. The British Journal of Criminology 47(5):728–745.
N.J. Henderson, C.W. Ortiz, N.F. Sugie, and J. Miller. 2006. *Law Enforcement and Arab American Community Relations after September 11th, 2001: Engagement in a Time of Uncertainty*. US: Vera Institute of Justice.
B. Hoffman. 1998. *Inside Terrorism*. New York: Columbia University Press.
B. Hoffman. 2003. The logic of suicide terrorism. *The Atlantic Monthly*, June.
ICM Research Marketing Communication, 2005 *Muslim Polls*. http://www.icmresearch.co.uk (accessed April 20, 2007).
M. Innes. 2006. Policing uncertainty, countering terror through community intelligence and democratic policing. *The Annals of the American Academy of Political and Social Science* 605:222–241.
A.L. Kamen. 2004. Will terror alert level show its true colours? *The Washington Post*, 13 October, A19.
R. Kaminski and W. Pelfrey. 2005. *South Carolina Law Enforcement Census 2004*. South Carolina: University of South Carolina, Department of Criminology and Criminal Justice, and the South Carolina Criminal Justice Academy.
G.R. Kerlikowske. 2006. Safe at home? Policing the hometown in the era of homeland security. In: *Presentation at John Jay College of Criminal Justice, New York*. November 2006. New York: John Jay College of Criminal Justice.

P. Klerks. 1999. The network paradigm applied to criminal organizations: Theoretical nitpicking or a relevant doctrine for investigators? Recent developments in Nederland's. *Connections* 24(3):53–65.

G. LaFree. 2002. Conceptual and methodological challenges to the criminological study of terrorism. In: *The Annual Meeting of the American Society of Criminology*, 14 November. Chicago: The American Society of Criminology.

C. Lum, L. Kennedy, and A. Sherley. 2006. Are counter-terrorism strategies effective? The results of the Campbell systematic review of counter-terrorism evaluation research. *Journal of Experimental Criminology* 2:489–516.

W. Lyons. 1999. Partnership, information and public safety: Community policing in a times of terror. *Policing: An International Journal of Police Strategies and Management* 25(3):530–542.

Mabat Daily News Television Report. 2002. *Television program*. Israel: Channel 1, July 31. [In Hebrew].

D.E. Marks. 2005. Policing and terrorism: *The impact of 9/11 on the organizational structure of state and local police departments in the United States*. MA Thesis, University of Delaware, USA.

A. Merari. 1993. Terrorism as a strategy in insurgency. *Terrorism and Political Violence* 5(4):213–251.

G.R. Murphy and M.R. Plotkin. 2003. *Protecting Your Community from Terrorism: The Strategies for Local Law Enforcement Series.* (Vol. 1) *Improving Local-Federal Partnerships*. Washington, DC: Police Executive Research Forum.

National Centre for Disaster Preparedness. 2004. *How Americans Feel about Terrorism and Security; Three Years after September 11th*. Columbia: Columbia University, Mailman School of Public Health.

W.M. Oliver. 2006. *Homeland Security for Policing*. New Jersey: Pearson Prentice Hall.

A. Perliger, A. Pedahzur, and Y. Zalmanovich. 2005. The defensive of the battle against terrorism. *Journal of Contingencies and Crisis Management* 13(2):79–91.

R. Rosenfeld and B. Buchner. 2002. The unanticipated contributions of criminology to *understanding terrorism*. In: *The Annual Meeting of the American Society of Criminology*, 14 November. Chicago: American Society of Criminology.

P. Rosenzweig. 2004. Civil liberties and the response to terrorism. *Duquesne University Law Review* 42:663–723.

R.J. Sampson and S.W. Raudenbusch. 2004. Seeing disorder: Neighbourhood stigma and the social construction of "broken windows". *Social Psychology Quarterly* 67:319–342.

W. Skogan and K. Frydl (eds). 2004. *Fairness and Effectiveness in Policing: The Evidence*. Washington, DC: National Academies.

E.L. Smith and M.R. Durose. 2006. *Characteristics of Drivers Stopped by the Police, 2002*. Washington, DC: Bureau of Justice Statistics.

D. Sobelman. 2002. The Taxi driver to his colleagues: Don't drive Palestinians in your taxis. *Haaretz Newspaper*, 1 January, p. 2. [In Hebrew].

W. Stuntz. 2002. Local policing after the terror. The Yale Law Journal 111:2137.

The Cost of Heightened Security in American Cities: A 192 City Survey. 2002. Washington, DC: US Conference of Mayors.

M. Traynor. 2006. Citizenship in a time of repression. *Stetson Law Review* 35:775–809.

T.R. Tyler. 2006. *Why People Obey the Law*. Princeton, NJ: Princeton University Press.

D. Weisburd, T. Jonathan, and S. Perry. (Forthcoming). The Israeli model for policing terrorism: Goals, strategies, and open questions. *Criminal Justice and Behavior: An International Journal*.

Chapter 8
Policing, Terrorism, and Beyond

Thomas E. Feucht, David Weisburd, Simon Perry,
Lois Felson Mock, and Idit Hakimi

Abstract In the US, Israel, and other democratic states, the police have been called to expand beyond their order-maintenance work to participate more and more deeply in the still-forming processes that are our societies' adaptive responses to terrorism. As the US and Israel work to achieve and maintain order and safety in an age of terrorism, these efforts must be understood in relation to the ongoing work dealing with other persistent challenges to public safety. Engaging the police in fighting terrorism raises some unresolved dilemmas for society. The chapters in this volume have begun the complex work of uncovering how this transformative engagement of the police is already making subtle but likely irrevocable changes in the nature and strategies of policing and the character of the bonds between police and community. This chapter summarizes the key findings of the volume, examines the broader context confronting the police in an age of terrorism and beyond, and identifies areas for future research.

Introduction

A social system's ability to respond and adapt effectively to changes and pressures from external conditions is a requisite for system functioning. Talcott Parsons' theory of social action names "adaptation" as one of the four functional imperatives of any social system (Parsons, 1937).[1] According to Parsons, adaptation occurs as a social system (or subsystem) and confronts the changing conditions in which it must function. As a requisite for solvent social systems, adaptation is not optional: in order to function, Parsons asserts, a system adapts and evolves or ceases to exist as it did before.

T.E. Feucht(✉), D. Weisburd, S. Perry, L.F. Mock, and I. Hakimi
National Institute of Justice, Washington, DC, USA
e-mail: thomas.feucht@usdoj.gov

---

[1] The other functional imperatives are goal attainment, integration, and order maintenance or latency.

Democratic societies today may face no greater adaptive challenge than terrorism. Increasingly, terrorism brings to bear international conflicts that pull nations into new and complex arenas of international relations, diplomacy, and armed conflict. It challenges fundamental assumptions about the separateness, relatedness, and interdependence of nation states. In addition, terrorism's roots in an absolute and violent rejection of core tenets of the prevailing political order undermine the fundamental procedures that a state would normally employ for resolving conflict and maintaining order (i.e., laws and legal recourse). Finally, even as a state responds to terrorist incidents, the networks and organizations of terrorists can form and re-form, seeming to disappear and reappear, making effective responses very difficult to establish and sustain.

Of course, the challenges posed by terrorism today are not new. Terrorism has plagued societies around the world for decades and longer. Considered side by side, the most recent US and Israeli experiences with terrorism help to underscore that our responses to terrorist events today are, in many ways, part of a much longer struggle played out in democratic and emerging democratic states in Europe, the Middle East, Latin America, Asia, and elsewhere around the globe. Even as the US and Israel struggle to achieve and maintain order and safety in their own communities, these efforts must be understood in the context of the larger global political order. Part of that context, in the US, in Israel, and elsewhere, is the need to develop effective responses to terrorism while at the same time continuing to deal with other persistent challenges to public safety, such as crime and disorder.

Comparisons between terrorism and crime, though imperfect, are compelling. Each is an assault on public order and public safety. We suspect that the organizations and networks that commit organized crime are similar in structure to organized terrorist networks, though this is far from certain. And like the fear of crime that can paralyze neighborhoods, the fear of terrorism can exact a very real and distinct cost in the communities affected.

Crime and terrorism are also linked in the way society responds to each threat. In particular, *the challenge to the social order posed by crime or by terrorism requires the state to at least contemplate using the most extreme forms of social control available against its own citizens or others, including the use of deadly force*. And this brings us to the police – the agents who, on behalf of the community, shoulder the work of preserving social order and protecting public safety. The "authority and mandate" for coercive force (see Skolnick and Fyfe, 1993, as cited in Greene and Herzog, in this volume), buttressed by the community's perceptions of police legitimacy, enable the police to intervene effectively in disputes and conflicts among citizens. In this way, the police constitute a unique - some would say essential – element of our society's response to terrorism as well as crime.

Engaging the police in fighting terrorism raises some unresolved dilemmas for society. Articulating and understanding these dilemmas are the central motivation for this volume. Fighting "ordinary" crime – what Brodeur (1983, 2007) would call "low policing," described here by Bayley and Weisburd – is part of what Parsons (1937) called society's "latency" or order-maintaining requisite. This kind of work is largely internal to the social system, focused on maintaining normative order in the institutions and processes within the society. But confronting terrorism entangles the police in the external, adaptive work of system response and adaptation to larger changes in the external sociopolitical framework that Brodeur (1983, 2007) would describe as "high" policing. As Bayley and Weisburd note, it may cultivate suspicion of citizens, rather than cooperation, and it is likely to focus police on large-scale strategic goals (e.g., defeating terrorism on a national scale) rather than on the crime-fighting needs of specific neighborhoods or local communities. This is police work of a very different order.

Police engagement in counter-terrorism creates tensions at the margins of the institution, Greene and Herzog point out. These include powerful tensions between the police and those who are policed. Greene and Herzog go on to say that, though all terrorism is likely criminal, the strategies, processes, and analytics of detecting and preventing crime may not be relevant to combating terrorism. Seen from Parsons' theory of social action, the engagement of the police in counter-terrorism creates a tension in the basic structural order of how a society organizes itself and how social action occurs. Viewed from this macrotheoretical perspective, it is no wonder that the dilemma of policing terrorism seems to tear at the very fabric of our communities and our societies.

And yet, here we are. There is no disputing that, in the US, in Israel, and in other democratic states, the police have been called upon to expand beyond their crime and order-maintenance work to participate more and more deeply in the still-forming processes than are our societies' adaptive responses to terrorism. In Israel and in many communities in the US, the police are now a central component of the counter-terrorism strategy and the response to terrorist events.

With time, engaging the police to combat terrorism may become increasingly normative. This is already the case, for instance, in Israel, where the police role in terrorism prevention and response is well established and generally acknowledged. In Israel, Greene and Herzog observe the distinction between the police and the military is less sharply drawn, making police involvement in counter-terrorism more readily accepted by both the police and those policed. Police in the US, in contrast, have only recently experienced the sudden and unexpected demand of responding to terrorist events and preventing subsequent terrorism. As a result, the functions and structures that flow from counter-terrorism work have not been fully integrated by the police – nor fully acknowledged or accepted by US communities and neighborhoods.

A timely examination of the terrorism work of the police can reveal the ways in which this work changes policing. Like the analysis of a sudden traffic collision, an examination of the forces and consequences of the "collision" between terrorism and the police is most profitably undertaken sooner rather than later, especially if there are lessons to be learned and changes to be contemplated.

This volume has begun the complex work of uncovering whether and how this transformative engagement of the police is already making subtle but likely irrevocable changes to the nature and strategies of policing and the character of the bonds between police and community. By examining the "point of the collision" between the force that is terrorism and the core institution that is the police, we begin to learn not only about the future of policing but also about the future of democratic societies in an age of terrorism, and beyond.

Each of the studies commissioned for this volume has examined a particular aspect of the juncture between terrorism and policing, providing a conceptual map for exploring the issue of terrorism and the police. In constructing this map, the authors have traversed three "vectors" that converge to form the intersection of the police and terrorism: the nature of terrorism itself; the community context within which policing and terrorism occur; and the role, structure, and functioning of the police. These vectors provide a useful framework for summarizing the key contributions of this volume and for understanding the broader issues at stake. This framework also helps to reveal the key tensions and unresolved policy issues regarding the policing of terrorism; these are discussed later in the chapter. A final section of the chapter describes areas of research that were not fully developed in this volume but could be profitably explored in the future.

Terrorists, Communities, and the Police: Crosscutting Themes

The Nature of Terrorism and Terrorists

The work of our authors sharpens our understanding of the phenomenon of modern terrorism and helps to reveal important aspects of terrorist organizations. In particular, we see that while terrorism is often highly organized, it is a constantly shifting phenomenon; that the organizational features of terrorist groups and their adherence to an ideology distinguish them from criminal groups; and that terrorist organizations often seek to develop, maintain, and exploit key strategic links with communities of citizens.

Terrorism As a Dynamic and Changing Phenomenon

Even a review limited to only contemporary terrorist events reveals the extensive variation and striking contours that have marked terrorism throughout the modern age. LaFree and Dugan's broad historical analysis confirms this and renders a wealth of important empirical findings; most of these findings underscore the dynamic and changing features of terrorism over time.

The data show how even the prevalence of terrorism and terrorist events has surged and receded over the last several decades. Within these shifts over time, scores of terrorist networks rise, thrive, and desist in what LaFree and Dugan's data show to be the relatively short lifecycle of most terrorist organizations: only about a fourth of terrorist organizations in LaFree and Dugan's data were operational for more than a year, and only a little more than 10% were operational for more than 5 years. Likewise, the types of targets attacked in terrorist events vary widely – government installations, private citizens, police agencies, transportation depots, and others.

Variations and changes in terrorist events over time are compounded by geographic differences in the prevalence and type of event.

The dynamic nature of these variations in terrorist organizations and actions may not be altogether surprising. By its nature, any effort to subvert social order may achieve a distinct advantage by minimizing predictability and maximizing the ability to evolve and change quickly. However, rapid adaptation and change can create internal instability, and this is almost certainly a contributing factor to the short lifespan of many terrorist organizations. Taken together, these features challenge simplistic notions of "terrorism" as a unidimensional, monolithic phenomenon. Like any social phenomenon, understanding and responding effectively to terrorism requires recognition that, like crime, terrorism is, in many ways, place and time specific. "All terrorism is local," at least in its consequences, Greene and Herzog declare.

This dynamism is further revealed in Ganor's focused examination of the Global Jihadi movement. This terrorist organization reveals a mix of persistent patterns and irregular, shifting features. LaFree and Dugan's comprehensive assessment of the means and weapons used (nearly half of their cases involved explosives) is placed in sharp relief in Ganor's essay on middle-east terrorism, where improvised explosive devices and roadside bombings are the primary (though by no means exclusive) means of the Jihadi terrorists.

The notion of change and evolution in terrorism and terrorist organizations is expanded further in Hasisi et al.'s distinction between "old" and "new" terrorism. New terrorism includes Global Jihad, discussed at length by Ganor, and is conducted in ways that "manufacture uncertainty." New terrorism maximizes unpredictability: terrorist attacks are rarely forewarned, in contrast to the "old"-style terrorism. New terrorism, Hasisi et al. tell us, selects targets that are more generalized in nature: where "old" terrorism more often targeted government sites, "new" terrorism more often targets urban areas and ordinary citizens. More than any other feature of the new, dynamic, and unpredictable terrorism, it is this feature that most challenges the police, to whom issues of citizen safety and urban patrol are paramount. In an "old regime" of terrorism, the police role was not essential. In the new terrorism regime, the police find themselves inextricably involved.

Terrorist Organization and the Use of Ideology

The US Department of State currently identifies 44 foreign terrorist organizations (FTOs) throughout the world (*Fact Sheet: Foreign Terrorist Organizations*, 2008). Until 2004, redesignation by the State Department of each FTO had been required every 2 years, or the designation would lapse. Changes introduced by the Intelligence Reform and Terrorism Prevention Act provide any designated FTO with the means for petitioning for revocation of the designation. It also extends the default period of designation to 5 years, though review and revocation can be made at any time.

What defines a terrorist *organization?* In addition to being foreign in nature and engaged in terrorist activities which threaten the security of US nationals or US national security, a designated FTO is on which, according to the State Department, has a capacity for *"planning and preparations"* for terrorist actions or *"retains* the capability and intent to carry out such acts" (emphasis added).

Beyond the idea of a persistent capacity or intent, there is little in the State Department's definition that helps establish a concise notion of what defines a terrorist *organization*. LaFree and Dugan's data on the short lifespan of most organizations suggest highly unstable organizations, due to internal or external factors which destabilize the organization. Other features – the degree of integration or autonomy among members and units, the centrality of authority and decision making, the depth of leadership and control within upper ranks, and so on – remain opaque regarding most terrorist organizations.

What Ganor presents in his depiction of radical Islamic terrorism confirms this. Even distinguishing unique "organizations" or separable factions is challenging. Ganor puts al Qaeda at the head of the Global Jihad movement and then lists separate suborganizations as parts of this movement under Osama bin Laden's umbrella organization. He includes Egyptian, Bangladeshi, and Afghan groups, and draws links to other terrorist organizations and activities in Jordan, Morocco, Indonesia, and elsewhere. Ganor would likely include under this umbrella organizations like HAMAS, Islamic Jihadi Group, Tanzim Qa'idat al-Jihad fi Bilad al-Rafidayn (al Qaeda in Iraq), al Qaeda in the Islamic Maghreb, and others – all which the State Department designates as distinct, differentiated FTOs.

Drawing precise boundaries around terrorist organizations is not a mere academic exercise, of course. The ties that link and the distinctions that divide groups of terrorists are keys to effective counter-terrorism.

Ganor's accounts summarize events that help us form a more precise sense of the changing features of the al Qaeda organization. An organization that was previously more centralized and hierarchical was significantly destabilized by the destruction of training camps and other facilities. It is clear from published accounts that the deaths of several key lieutenants in the organization contributed to further destabilization. The result is that recent terrorist actions conducted under the al Qaeda banner have been carried out, Ganor says, by the increasingly loosely affiliated subnetworks of al Qaeda, functioning as "proxies of al Qaeda."

In al Qaeda, as in other terrorist organizations, it is the allegiance to a persistent, overarching ideology with the power to unite and motivate that is the distinguishing feature of terrorist organizations. The key link among al Qaeda affiliates has been – and appears to continue to be – their subscription to the al Qaeda world view, what Ganor calls the "one divine mission" of establishing a radical Islamic caliphate.

However, the continued strength of this ideology – and of al Qaeda's power of control and allegiance within the parts of the jihadi movement – is the subject of considerable debate in counter-terrorist policy circles. One view is that the ultrafundamentalist ideology of al Qaeda no longer reflects nor has in harness the ambitions and motivations of the fractured subgroups Ganor says serve as proxies for al Qaeda. The result, according to Marc Sageman, is a new "third wave" of terrorism, a "leaderless jihad," that will burn itself out over time (Ignatius, 2008).

Predictably, this view is not unanimous. Hoffman (2008) asserts that "al Qaeda is a remarkably agile and flexible organization that exercises both top-down and bottom-up planning and operational capabilities." And while the notion of "leaderless jihad" may persuade some in the US intelligence community, it is likely met with greater skepticism in Europe (especially the UK), where the reported number of thwarted or failed terrorist plots continues to mount (MI5 tracking '30 UK terror plots', 2006).

If terrorist organizations like al Qaeda decentralize and fragment, this has important implications for the role of the police in counter-terrorism. Smaller bands of terrorists, operating autonomously on a more local scale, present the police with a range of investigative, preventive, and reactive challenges for which they might reasonably draw upon current policing strategies and experiences gained in combating street gangs or illegal drug markets. Undeniably, more localized operations of highly fragmented terrorist groups can have profound national and international consequences. But as a terrorist organization separates into fragments and subunits, the threat of terrorism may take on a local reality for which the police may be uniquely well-suited.

The Need to Examine Terrorist Organizations' Links to "Host" Communities

Finally, no terrorist organization can be accurately characterized or adequately understood apart from its social context. At its base, this requires an appreciation for the way in which terrorists and terrorist organizations are rooted in specific places, specific communities, and even specific neighborhoods. Even large, highly organized international networks of terrorists seek to cultivate and maintain local affiliations and community ties, especially when ethnic or regional identity or separatism is part of the ideological foundation of the terrorist movement. Hasisi et al. discuss the way in which sectors of the Arab minority community in Israel provide terrorists with a foil against detection and counter-terrorist measures. Partly due to a community's genuine sympathies for the terrorists and partly due to an underlying distrust of the police, the obstacles created by terrorists' intentional links to the community can effectively thwart police efforts to gather counter-terrorist intelligence. Hasisi et al. note data from community surveys of British Muslims as additional evidence of the way in which the community context of terrorists can shroud their actions from detection and effective preventive measures.

Communities also serve as the context from which terrorist recruits are obtained and within which strategies and propaganda can be shaped and tested. The exploitation of links to host communities by terrorist organizations poses substantial obstacles to the police, not only in combating terrorism but in doing the work of "ordinary" policing. The next section explores the role and context of the community further.

Communities: The Social Context of Terrorism and Policing

The urban community, Hasisi et al. state, has become the primary context – and target – for "new" terrorism. Population centers hold choice targets for terrorists such as businesses, transportation centers, and government facilities. They also provide dense media coverage, giving terrorists the publicity they often seek for their actions.

And urban communities provide situations in which large numbers of citizens can be attacked in the most disturbing and spectacular forms of terrorist violence. Yet, our authors reveal, the community is more than a battlefield on which terrorism occurs. It is the social context in which terrorist organizations thrive, hide, and cultivate sympathy and support. It is also the context in which expectations for the police are defined.

Hasisi et al. and others in this volume have underscored the multinational character of communities and what this means for terrorists and for the police. Other key points by the authors touch on the nature of the community's expectations for the police and the evidence regarding effective police engagement with the community in combating terrorism.

The (New) Challenge of Multinational Communities

Even absent from the threat of terrorism, the changing ethnic composition of communities challenges much of "policing as usual." Immigrants, Hasisi et al. point out, bring to their new communities varying levels of distrust of public officials, including the police. Language barriers and other cultural differences present new obstacles to policing effectiveness. Community residents of longer tenure often harbor suspicions against immigrants, and these suspicions form the basis for some unrealistic expectations for (unjustified) police actions against minorities.

All these complexities are compounded, Hasisi et al. point out, in a context of terrorism and terrorist networks, where efforts by the police to establish bonds with the community can conflict with the need to gather covert intelligence about potential terrorist threats. In this context, police work on public safety has a new metric, evaluated against and balanced by the fear of lost privacy and liberty. In the end, reciprocal trust is simply harder to establish and maintain in an age of terrorism.

A post-9/11 study on policing in Arab-American communities confirms these complexities. Following the terrorist attacks of September 11, 2001, residents in Arab-American communities were found to be less trustful and more fearful of law enforcement. Residents reported a heightened sense of scrutiny by the police and a more acute sense of the cultural and language differences between residents and police (Henderson et al., 2008). As Bayley and Weisburd point out, this is one of the consequences of the shift to "high policing." As the police begin to involve themselves in counter-terrorism efforts, these communities are viewed as neither key constituencies nor partners of the police (as they are in community policing models) but as havens for citizens who are regarded with suspicion and who need to be carefully observed and controlled.

The Community's Expectations for the Police

Beginning in 1993, Gallup has reported annually on Americans' levels of confidence in the police, the broader criminal justice system, and other institutions. Of the 14 institutions tracked annually by Gallup, the police consistently have ranked in the top two or three institutions engendering the greatest confidence (Newport, 2008).[2] The percentage of Americans expressing "a great deal" or "quite a lot" of confidence in the police is consistently high, ranging between 52% (1993) and 64% (2004). While Sherman (2002) notes with concern the significantly lower level of confidence in the police among blacks in the US, more dramatic (and troubling) differences are found in the international comparisons of Gallup's World Poll (Rheault, 2007). Respondents in Finland, New Zealand, and the UAE expressed much higher levels of confidence in the police than respondents in places like Russia, Kenya, Bolivia, and Chad.[3] Given the extreme levels of distrust in some countries, it is not at all surprising to find that these beliefs persist when individuals emigrate, as Hasisi et al. assert.

A community's expectations for the police include not only how they are to conduct themselves but also *what they are to do*. The era of community policing has raised fundamental questions regarding what the work of the police should be about. Are they to prevent crime? Are they to engage the community as partners in coproducing safety? Does their work include matters of public order? The era of terrorism introduces a new set of potential expectations: gathering intelligence on terrorist and preterrorist activities. With these come the potential for more complex expectations and deeper disagreement about *what* the police should do and *how well* they do it.

Skogan's work with the Chicago Police Department (Skogan et al., 2002) and its community policing efforts provides important lessons about community expectations for the police. His analysis of Chicago's Latino neighborhoods is particularly pertinent. Skogan found that while Latinos were much more likely than white residents to register concerns about crime in their neighborhoods, particularly gang violence, their confidence in and engagement with the police was significantly lower than in non-Hispanic neighborhoods. Latinos were significantly less likely to attend meetings with the "beat" police officers – a hallmark of Chicago's community policing strategy known as Chicago Alternative Policing Strategy (CAPS). They were also more likely to report that police behaved in ways that were unfair, impolite, or insensitive to Latinos' problems. Results from Skogan's evaluation of CAPS suggest that language barriers may have contributed to some of these obstacles for effective policing and community engagement in Latino neighborhoods.[4]

Hasisi et al. discuss the importance of "mutual trust" between the police and the community for effective police work. In the context of community policing, this implies an open relationship with the community, where beat meetings and other

---

[2] Though Gallup's "confidence" opinion polls date back to the 1970s, questions about the police, the criminal justice system, and other institutions were added later. The military and, in some years, the church rank ahead of the police. In contrast, the criminal justice system has been consistently among the institutions in which respondents express the least confidence.

[3] In only 33 of 86 countries were respondents more likely than not to express confidence in the police with respect to returning a lost wallet.

[4] Skogan et al.'s research also determined that Latinos of longer residence were more favorable toward the police.

activities provide the community with a transparent view into the plans and activities of the police. Skogan's evaluation suggests that even concerted outreach activities by the police may not overcome the underlying distrust that some minority communities may harbor against the police. And this distrust is only exacerbated in a context of terrorism.

Gathering intelligence on terrorism and terrorist organizations is not a function the police have historically embraced. A 2001 survey of police agencies to assess police preparedness in confronting terrorism indicated that a chief concern was the challenge of developing a capacity for gathering intelligence. Police concerns were linked to the perception that federal agencies were unwilling to share their intelligence information with local police. However, the survey also surfaced concerns that local police needed to establish new intelligence policies and protocols within their own agencies (*Local Law Enforcement*, 2001).

The implication for intelligence work in minority communities was a focus of subsequent discussions and a series of working papers on police and terrorism produced by the Police Executive Research Forum.[5] "Working with Diverse Communities" describes the context of community expectations within which the police work to combat terrorism. For Muslim communities, these "routine" expectations for the police center on a fluency in and a respect for what is culturally distinctive in the community. This includes respectful appreciation by the police for places (such as mosques) and dates (particularly holy days) of significance to the Muslim communities; respecting Muslim norms regarding women or entering the home of a Muslim; and avoiding other potential actions that might signal disrespect (Davies and Murphy, 2004).

The pitfalls are myriad, reflecting the diverse apprehensions of the minority community. Particularly in minority communities, where fear of crime is high, the police tread a fine line between effectiveness and distrust – or worse. Since the events of 9/11, Arab-American communities have sought police protection from "backlash" crimes committed against them by those intolerant of their religious or ethnic affiliation; this expectation is over and above the community's desire for prevention of "ordinary" crime. Preventing ethnic hate crimes is probably at least as difficult as preventing crime generally; and police prevention efforts often get lost – or misperceived – against the backdrop of aggressive intelligence work and threat assessment efforts that concentrate police resources on identifying plausible terrorist threats *within*, rather than against the minority community. In this way, police failure to prevent backlash crimes against ethnic minorities, coupled with heightened police intelligence activity in minority communities, is likely viewed by many in minority communities as a double failure by the police.

Ganor and Hasisi et al. discuss the community's expectation that the police will relieve not only the threat of crime and terrorism but also the *fear* of it. Actively seeking to gather intelligence on subsequent threats may give the larger community a sense of restored confidence and may alleviate fears of additional terrorist events. However, minority communities will view this through the lens of their different

---

[5] See a full inventory of the PERF symposium papers at: http://www.policeforum.org/library.asp?MENU=346.

experience with the police. If the police fail to prevent follow-on crimes of racial hatred *and* are perceived as biased or unduly suspicious against minorities in their intelligence work, fear in the minority community is compounded, not relieved, by the police.

While policing terrorism may have special influence on minority communities, especially those minority groups that might have ethnic, religious, or national ties to groups that are involved in terrorism, it also influences the attitudes in majority groups regarding the police. Bayley and Weisburd argue that majority groups may support and praise police counter-terrorism activities during heightened periods of terrorism, but as the police focus shifts away from local community crime problems, the majority communities may begin to lose their trust in the police. This "rallying" effect and subsequent decline in trust was detected by Tal Jonathan. Her analysis of data from the Israeli Ministry of Public Security showed that public support and trust for the police increased at the height of the Second Palestinian Intifada in Israel, but once terrorist activities had subsided, trust for the police actually declined. (Jonathan, forthcoming)

Evidence Regarding Police Efforts to Engage the Community Following Terrorist Events

Lum et al. make a critical observation regarding community ties to the police and the potential for these ties to foster effective terrorism prevention strategies. Their review of counter-terrorist strategies turns up no empirical evidence whatsoever as to what form effective engagement for counter-terrorism should take or whether the police are doing this in ways that have any measurable consequences. In fact, evidence is lacking that would show the effectiveness of *any* particular policing strategy – including community policing – in preventing terrorism. As Bayley and Weisburd suggest, policing terrorism *could* benefit from community policing because of its ability to provide the police with essential intelligence about what is going on in local contexts; and these community ties could prove most valuable in communities where terrorists may "blend in" or seek support from like ethnic, religious, or national groups. But a shift to "high policing" focused on counter-terrorism in these communities is likely to reduce positive contacts between the police and the public. Thus, the outcome of attempts to exploit community ties for purposes of counter-terrorist intelligence is uncertain: it may have immediate positive outcomes in terms of preventing terrorism, but it might also imperil effective community ties in the long term.

The Police: Their Role, Structure, and Functioning

Terrorism, played out in a context of communities and targeting citizens going about the routine activities of daily life, raises questions regarding the defining role of police. Threats of a sort more consistent with military actions beyond society's borders suddenly encroach on the streets and neighborhoods of ordinary life, where the police are the guardians of public safety. How the police are organized, what we expect of the police, and how the police carry out their sometimes competing functions have been inexorably changed by the intrusion of terrorism into everyday life.

Centralization Versus Decentralization

The fundamental questions of police organizational structure take on a new urgency in an age of terrorism. For instance, each of the chapters in this volume has considered the issue of centralization of police agencies and its advantages and liabilities in confronting terrorism. Indeed, the contrast between the unified national police force of the State of Israel and the 18,000 independent (yet interdependent) law enforcement agencies in the United States – and the differences in police operations that flow from these structures – provides the context for this entire volume.

While it may be overly simplistic to state that "all crime is local," the particular contours of crime, the identity of its victims, and the impact on their lives occur in a relatively limited frame. This is true even for many large-scale crimes involving scores of victims. Even the tragic events of 9/11 were felt and are remembered as linked to very specific places.

Police work, too, is overwhelmingly local, at least in the US, or so it is perceived through the lens of international comparison. How else to explain the existence of 18,000 independent law enforcement agencies? Like the response to "ordinary" crime, the police response to 9/11, though relying on important federal resources through the FBI and other federal agencies, drew primarily upon the officers and resources of specific *local* law enforcement agencies with responsibility within distinct jurisdictions. Moreover, the policing strategies with the best supporting research evidence to date are strategies linking police to specific places, like hot spots policing (Sherman and Weisburd, 1995; Weisburd and Braga, 2003), problem-oriented policing, (Weisburd and Eck, 2004), and others where the police focus on the specific locations where crime occurs or may occur.

Increasingly, however, individual agencies find themselves enmeshed in a web of extensive interjurisdictional ties. Task forces forge federal-state-local partnerships that redraw the lines of authority, operations, and resource allocation. National data systems penetrate deep into local police operations, overlaying each suspect identification or vehicle check with the potential for national or international significance.[6] The world has become smaller, and the corollary may be that police

---

[6] A story from Germany is apocryphal. A German police officer, upon stopping a vehicle for traffic violation, discovered the car was carrying individuals on a federal terrorist suspect "watch list." Loud comments by the police officer, including his exclamation that individuals were on the watch list, were audible to federal investigators who had bugged the vehicle and had the suspects under surveillance for months. The suspects, who were released at the time, may have been tipped off by the police officer; they were apprehended days later while preparing explosive devices (*Terror Suspects were Tipped Off*, 2007).

work has become *larger*. Within the finite resources of the police, these larger efforts redirect equipment, time, and funds that might otherwise be applied to local policing. It may be that countries like Israel, with national police agencies, have an advantage in dealing with the macronature of many terrorist threats. But at the same time, the relative advantage that national police forces have in coordinating intelligence and allocating resources for responding to terrorism, is offset by the disadvantage they have in connecting with local communities and their problems.

It is important to note what Ganor and others assert: that "local policing vs. national security" is something of a false dichotomy. In fact, Ganor states, national security *depends on* neighborhood security; police work to combat terrorism is inexorably linked to fighting "ordinary" crime. Hasisi et al. echo this sentiment, and Greene and Herzog describe the evolution of the Israeli National Police into a "dual mission" police force. There is certainly potential for integrating functions and perhaps even achieving greater efficiencies by combining ordinary policing and counter-terrorist work. Activities aimed at preventing ordinary crime may simultaneously prevent terrorist activities. Police resources may serve dual purposes, and data systems can be scoured for intelligence on criminal as well as terrorist networks and planning (Hollywood et al., 2008). However, the costs – explicit and hidden – of combining these efforts, as well as the dividends achieved in terms of crimes and terrorist events averted, remain elusive.

The question of police centralization is especially salient to Greene and Herzog and Bayley and Weisburd. The nationalized police model in Israel, Greene and Herzog observe, contributes to a blurred distinction between the roles and functions of the police and those of the military.[7] In contrast, Greene and Herzog observe, the US organization of the police into local agencies is what drives US police to fix their attention on local safety issues, like local crime. Despite their assertion that "all terrorism is local," US police, as Bayley and Weisburd observe, are not disposed to engage it as readily – or as effectively – as they engage ordinary, local crime. The tension, Greene and Herzog propose, is between the "war" and "criminal justice" models of policing. Given their roots in local governance and their traditional focus on local crime problems, it is unlikely that many US police agencies have found a comfortable balance point in the middle, embracing what Greene and Herzog call the "widened criminal justice model."

Bayley and Weisburd draw upon an even wider theoretical palette of police organizations, introducing the role of specialized counter-terrorist agencies. They note the existence in every country of a national agency responsible for intelligence gathering regarding threats of subversion or terrorism; however, these agencies are not charged with routine policing responsibilities. Nearly everywhere around the globe, a national police force is paired with a separate national agency responsible for intelligence and terrorism surveillance. Where policing is organized at the local

---

[7] The easy comparability of the police to the military in Israel is partly due to other factors besides the decades-long fight against terrorist actions initiated from both within and outside Israel. (See Weisburd et al., forthcoming.)

or regional level, however, there is typically no dedicated local or regional intelligence and counter-terrorism agency. This creates a vacuum into which local police agencies are drawn. Bayley and Weisburd note that *all* police – local, state, or national – engage in covert surveillance for crime control (a form of "high" policing). The question is whether the work of counter-terrorism intelligence and the forms it takes, such as counter-terrorism task forces, fusion centers, or regional data-sharing systems, contorts the police in new and ineffective ways.

For Bayley and Weisburd, police form and police function are inextricably intertwined within the question of police counter-terrorist work. The question turns on the degree to which a police force is centralized (or nationalized) as well as whether the capacity for counter-terrorist intelligence gathering lies with the police or with a separate agency. But it also turns, Bayley and Weisburd say, on how resources for counter-terrorism (including funding) are allocated to the police and managed by the police; how traditional police operations, such as the use of informants and work on preventing crime are affected; the extent of planning and collaboration with other law enforcement agencies; the acquisition of equipment designed or dedicated solely for counter-terrorist purposes; changing expectations – and laws – regarding the police, human rights, and procedural guarantees; and other factors.

Police Involvement in Counter-Terrorism: Pros and Cons

Certainly, there are limits to what the police can achieve in combating terrorism. Yet, there are specific benefits and advantages in asking the police to become more centrally involved in counter-terrorism, as Bayley and Weisburd point out. They detail a series of benefits of having local police involved in society's responses to terrorism. Uniformed police have more opportunities to observe activities that may be associated with terrorism than do outside specialists, particularly specialists not deployed routinely in local areas. Police have access to information within communities that cannot be obtained by more remote, specialized intelligence agents. Analysis of ordinary crime patterns may reveal activities associated with terrorism. Local police are best positioned to develop partnerships in terrorism detection and protection with businesses and the growing private security industry. By drawing on local knowledge, intelligence specialists can narrow their surveillance, interrogations, and penetration more quickly on likely suspects. Local police may also be better able to work undercover without detection than agents brought in from afar. Finally, because of their leverage over criminals, local police can recruit and monitor informants better than outside agents.

But the costs of policing terrorism are also significant, Bayley and Weisburd say, though they have often been overlooked as Western policing agencies seek to respond to terrorist threats. Because police resources are limited, enhancing intelligence-gathering capability by general-duties police through surveillance, covert penetration, and the use of informants may lead to the neglect of other important police responsibilities. In turn, although "high" policing is undoubtedly needed in the war on terror, its injection into local policing can produce tunnel vision that undermines creativity in traditional areas of policing. Previous campaigns of counter-espionage have shown, moreover, that high policing is difficult to control. Finally, as we have already noted, high policing changes the mindset of officers from service to suspicion, where people are viewed as suspects to be watched rather than individuals to be helped.

Bayley and Weisburd suggest that democracies like the United States with strong local policing cultures, should be reluctant to adopt "high-policing" roles such as counter-terrorism policing. They argue: "Taking stock of the advantages as well as the disadvantages of using general-duties police in counter-terrorism, we believe that [the police] can contribute more by focusing and fine-tuning their standard operations than by creating specialized high policing capabilities."

The Evidence Base for Policing Terrorism: Data Rich, but Evidence Poor

As Lum (2005) notes, there are a lot of "data" available, but not much "evidence" to guide the strategies and tactics of policing to counter terrorism. Currently, the police are doing more to compile law enforcement data, create networked data systems, and compile vast arrays of data to be mined for intelligence in order to fight crime. Some early studies have shown that techniques can be employed to comb through these vast data arrays for information relevant to terrorism as well (Hollywood et al., 2008). However, the degree to which useful counter-terrorism intelligence can be sifted out by law enforcement remains largely unknown. On balance, it might be more effective to engage more fully in the process of building rigorous "evidence" of what works, in the same way that police agencies have sometimes engaged in research to find out "what works" in fighting crime and disorder.

Lum and colleagues remind us that part of the work of "ordinary" policing has been the active participation by the police in research work to build needed evidence of what works, what is effective, and what does not work in controlling and preventing "ordinary" crime. They argue that an important benchmark of the police commitment to effective counter-terrorism will be their participation in research on what works and what does not in response to terrorism. This participation in research is essential to fill the void that Lum et al. so expertly define regarding evidence for policing counter-terrorism. It will also signal that the police embrace the need for research on counter-terrorism policing just as they have embraced and advanced research on other aspects of policing.

Terrorism – and Beyond

This volume focuses on terrorism and its influence on the work of the police. Terrorism is likely to continue to be a major force in shaping police organizations and the work of the police. Other factors, however, will also exert substantial influence on the police and policing in the future. While our volume does not deal specifically with these challenges, we think that any understanding of the future of policing terrorism must recognize that there are other forces that are influencing development and change in policing. Accordingly, before concluding we discuss some examples of specific challenges that are already emerging and consider how they might affect the ways in which the police respond to terrorism.

Budgets, Management, and Accountability

Management sciences continue to evolve, and business practices require public agencies to adopt improved management practices in order to remain efficient and effective. This is equally true for all public sectors, including the police. As agencies of the people, the police are accountable to their public managers. This accountability includes demonstrating effectiveness and achieving efficient use of scarce resources – resources that might otherwise have been allocated to support other public services with soaring costs, such as education, public utilities, infrastructure, and health care.

Concerns about how best to organize the functions and manage the personnel in a police organization are not new. What is new is the competitive environment in which the public police find themselves. The costs of public policing have been rising at unprecedented rates, as personnel, training, and management have become more and more expensive. Foglesong and Gascon (2008) document a dramatic increase in the costs associated with public policing, at the same time that there is evidence of an explosion in the public's use of private policing (Bayely and Nixon, 2008). Some have begun to argue that public policing is "pricing itself out of business." How will policing terrorism affect this trend?

On the one hand we might expect that the critical nature of policing terrorism would lead to greater investment in public police. Certainly, terrorist threats have led to increases in public support in the United States for homeland security programs in local jurisdictions. However, many have argued that the increased funding for homeland security has come at the expense of funding for traditional crime prevention programs (*To Protect and Defend*, 2008). It would also seem that private police would be less appropriate for homeland security functions, thus demanding greater investment in public police services. However, in Israel for example, police have come to play a supervisory and licensing role for private security at malls, restaurants, and other public institutions. Does this example suggest that more and more policing roles will be taken by private security, and the police will become more of a licensing authority?

We have no way to answer such questions, but we think it important to note that the costs of public policing will be affected by greater involvement in homeland security and counter-terrorism. To date, we are not aware of any definitive examination of there questions, though they are critical to understanding the future of policing and policing terrorism.

Technological Change

Another area that is critical to consider is the accelerated pace of technological change. Technological advances touch every aspect of society, and policing is not exempt. For example, communication has become more rapid and more pervasive, placing all public agencies under more intense public scrutiny. As we have already noted, policing terrorism emphasizes "high-policing" functions and often requires operation in secrecy. In what ways will advances in communications hinder policing terrorism? In what ways will it facilitate the investigation and tracking of terrorist suspects? Will advances in communications make the police more accountable to the public, or in combination with the high-policing functions demanded by counter-terrorism policing, will it lead to less freedom and more covert observation of the public by the police?

Automation has replaced many face-to-face encounters, and this too will influence the face of policing in the future. ATMs have replaced bank tellers; machines dispensing fare cards and tokens have taken the place of train conductors and subway agents. Technology has eliminated many place guardians (Eck, 1994), and the overall context for crime and public safety is altered as face to face interaction becomes more fleeting. Will this hinder the police in their ability to police terrorism? Or will such devices as closed circuit television aid the police in identifying and preventing terrorism? There is initial evidence that CCTV is effective in preventing crime (Welsh and Farrington, 2003a,b), and some have argued that it has facilitated tracking and identification of terrorists (Fussey, 2007; Segell, 2006). But the full implications of automation both for facilitating policing and for reducing freedoms of the general public have not been studied.

Advances in forensic science provide another important example of technological change that is influencing policing. A recent study supported by the National Institute of Justice shows that the collection of DNA evidence provides a more effective response to burglaries than traditional investigative approaches (Roman et al., 2008). Clearly, policing terrorism will also be strongly aided by advances in forensic science. Will these advances fundamentally alter the police role in counter-terrorism? Will the traditional roles of investigators become less important as forensic evidence becomes more critical in investigations? Is this, like private policing, a threat to the traditional importance of the police in investigations more generally, and in investigations of terrorism more specifically?

More generally, "smart" identification cards, driver's licenses, and passports, DNA, and other biometric tools add a new dimension – and new challenges – to policing and policing terrorism. In Europe today, large biometric databases are being collected with millions of individuals identified (Neyroud and Disley, 2008). Policing is being changed in critical ways by the availability of such data and communications and computer technologies that make it possible to manage, analyze, and disseminate the data. Unfortunately, we still know little about the effects of these tools on policing, and as Lum et al. show, we have not examined them systematically.

In developing our volume we tried to identify scholars who could examine critically the influence of technology on policing and its impact on policing terrorism. But we discovered quickly that the "science of technology" and the "science of policing" remain largely disconnected. Scholars concerned with policing generally have not researched changes in technology, and those researching innovations in technology have not studied the social and organizational impacts of this technology. As the intersection of these lines of research receives greater attention, we will certainly know more in the future.

Globalizations and Cultural Diversity

Of course, technology is not the only element in the world of policing that is changing rapidly. We live on a "smaller" planet, and boundaries between nations have become very porous. The ease of transportation and the advances in communication technology have increased the opportunities and the motives for international mobility. This, in turn, has led to greater immigration, both legal and illegal, from poorer, less developed nations – some experiencing substantial turmoil and economic deprivation – to more prosperous and democratic nations.

Immigrants, documented and undocumented, vary widely in both their experience with democratic governance and in their expectations for democratic rule. Their first-hand and indirect exposure to democratic policing varies likewise. Thus, immigration and globalization have created an evolving social environment to which policing must be attentive. Policing terrorism, as we have already noted, is very much a part of these social changes.

Societies are becoming increasingly diverse due to increasing globalization and immigration. This creates difficulties in culture clashes and violent incidents, especially in youth gangs and groups. In addition, this diversity creates havens for terrorists infiltrating countries they have targeted. There is a growing need for multilingual police officers and those who understand the cultures and needs of large immigrant groups. How will police agencies recruit and train officers to develop all the requisite skills for policing in these communities? Are police agencies well advised to establish cultural competencies within specific liaison units within the department that focus on specific ethnic or immigrant segments of the community?

Often, new immigrants constitute an especially vulnerable group of potential crime victims, due in part to their unfamiliarity with routine activities in their new country, unable to distinguish suspicious or threatening behavior or activity by others. In addition, some may come from countries where the police are unresponsive to victim reports or are simply not trusted. How should police agencies help prevent victimization among immigrant groups? How can the police most effectively cultivate the trust and confidence of immigrant communities? This is especially urgent in the case of undocumented aliens for whom the security of conventional institutions, such as banks, may be less accessible. Forced to deal more often in cash, they can become easy crime victims; when victimized, they may be more reluctant to contact the police, fearing discovery of their illegal status.

The challenge of policing multicultural and immigrant communities is magnified in the age of terrorism, when immigrants could be covert terrorists, or where immigrant communities can (even inadvertently) serve as havens for terrorist cells plotting violent incidents. Certainly, immigrant groups must be viewed as essential partners in preventing terrorist incidents, serving as a crucial source of information to police about suspicious and potentially dangerous people and situations in their neighborhoods. All of this puts added strain on law enforcement as departments try to serve their communities effectively. How are police to balance police work in immigrant communities against the need to gather intelligence about possible terrorist cells or terrorist activities?

Finally, we think it important to consider not only the globalization of peoples but also the globalization of crime. Sometimes, "it takes a village" – or a global network – to commit a crime. Today, crime networks may easily span the globe, using global communications to link resources and criminal cells. "Crime is still local," but an increasing share of what surfaces as a local crime incident – a case of fraud, extortion, sexual victimization, or trafficking in persons or illegal goods and drugs – has roots that reach around the globe. Terrorism is very much a part of this global network, as identified by Boaz Ganor in his chapter. Are local police prepared to confront national and international criminal networks? How can police best assemble information about local crimes to combat underlying criminal networks? How will police distinguish between "local crime" and national or international criminal enterprises? Policing terrorism in this case may actually aid the police in responding to the globalization of criminal networks. High policing in this case provides an important context for dealing with strategic criminal threats that span national boundaries. But once again, we caution that this advantage may come at the expense of the benefits associated with a focus on local policing.

Conclusions

This volume responds to the specific challenge of policing in an age of terrorism. The motive for its development lies in the terrorist events that have recently transpired in Israel, the US, and elsewhere—events that may change forever the form and function of policing. A longer view, however, suggests that change and adaptation have been the work of policing organizations from the beginning. If terrorism is only the latest lesson from which we must learn and to which the police must adapt, what will be the next challenge? More importantly, how are the police to be organized, equipped, and led in order to remain effective in a constantly changing world: in the age of terrorism – *and beyond?*

As Lum reminds us, police agencies have often established themselves as active participants in the work of research. More than any other criminal justice institution, the police have allowed their operations, procedures, and strategies to be scrutinized and strategies to be scrutinized and tested. This was not always their orientation, and police agencies elsewhere vary significantly in their commitment to research. And though community policing and problem-solving approaches to policing have done much to entrench the spirit of empiricism among police, specific practices persist without evidence to support them, and new circumstances are sometimes met with unproven hunches of what "will work" or what might constitute a "best practice." Our response to terrorism has been no different in this regard. But the challenges of terrorism and what lies beyond require flexible, research-ready police organizations that will be led by evidence and committed to strategic adaptation.

The exploration of any frontier requires a map. Our authors have provided a conceptual map that examines the theoretical contours of policing counter-terrorism. How the police ought to traverse this terrain in ways that maximize public safety remains an empirical question. As we move forward with the important work of policing in the age of terrorism, we must continue to assemble the most rigorous research evidence we can muster. Police agencies will best thrive when they actively seek and carefully process information about emerging challenges and are willing and able to learn from that information and adapt in response to it. In this sense, if police agencies are to be successful in responding to terrorism they must become "learning organizations," capable of rapid, timely, and effective self-study; able to modify policies, practices, and priorities based on evidence; willing and capable to evaluate actions for effectiveness and efficiency, weighing costs and advantages against alternative options; and continually seeking better, more concise evidence and measures of their effectiveness.

Specific challenges facing the police should be the priority work of researchers and police, working in partnership. How will successful police organizations use information and intelligence, balancing public security with public trust? What is the most effective way to get intelligence up from the line officers to make strategic policy changes for the organization - including its response to terrorist intelligence? What are the strategies through which the police should engage minority communities in confronting and preventing terrorism? As more and more data become available to the police, how are they to make sense of available data (including local and international intelligence) to effectively distinguish "signal" from "noise?" As terrorist organizations and tactics change and evolve, how do the police effectively adapt? What are the costs and benefits of centralized police structures and strategies or of specialized terrorist units? How are policing resources best applied in engaging private security partners? Which among the available technological advances will prove most effective – and cost effective? These are just some of the questions of police practice and policy that can only be answered with more evidence.

The threat of terrorism will remain with us for the foreseeable future, and our expectations for what the police should do in response to this threat are unlikely to diminish. We think this volume takes an important step in providing the types of data and discussion that can help to inform police organization and strategy and help the police to adapt to a changing and challenging environment. Only as learning organizations can the police sort out and prioritize competing claims of urgency or effective strategies. The pace of research must quicken, the quality of the evidence must continue to improve, and the police must remain committed to the continual work of testing, refining, adapting, and evaluating its efforts if we are to overcome the threat of terrorism and move beyond in preparation for the next assault on the security, the safety, and the quality of life in our neighborhoods, our communities, and our nations.

References

Bayley, D., and C. Nixon (forthcoming). The changing environment for policing, 1985–2008. *New Perspective in Policing* Harvard Kennedy School and the National Institute for Justice Executive Session on Policing.

Brodeur, J.-P. 1983. High and low policing: Remarks about the policing of political activities. *Social Problems* 30(5):507–520.

Brodeur, J.-P. 2007. High and low policing in post-9/11 times. *Policing* 1(1):25–37.

Davies, H. J., and G. R. Murphy. 2004. *Protecting Your Community from Terrorism: Strategies for Local Law Enforcement, Vol. 2: Working With Diverse Communities.* Washington, DC: Police Executive Research Forum. http://www.policeforum.org/upload/wp2_925579737_322006144428.pdf (accessed November 6, 2008).

Eck, J. E. (1994). Drug markets and drug places: A case-control study of the spatial structure of illicit drug dealing. PhD dissertation, University of Maryland, College Park, MD.

Fact Sheet: Foreign Terrorist Organizations. 2008. Washington, DC: State Department, Office of the Coordinator for Counterterrorism.http://www.state.gov/s/ct/rls/fs/08/103392.htm (accessed April 8, 2008).

Fussey, P. 2007. Observing potentiality in the global city: Surveillance and counterterrorism in London. *International Criminal Justice Review* 17(3):171–192.

Gascon, G., and T. Foglesong (forthcoming). Are police departments pricing themselves out of (the) business? *New Perspective in Policing* Harvard Kennedy School and the National Institute for Justice Executive Session on Policing.

Henderson, N. J., C. W. Ortiz, N. F. Sugie, and J. Miller. 2008. *Policing in Arab-American Communities after September 11.* Washington, DC: National Institute of Justice. http://www.ncjrs.gov/pdffiles1/nij/221706.pdf (accessed November 6, 2008).

Hoffman, B. 2008. The myth of grass-roots terrorism: Why Osama bin Laden still matters. *Foreign Affairs,* May/June. http://www.foreignaffairs.org/20080501fareviewessay87310/bruce-hoffman/the-myth-of-grass-roots-terrorism.html (accessed November 6, 2008).

Hollywood, J., K. Strom, and M. Pope. 2008. *Developing and Testing a Method for Using 911 Calls for Identifying Potential Pre-Planning Terrorist Surveillance Activities.* Washington, DC: National Institute of Justice. http://www.ncjrs.gov/pdffiles1/nij/grants/222911.pdf (accessed November 6, 2008).

Ignatius, D. 2008. The Fading Jihadists. *Washington Post,* February 28.

Jonathan, T. (forthcoming). The relationship between police involvement in counter-terrorism and public attitudes toward the police among majority communities in Israel: 1998–2007

Local Law Enforcement's Role in Preventing and Responding to Terrorism, Discussion Draft. 2001. Washington, DC: Police Executive Research Forum. http://www.policeforum.org/upload/terrorismfinal%5B1%5D_715866088_12302005135139.pdf (accessed November 6, 2008).

Luna, C. 2005. *Tip Line Technologies, Intelligence Gathering and Analysis Systems: Phase I Final Report and Executive Summary.* Washington, DC: National Institute of Justice. http://www.ncjrs.gov/pdffiles1/nij/grants/211677.pdf (accessed November 6, 2008).

MI5 tracking '30 UK terror plots'. 2006. *BBC News*, November 10. http://news.bbc.co.uk/1/hi/uk/6134516.stm (accessed November 6, 2008).

Newport, F. 2008. Confidence in institutions. *Gallup*. http://www.gallup.com/poll/1597/Confidence-Institutions.aspx (accessed November 6, 2008).

Neyroud, P., and E. Disley. 2008. Technology and policing: Implications for fairness and legitimacy. *Policing* 2(2):226–232.

Parsons, T. 1937. *The Structure of Social Action*. New York: McGraw-Hill.

Rheault, M. 2007. Many world citizens trust neighbors more than police. *Gallup*. http://www.gallup.com/poll/102346/Many-World-Citizens-Trust-Neighbors-More-Than-Police.aspx (accessed November 6, 2008).

Roman, J. K., S. Reid, J. Reid, A. Chalfin, W. Adams, and C. Knight. 2008. *The DNA Field Experiment: Cost-Effectiveness Analysis of the Use of DNA in the Investigation of High-Volume Crimes*. Washington DC: US Department of Justice. http://www.ncjrs.gov/pdffiles1/nij/grants/222318.pdf (accessed November 6, 2008).

Segell, G. M. 2006. Terrorism on London public transport. *Defense & Security Analysis* 22(1):45–59.

Sherman, L. W. 2002. Trust and confidence in criminal justice, *National Institute of Justice Journal* 248:22–31.

Sherman, L. W., and D. Weisburd. 1995. General deterrent effects of police patrol in crime "hot spots": A randomized, controlled trial. *Justice Quarterly* 12(4):625–648.

Skogan, W. G., L. Steiner, J. DuBois, E. J. Gudell, and A. Fagan. 2002. *Community Policing and "The New Immigrants": Latinos in Chicago*. Washington, DC: National Institute of Justice. http://www.ncjrs.gov/pdffiles1/nij/189908.pdf (accessed November 6, 2008).

Terror suspects were 'tipped off'. 2007. *CNN News*, September 10. http://www.cnn.com/2007/WORLD/europe/09/10/germany.terror/index.html (accessed November 6, 2008).

To Protect and Defend: Challenges to Public Safety and Homeland Security Facing the Next US President. US: The International Association of Chiefs of Police. http://www.theiacp.org/documents/protectdefend.pdf (accessed August 28, 2008).

Weisburd, D., and A. A. Braga. 2003. Hot spots policing. In *Crime Prevention: New Approaches*, eds. H. Kury and O. Fuchs, Mainz, Germany: Weisner Ring.

Weisburd, D., and J. Eck. 2004. What can police do to reduce crime, disorder, and fear? *Annals of the American Academy of Political and Social Science* 593:42–65.

Weisburd, D., T. Jonathan, and S. Perry. (forthcoming) The Israeli model for policing terrorism: Goals, strategies, and open questions. *Criminal Justice and Behavior*.

Welsh, B. C., and D. P. Farrington. 2003a. Effects of closed-circuit television on crime. *Annals of the American Academy of Political and Social Science* 587:110–135.

Welsh, B. C., and D. P. Farrington. 2003b. *Effects of Closed Circuit Television Surveillance on Crime: Protocol for a Systematic Review*. Campbell Collaboration Crime and Justice Group. http://www.campbellcollaboration.org/campbell_library/index.php (accessed December 8, 2008).

Index

A
Al-Qaeda, 27, 29–32, 35, 67, 178
American policing, 2, 103, 115

B
Bomb-Disposal unit, 151
British Mandatory Police (BMP), 161
Broken windows policing, 2

C
Closed-circuit television (CCTV) monitors, 111, 116–117, 119, 126, 137, 219
Combatants, 22, 23, 155
Commercial Equipment Direct Assistance Program (CEDAP), 120–121
Community policing, 2, 5, 90, 92, 94, 122, 123, 126, 128, 133, 150, 161, 181, 211, 213, 222
Continuation of Government (COG), 179–180
Contra rebels attacks, 19
Cops and spooks
   advantages and disadvantages
      community policing, 94
      counterterrorism, 93
      intelligence bureau (IB), 94
      London Metropolitan Police, 92
      Michigan State Trooper, 91
      police agencies, 94
      Police-Community Service Officer (PCSOs), 92
   counterterrorism
      communist party, 90
      high-policing functions, 88, 89
      International Association of Chiefs of Police (IACP), 87, 89
      law-enforcement agencies, 87
      national security service, 86
      police agencies, 90
      Red Scare, Russian revolution, 89
      united farmworkers party, 90
   national models
      counterterrorism, 83–86
      domestic organization, 84, 85
      federal systems, 86
      foreign intelligence, 83
      police agencies, 83, 84
Council of State Governments and Eastern Kentucky University (CSG/EKU study), 105
Counterterrorism
   CEDAP, 120–121
   Civil Guard Bases, 150–151
   communication and information-sharing barriers, 167
   communist party, 90
   crime analysts, 169
   Criminal Justice Model, 147–149
   CSG/EKU study, 105–106
   in Europe, 124–125
   hazmat training activity, 114
   high-policing functions, 88, 89
   information and intelligence activities, 114–115
   intelligence approach, 160
   International Association of Chiefs of Police (IACP), 87, 89
   in Ireland, 126
   in Israel, 130–131
   lack of empirical information, 102
   law enforcement agencies and activities, 87, 101–102, 104–105
   LEMAS survey, 106–109
   major intelligence providers, 165
   national security service, 86
   in Netherland and Sweden, 127
   patrol activities, 170

Counterterrorism (*cont.*)
    philosophies and strategies, 145–146
    police agencies, 90
    Red Scare, Russian revolution, 89
    response areas, 110–112
    in Spain, 127–128
    strategic planning, 113–114
    strategies and structure, 157–159
    survelliance, 116–117
    technologies, 115–116
    in Turkey, 128–129
    United Farmworkers Party, 90
    in United Kingdom, 125–126
    War model, 146
Criminal Justice Model
    law enforcement mechanisms, 147
    special counter-terrorist divisions, 148

D

David-and-Goliath style confrontation, 33
Department of Homeland Security (DHS), United States, 48, 104, 108, 110, 112, 118, 120, 122, 150, 161–162, 189–190

F

FBI's Uniform Crime Report, 44
Federal Bureau of Investigation (FBI), United States, 44, 47, 84–86, 91–93, 105, 149, 163, 164, 167, 214
Foreign terrorist organizations (FTO), 207
Formal and social organization, policing systems
    bending granite, 144
    Border Guard, 160
    British Mandatory Police (BMP), 161
    Color-Coded Advisory System, 163
    community-based responses, 163
    counter-intelligence structures, US, 163
    counter-terrorism, philosophies and strategies, 145–146
    Criminal Justice Model
        Israeli National Police (INP), 148–149
        law enforcement mechanisms, 147
        special counter-terrorist divisions, 148
    Fusion Centers, 164
    ground behavior, 144
    Homeland Security Information Network (HSIN), 164
    NYPD Shield, 162
    PATRIOT Acts, 162
    US and Israel, comparison of
        Bomb-Disposal unit, 151
        Civil Guard, 150–151
        communications and information-sharing barriers, 167
        community policing officers, COPS programs, 150
        core areas, 159
        crime analysts, 169
        crime rates, 156–157
        generalized patrol activities, 170
        institutions, 152–153
        intelligence approach, 160
        major intelligence providers, 165
        organizations and problems, 153, 155, 164
        police intelligence gathering, 165–166
        staffing, 168–169
        strategies and structures, 157–159
        structural and operational differences, 150
    War Model, 146
French civil war, 25
Fusion Centers, US, 118, 119, 164, 166, 170, 216

G

Gendermarie, Turkey national security agency, 129
General Security Service (GSS), 189, 191
Global Jihad organizations
    Al-Qaeda, 30–31
    definition, 12
    developmental process, 31–32
    Global Jihad organizations of nonconventional measures (CBRN), 32
    homegrown terrorism, 29–30
    Islamic terrorism, 29
Global Terrorism Database (GTD), 44, 47–48
    current status, 49–50
    data collection since 2005, 49
    definitions of terrorism, 47
    original PGIS data, 48
Global terrorism trends, tracking
    characteristics of terrorism, 50
    country-level comparisons, 67–72
        countries with most terrorist attacks, 67–68
        democracy and terrorism, 68–70
        revolutionary wars, 71
        state failure, 71
    attacks attributed to specific group, 53
    attacks with more than ten fatalities, 52–53
    average fatalities per attack, 53–55

distribution of weapon types, WMD
   attacks, 58–59
 fatalities per attack, 57–58
 target types, 56
 total attacks and fatal attacks, 51–52
 types of attack, 55–56
 weapon types, 56–57
lack of data, 43
measuring illegal violence
 media and crimes, 46
 official data on common crimes, 45
 self-report survey data, 44, 46
 victimization data, 44, 45–46, 73
regional variations
 attacks and fatalities, 60–61
 target types, 61–62
 weapons, 62–63
terrorism and violent crime, 72–73
terrorist organizations
 list of groups, 65–67
 longevity of groups in attacks, 63–64
 total fatalities by, 65
Guarda's Intelligence Unit, Dublin, 126
Guided missiles, 58, 67

H

Hamas terrorist group, Palestine, 28, 66, 67, 208
Hezbollah terrorist group, Lebanon, 17, 27, 28
Homegrown terrorism, 29–32
Homeland Security Information Network (HSIN), 164
Homicide, 44, 46, 71, 73–75
Hot spots policing, 2, 214

I

Immigration and terror, minority community
 antiterrorism efforts, 186
 Arab American communities, 185
 foreign elements, 186
 law enforcement, 184, 186
 muslim community, 186, 187
 national security agenda, 185
 policing terrorism, 187
International Association of Chiefs of Police (IACP), 81, 87, 89, 95, 122
International Criminal Police Organization (Interpol), 44, 73
International terrorist organizations
 Al Qaeda, 27, 29–32, 33, 67, 178
 Hezbollah and Hamas, 17, 27, 28, 66, 67, 208

Red Brigades, 27
Israel Defense Forces (IDF), 21, 160, 166
Israeli Internal Security Service (SHABAK), 131
Israeli Model, Counterterrorism by Police, 131
Israeli National Police (INP), 148, 150, 151, 158, 160, 161, 166, 168

J

Joint Terrorism Task Forces (JTTFs), 86, 105, 118, 167, 193

K

Khomeini's revolution, Iran, 37–38

L

Law Enforcement Management and Administrative Statistics (LEMAS)
 Campbell systematic review and meta-analysis, 109
 community-oriented tactics, 108
 personal allocation and cooperative agreements, 107–108
 US Department of Justice, 106

M

Ministry of Public Security (MoPS), State of Israel, 2–3, 131, 182, 196, 213
Modern international terrorism
 academic approaches, 12
 democratic state and, 33–34
 dynamic terrorist phenomenon, 13
 economic ramifications, 34–36
 explanatory disciplines
  criminology, 17
  economics and sociology, 17
  political science and international relations, 18
  psychology, 16
  theology, 18
 Global Jihad organizations, 12
  Al-Qaeda, 30–31
  definition, 12
  developmental process, 31–32
  Global Jihad organizations of nonconventional measures (CBRN), 32
  homegrown terrorism, 29–30
  Islamic terrorism, 29
 political-rational school

Modern international terrorism (*cont.*)
  decision-making process, 15–16
  rational choice theory, 15
  psychological–sociological school
    political psychology, 14
    psychological characteristics, 13–14
    terrorist psycho-logic, 14–15
  recommendations, 36–38
  research implications, 39
  schools of thought, 12
Muslim World League, 20–21

N
Narco-terrorism, 27
National Institute of Justice (NIJ), 2–3, 48, 103, 124, 219
National models, counterterrorism
  domestic organization, 84, 85
  federal systems, 86
  foreign intelligence, 83
  police agencies, 83, 84

O
Operation Rainbow, United Kingdom, 129

P
PATRIOT Acts, US, 162
Patterns of Global Terrorism, 50
Pinkerton Global Intelligence Service (PGIS), 47–50
Police Antiterrorist Unit (Ya'mam), 151
Police-community relations
  American law enforcement community, 179
  Basque separatist movement, 178
  Bin Laden's campaign, 179
  defensive methods, 180
  immigration and terror
    antiterrorism efforts, 186
    Arab American communities, 185
    foreign elements, 186
    law enforcement, 184, 186
    minority community, 184
    muslim community, 186, 187
    national security agenda, 185
    policing terrorism, 187
  intelligence
    arab minority, 183, 184
    community policing projects, 181
    Israeli society, 182
    law enforcement, 184
  Islamic fundamentalists, 178
  policing terrorism, 178–179
  proactive measures, 180–181
  reactive measures
    Civil Guard, 191
    color code system, 190
    federal government, 193
    General Security Service (GSS), 189
    Katarina disaster, 188
    law enforcement agencies, 192, 193
    police organizations, 192
    policing agencies, 189
    private security companies, 193
    resources drain, 188
    Security Advisory System (SAS), 189
  terrorism
    federal government, 194
    Israel police, 195
    psychological effect, 194
    research proposals, 196–197
  terrorist organizations, 180
Police counterterrorism activities
  Aliens Police Unit of the National Police Service (KLPD), 127
  Community Policing Unit, 128
  Council of State Governments and Eastern Kentucky University, 105–106
  in Europe, 124–125
  Euskadi Ta Askatasuna, Basque national separatist organization, 128
  future action and research, 132–133
  Gendermarie, Turkey, 129
  Guarda's Intelligence Unit, Dublin, 126
  in Ireland, 126
  in Israel, 130–131
  information, lack of, 102
  Israeli Internal Security Service (SHABAK), 131
  law enforcement agencies and its response, 101, 134
  Law Enforcement Management and Administrative Statistics (LEMAS)
    Campbell systematic review and meta-analysis, 109, 135–136
    community-oriented tactics, 108
    personnel allocation and cooperative agreements, 107–108
    US Department of Justice, 106
  Metropolitan Police Service (MPS), London, 125
  Ministry of Public Security, Israel, 131
  MI5 security agency, England, 125–126
  multilayered level, 102
  Muslim Contact Unit (MCU), 125
  National Institute of Justice project, 103
  in Netherlands, 127

Index

Operation Rainbow, United Kingdom, 129
Rainbow Unit, England, 126
RAND Corporation
  Federal Bureau of Investigation or Joint Terrorism Task Forces, 105
  interagency cooperation, 105
  main areas, law enforcement activity, 104
  reallocating personnel and resources, 105
  state and local law enforcement preparedness, 104–105
  US Department of Homeland Security, 104, 108
research infrastructure
  evidence-based decision making, 136
  metal detectors, 137
  prevention matrix, 136
in Spain, 127–128
Specialist Operations 13 (SO13) branch, 125
state highway patrol agency, 133
in Sweden, 127
thematic perspective, advantages of, 102–103
in Turkey, 128–129
Turkish National Police (TNP), 128–129
in United Kingdom, 125–126
in US
  closed-circuit television (CCTV) monitors, 111
  Commercial Equipment Direct Assistance Program, 120–121
  common deterrence tactics and surveillance, 116–117
  community-based interventions, 122–123
  Fusion Centers, 118
  hazmat training activity, 114
  information and intelligence activities, 114–115
  interagency cooperation and coordination, 112–113
  low use of technologies, 120
  Office of the Inspector General (2005), 119
  on-the-ground tactics, 119
  response areas, 110–111
  strategic planning, 113–114
  technologies, 115–116
Policing
  Aliens Police Unit, Netherlands, 127
  American organization, 215
  Campbell systematic review, 135
  centralization vs decentralization, 214–216

counter-terrorism, 205, 216–217
crosscutting themes
  police, 213–217
  terrorism and terrorists, 206–209
  urban community, 209–213
CSG/EKU study, 105–106
federal agencies, 214
Guarda's Intelligence Unit, Dublin, 126
information and intelligence activities, 114–115
interagency cooperation, 105
interagency coordination, 112–113
Israeli Model, 131
Israeli National Police, 215
law enforcement agencies, 101–102, 214, 216
LEMAS survey, 106–109
metal detectors, 137
MI5 security agency, UK, 125
prevention matrix, 136
RAND Corporation, 104
response areas, 110–111
social systems, 203, 204
strategic planning, 113–114
Talcott Parsons' theory, 203
technologies, 115–116
terrorism
  budgets, management, and accountability, 218
  forensic science, 219
  globalizations and cultural diversity, 220–221
  high-policing functions, 219
training, 114
US and Israel
  communication and information-sharing barriers, 167
  community policing officers, 150
  core areas, 159
  counter-intelligence structures, 163
  crime rates, 156–157
  FBI, 149
  institutional dimensions, 152–153
  intelligence gathering, 165–166
  major intelligence providers, 165
  operational dimensions, 154–156
  organizational dimensions, 153
  patrol activities, 170
  special counter-terrorist divisions, 148
  staffing, 168–169
  strategies and structures, 158–159
  structural and operational differences, 150
US communities, 205

Political Instability Task Force (PITF), 71
Problem-oriented policing, 2

R
RAND Corporation, United States, 74, 104–108, 110, 113, 117
Rational choice theory, 15

S
Sharia law, 30
State failure, global terrorism, 71–72
Study of Terrorism and Responses to Terrorism (START), 4, 49
Substate actors, Modern asymmetric warfare, 23

T
Terrorism
 al Qaeda organization, 208
 Arab minority community, 209
 bad *vs.* good, 24
 budgets, management, and accountability, 218
 Contra rebels attacks, 19
 criminal acts *vs.* acts of war, 21–22
 FBI definition, 47
 fear and anxiety element, 25–26
 federal government, 194
 foreign terrorist organizations (FTO), 207
 forensic science, 219
 freedom fighters, 20
 French civil war, 24–25
 Geneva and The Hague conventions, 22
 globalizations and cultural diversity, 220–221
 Global Jihadi movement, 207, 208
 high-policing functions, 219
 LaFree and Dugan's data, 206, 208
 Muslim World League, 20–21
 national liberation, 19–20
 non-combatants, U.S. State Department, 23
 Pinkerton definition, 47
 psychological effect, 194
 research proposals, 196–197
 terrorist organizations aim, 26–27
 umbrella organizations, 208
 US intelligence community, 209
 US national security, 207
Tri-border area (TBA). *See* Hamas; Hezbollah

U
United Kingdom, Counterterrorism by Police
 M15, security agency, 125
 Muslim Contact Unit (MCU), 125–126
 Rainbow Unit, 126
Urban community
 Arab-American communities, 210, 212
 Chicago Alternative Policing Strategy (CAPS), 211
 counter-terrorism, 213
 minority communities, 212, 213
 policing terrorism, 213
 terrorist organizations, 210

W
War criminals, 22, 23
Weapons of mass destruction (WMD), 4, 32, 58–59, 66, 67, 87
Helsinki Accords, 38
World Health Organization (WHO), 44, 73, 75

Printed in Great Britain
by Amazon